MICHIGAN STUDIES ON CHINA 

China's Economic Development: The Interplay of Scarcity and Ideology, by Alexander Eckstein

The Chinese Calculus of Deterrence: India and Indochina, by Allen S. Whiting

The Presidency of Yuan Shih-k'ai: Liberalism and Dictatorship in Early Republican China, by Ernest P. Young

The Outsiders: The Western Experience in India and China, by Rhoads Murphey

The Concept of Man in Contemporary China, by Donald J. Munro

China Enters the Twentieth Century: Chang Chih-tung and the Issues of a New Age, 1895–1909, by Daniel H. Bays

The research on which these books are based was supported by the Center for Chinese Studies of The University of Michigan.

CHINA ENTERS THE TWENTIETH CENTURY

Michigan Studies on China
Published for the Center for Chinese Studies
of The University of Michigan

The Viceroy Chang Chih-tung

China Enters the Twentieth Century

Chang Chih-tung and the Issues of a New Age, 1895–1909

DANIEL H. BAYS

Ann Arbor The University of Michigan Press

Published in the United States of America by
The University of Michigan Press and simultaneously
in Rexdale, Canada, by John Wiley & Sons Canada, Limited
Manufactured in the United States of America

Published with the assistance of a grant from the University of Kansas and the Center for Chinese Studies of The University of Michigan.

Library of Congress Cataloging in Publication Data

Bays, Daniel H
China enters the twentieth century.

(Michigan studies on China)
A revision and expansion of the author's thesis,
University of Michigan, 1971.
Bibliography: p.
Includes index.
1. China—History—Kuang-hsü, 1875–1908. 2. Chang, Chih-tung, 1837–1909. I. Title. II. Series.
DS764.B34 1978 951′.03 77-14261
ISBN 0-472-08105-5

To my father and my mother

Acknowledgments

It is a pleasure to pay tribute to those who have directly and indirectly helped to make possible the publication of this volume.

Claude Buss and Lyman P. Van Slyke of Stanford University first ignited a passion for China during my undergraduate years there. The Horace H. Rackham School of Graduate Studies and the Center for Chinese Studies of the University of Michigan gave me generous support during my years of graduate study. The Center, in particular, made possible both the initial incarnation of this manuscript as a dissertation in 1971 and its present publication in revised and expanded form. The National Endowment for the Humanities supported a stay in London in 1973, during which I completed the research on Chang Chih-tung's last years. That research was enriched greatly by the holdings of the Public Record Office. The University of Kansas supported the rewriting of the manuscript in 1974 and 1975, and has made a further contribution toward its publication. My colleagues here in the Department of History have provided me with a stimulating and congenial atmosphere within which to pursue my research and writing.

Over the years, Albert Feuerwerker and Ernest P. Young have been faithful and encouraging friends, and conscientious and perceptive critics as well. I am happy to acknowledge the intellectual obligations which I have to each of them, while at the same time absolving them of any responsibility for errors of research or interpretation which exist in this study.

All these debts to others notwithstanding, it remains a fact that the writing of a book can be a lonely, and at times a discouraging, endeavor. An uncompleted manuscript inevitably competes for time with the demands of a fledgling teaching career and the needs of a young family. In all truth, this study would never have broken through the surface of my cluttered day-to-day existence, had it not been for the unswerving love and support I have always received from my wife, Janny. For that she deserves, and hereby is given, a very special word of appreciation.

Contents

Introduction

Sometime between 1895 and 1911, there came into being forces which would help to shape the course of Chinese history for several ensuing decades. It might be argued that these years set the course for most of the first half of the twentieth century; or at least that the historian can better understand the basic issues of that half-century by extending trends forward from this period. Without necessarily making so sweeping a claim, I do believe that systematic analysis of several aspects of the 1895–1911 period, besides being important itself, illuminates some of the main political, social, and intellectual configurations of the post-1911 era as well. This was a time of rapid, and rapidly accelerating, change, very different in mood from the half-century of relative lethargy in institutional and value change which preceded it. During these years, several themes emerged which were of profound concern to increasing numbers of Chinese, and basic structural changes in the political system were begun for the first time in the modern age.

One of those themes was what might be called, for lack of a more appropriate term, "reformism." After 1895, a progressively broader acceptance of the need for a systematic national reform program spread through government and society, until by 1909 proposals which a decade previous had been considered excessively radical were now commonplace, and even assumed as necessary. Another theme, closely associated with the first, was the motivating force of nationalism. A growing determination to reassert China's dignity in the world drove the politics of dynasty, bureaucrats, gentry, and revolutionaries alike during these years.

Each of these large, elemental currents, reformism and nationalism, had a variety of separate cross-currents and minor eddies swirling within it, ranging from cautious, incremental reform and gradual assertion of national rights to radically totalistic schemes advanced as solutions to China's foreign and domestic problems.

In addition to the above themes, the years before 1911 occasioned a great deal of concrete structural change in the forms and instruments of political power in China, more than many observers before 1895 would have dreamed possible. The central government underwent significant reorganization, and most important, after 1905 it began the step by step introduction of a constitutional system. The modern student class, at home and especially in Japan, developed into an important political factor. The traditional gentry class rapidly mobilized itself as a series of provincial interest groups after 1900, and was a major new claimant for a share of power in the last years of the dynasty. These groups and others expressed their views in newspapers and journals which came to constitute a potent new force of "public opinion" in the early twentieth century. Thus political structures and activities, as well as the expectations for politics, were undergoing considerable change.

There are many possible methods of approaching this period, but I have utilized that of studying the political career of one of China's major officials, Chang Chih-tung (1837–1909), as a means of highlighting some of the important themes I have touched on above. Over the entire period from 1895 to his death in late 1909, Chang was one of the two or three most important political figures below the throne itself. He had stature both as a leading provincial official and as one who occasionally played an important role at court as well. He was what we should call a "national bureaucrat," perhaps because, despite his long tenure as a governor-general, he never lost his national perspective and instinctively approached issues and problems with this perspective foremost; moreover, he spent his last two years at the center of power in Peking. Nevertheless, through most of his career Chang dealt extensively with the growing provincial forces which were such an important part of the national political scene by the time of his death, and his attitudes toward them are of considerable interest. Chang at one time or another addressed himself not only to all other important actors on the political stage, but also to most of the important issues which China as a nation and the Ch'ing dynasty as a political regime faced. His attempts to gain a hearing for his views on various questions, and to deal with opposition from other quarters, shed light on the practical realities of change and reform within the traditional dynastic political structure.

I will make no attempt to idealize Chang either as a visionary or as a politician. He left no profound legacy of ideas or eternal monument of statesmanship, although aspects of his thought and achievements remained visible in later decades. He was not an easy man to work with or for, and he had deep prejudices on some matters which limited his horizons. He tended to be overambitious in setting up new programs and projects, which were left stranded and vulnerable to minor malfunction because of faulty planning. He was not, on the whole, politically courageous, although on some occasions he took action on the basis of moral conviction rather than political expediency. Yet Chang was touched by his times. He felt the pressures of the post-1895 era, and he responded in a substantive way, though always from his vantage point as a national bureaucrat. During these years when reformism was on the rise, Chang articulated his own program of what I would call "bureaucratic reformism." In an increasingly nationalistic age, Chang himself became a proponent of what might be termed "bureaucratic nationalism." How his own variety of these themes differed from that of others of his day will be apparent, I trust, from this study. And the changing nature of Chang's political career between 1895 and 1909 will help in understanding just what was important about this key period of transition in modern China.

One of the particular ways in which this study might be useful is in relation to the process of conceptualization and reevaluation of China's overall fabric of political life in the late nineteenth and early twentieth century, including its local and provincial, as well as its central, elements. In the spectrum from throne down to village, in other words, where was the center of gravity, or the point of equilibrium, and was it changing? In years past, in the initial steps toward dealing with this problem, some scholars tried to outline a phenomenon of "regionalism," which tied the fate of

China's political structure to a constantly declining ability of the central government to shape events from the time of the Taiping Rebellion down to the dynastic collapse of 1911 and on into the succeeding warlord era. This allegedly was due to the manner in which newly established provincial armies, under the direction of governors-general and governors, suppressed the Taiping rebels and in the process acquired prerogatives and power for these provincial officials which Peking was never able to recapture.[1] The warlords, to put it crudely, were the logical outgrowth of Tseng Kuo-fan's Hunan Army.

More recent research has shown this initial theory of regionalism to be unsatisfactory.[2] Governors, and in particular governors-general, did have greater powers within their areas of jurisdiction near the end of the dynasty than, say, in the heyday of the Ch'ien-lung emperor. But these functions were not necessarily a subtraction from the imperial power. They were largely extensions of government authority into new areas of activity (educational, military, and economic enterprises, new tax sources like *likin*). In the process, the chief official in the province tended to concentrate control of these activities in his own hands, largely through a personal and technically unofficial secretariat (*mu-fu*).[3] However, these officials, including powerful ones like Li Hung-chang, Chang Chih-tung, and Yüan Shih-k'ai, operated primarily as extensions of central power, not as foci for decentralizing tendencies; they were under the threat and sometimes the reality of restraint and discipline from the throne, and always submitted to it.[4] Moreover, to the extent that rationalization of activities and extension of control downward from the top of the provincial administration did in fact occur (and the record was spotty at best), there is still no compelling reason why it could not have been put to advantageous use by a central government committed to a clear program of national action.[5]

There were problems encountered in administering new affairs, and some provincial officials were at times undoubtedly hostile or indifferent to the tasks expected of them. But after 1895, when for the first time large numbers of officials both in the provinces and Peking desired some kind of nationwide, coordinated institutional reform, it was not "regionalism," with provincial officials thwarting central directives, which was the main barrier to success. Indeed, there was a fairly wide consensus on the need for an integrated, nationwide approach to the task of increasing national strength. The most intractable problems were rather encountered in deciding which programs to follow, what pieces of the traditional system to keep or discard, and eventually how to integrate into the political system the new forces, especially the provincial gentry and the modern student class, which were emerging rapidly after 1900.

The theory of regionalism, in other words, has misplaced the political center of gravity in traditional China by ascribing the major dynamic of the late Ch'ing political structure to the central-provincial balance, with the top provincial officials standing on the fulcrum. In actuality, throughout the most recent centuries of Chinese history, the crucial dividing line in the political system has not been that between throne and provincial official. In the Ch'ing period, top-ranking provincial officials, and even those down to the district (*hsien*) level, almost invariably came from a select group which Philip Kuhn calls the "national elite."[6] These individuals drew their status from the upper reaches of the national bureaucratic-academic system, supported and maintained by the dynasty, and as a result were characterized both by an instinctive supraprovincial sense of identity and by a set of interprovincial personal friendships and connections which enabled them to cooperate across provincial boundaries. For members of this group, as governors-general and governors, to amass broader functions in the latter nineteenth century by no means removed them from their basic identification with central government interests.

The real political watershed which is relevant for our understanding of the late nineteenth and early twentieth centuries is that between the entire formal apparatus of government and the informal system of local administration below the level of the district magistrate. This informal system depended upon the quasi-governmental functions of the gentry class in local society. A degree-holding individual, when appointed to office, was part of the central apparatus; when not in office, and living at his provincial home, he was a key part of the local system of government, complementary to the central one.[7] The balance between these two separate but vitally linked polities began to change in the late nineteenth century, and by 1911 it had shifted so drastically that the dynasty itself could be sloughed off. The reason for this was the mobilization of the gentry class, in particular at the provincial level, and its willingness to act as an interest group outside the old formal structures linking it to central dynastic authority.

Behind this phenomenon, as Philip Kuhn has so ably shown, were several decades of development and expansion upward from the local level of the militia and tax collection functions of the gentry class.[8] These first began to grow in response to conditions of unrest earlier in the nineteenth century, especially as an adaptation to the challenge of the Taiping Rebellion. But after the suppression of the major rebellions these activities took on a continuity of their own, until by the end of the century they almost could operate on a province-wide basis. Here was an incipient "provincialism" arising from the bottom of the political structure, one which eventually proved far more destructive of central authority than that represented by the power position of top provincial officials. As governor-general of Hupeh and Hunan, Chang Chih-tung found himself dealing with the developing forces which would in 1911 help to topple the dynasty and usher in a period of political particularism based on provincial associations. His own perceptions of these forces, and his attempts as an agent of central authority to deal with them, are, in addition to the elucidation of the broad themes of reformism and nationalism, some of the most important aspects of this study.

Chapter 1

Chang Chih-tung and the Shape of National Politics in the 1890's

In this first chapter I will summarize the major events of Chang's previous political career, and the most important aspects of his power position, on the eve of the Sino-Japanese War of 1894–95. I will also attempt to evaluate the impetus toward political change which was apparent even before the war was concluded, and what this meant for Chang as an official and as a politician. Finally, I will lay out the basic elements of Chang's perceptions, at this early stage, of the relationship between the central government and the elite class of the nation.

Early Career

Chang Chih-tung (1837–1909) was a native of Nan-p'i, Chihli.[1] His career remained in the educational bureaucracy until 1879, with alternating tours of duty in the Hanlin Academy and as educational commissioner in Hupeh and Szechuan. In 1879, he and a number of other fairly young scholars emerged to speak out on national political issues and soon became known as the *ch'ing-liu* party. They were distinguished by their cultural conservatism and belligerence in foreign affairs, and maintained considerable influence, though its real extent is hard to determine, until the end of the war against France in 1884–85.[2] Chang himself was appointed governor of Shansi in 1882. As tensions rose on the Sino-Vietnamese border during 1883–84, he sent in several long, detailed memorials concerning war preparations in the south; in May, 1884, he was made governor-general of Kwangtung and Kwangsi.

As governor-general, he seems to have performed well his job of logistical support of the armies at the front during the Sino-French War of 1884–85; he received explicit imperial praise for these efforts. Visibly affected by the magnitude of the Chinese defeat, especially the debacle at Foochow harbor where the southern fleet was almost entirely destroyed, Chang joined the ranks of provincial "self-strengtheners" like Li Hung-chang for the rest of his tenure at Canton. He displayed great energy and perseverance in establishing new military forces and educational institutions around Canton. He also began the development of industrial installations such as a new arsenal, an ironworks, a cotton mill, and a modern mint. These enterprises and projects, in their variety and scope, altogether constituted an extremely ambitious program which foreshadowed many of the goals of the reforms of the late 1890's.[3] Just as these industrial projects were getting underway, however, Chang found himself transferred to the governor-generalship of Hupeh and Hunan in August, 1889.

The circumstances of his transfer had to do with the politics of the abortive Tientsin-Peking Railroad project sponsored by Li Hung-chang. Chang suggested a great interior trunk line from Peking to Hankow as an alternative to Li's plan, and he was ostensibly sent to Hupeh to administer its construction.[4] The effects of his move, however, were deeply felt by the institutions and enterprises which he had been developing at Canton during the late 1880's. Those left behind did not prosper under the hand of Chang's successor, Li Han-chang, and especially not during the term of office of Kang-i, a reactionary Manchu, as governor of Kwangtung in the early 1890's.[5] Those projects which were transferred to Hupeh, partly because of Li Han-chang's indifference to their fate, included the ironworks, the arsenal, and the textile mill. These enterprises undoubtedly also suffered because of the difficulties and delays Chang found in relocating them, providing them with new sources of capital, and in some cases finding new management personnel. Viewed broadly, the inefficiencies and drawbacks of provincially based "self-strengthening" efforts, in the absence of overall national planning, coordination, and mobilization of resources, are clearly shown by the transfer of Chang from Canton to the Wuhan cities in 1889.

Chang's activities in Hupeh for the first few years consisted largely in establishing the three enterprises which he had brought with him from Canton. This he did manage to do before the Sino-Japanese War began in 1894, scraping together financing wherever he could and often using members of his own secretariat as supervisors or administrators. In November, 1892, the Hupeh Textile Mill started production. Just a year later, Chang was able to report the completion of the Hanyang Arsenal, which was located on the same site as the Hanyang Ironworks. The Hanyang Ironworks, largest and most ambitious of these enterprises, had a poorer record. Its first blast furnace was started up in June, 1894, but it was shut down in November and not fired again until late 1895.[6]

More important than these activities, for the purposes of this study, is consideration of the manner in which Chang Chih-tung operated in the overall political system of the day. While he was at Canton in the 1880's, Chang more than once clashed with the lower levels of the provincial administration and with the local gentry class which was often intimately associated with local officials. He dealt harshly with excessive corruption, and he did not hesitate to pressure local officials and gentry for contributions to his educational, military, or industrial projects. Other gentry grievances against Chang, besides these forced "contributions," included resentment of his unceasing efforts to assess full land taxes on reclaimed delta and riverbank property that had long escaped the proper levies. There is some evidence that only strong and consistent support from the court, then dominated by the Empress Dowager Tz'u-hsi, permitted Chang to retain his effectiveness in the face of local resistance to his endeavors. At one point, chafing under the demands put upon them to pay the province's debts from the war with France, the local officials and gentry assiduously circulated vicious rumors of Chang's incompetence. Even the governor lined up against Chang, and in a test of strength, the governor was removed by the throne.[7]

Chang's relationship with Tz'u-hsi was solid and of long standing. It began in 1863, when she personally advanced his rank in the palace examination because she liked his essay; Chang thus finished almost at the top of his *chin-shih* class. In the late 1870's, the members of the *ch'ing-liu* group supported Tz'u-hsi with their literary and argumentative skills when she was under attack for the crude tactics employed in installing the infant Kuang-hsü emperor, her nephew, on the throne. Chang was a major beneficiary of this support; he received several honors and promotions between 1880 and 1882, and in the latter year he was made governor of Shansi.[8] When Chang was promoted to be governor-general at Canton in 1884, his appointment and those of others favored by the empress dowager were announced on the same day that Prince Kung and his followers were purged from the Tsungli yamen; this consolidated Tz'u-hsi's political position at the time.[9]

Despite Chang's strong ties to Tz'u-hsi, in March, 1889, there occurred an important change in his relationship (and that of others as well) to the throne. At that time the empress dowager formally turned over ultimate state authority to the Kuang-hsü emperor, and "retired" to the Summer Palace outside of Peking. Though she continued to maintain general surveillance of state affairs, and probably made the final decision on many important matters, the young emperor, then only seventeen years old, became for the first time a significant factor on the political scene. Chang Chih-tung had no direct ties with Kuang-hsü. Moreover, it soon became clear that Weng T'ung-ho, the emperor's tutor and by all accounts his trusted friend, now was determined to play an important role in national politics. As Chang became involved in court politics again through the railroad dispute in 1889, Weng began to view him as a rival. There was distinct harassment of Chang during the last few months at his Canton post, much of it originating in the Board of Revenue, of which Weng was president.[10] Thus it may be that in the early 1890's, Chang was somewhat less than sure of his position vis-à-vis the throne. He had never had an audience with the young emperor, and the emperor's closest adviser seemed unfriendly toward him.

On the eve of the Sino-Japanese War, therefore, Chang was an important provincial official with a good record of diligent service. He was deeply engaged in provincially based enterprises, but for purposes which would benefit the dynasty and nation as a whole. He functioned as an integral part of the central government administration, he was sensitive to power constellations in Peking, and he depended upon his ties to the throne. However, these ties were now somewhat ambiguous because of the duality of power between the empress dowager and the emperor.

The Sino-Japanese War

It is universally recognized that the Sino-Japanese War of 1894–95 was one of the major turning points in the history of modern East Asian international relations. The war resulted in significant changes on the Chinese domestic political scene as well. While the war and the trauma of defeat occasioned the humiliation of Li Hung-chang and the broad power position he had long held in the north, it resulted in a somewhat more integrated and unified approach to the problems of defense and national development in the Yangtze Valley. Moreover, Chang Chih-tung himself emerged from the war as perhaps the most important of provincial officials.

At the beginning of the war in August, 1894, Chang was ordered to cooperate with the officials of the other Yangtze provinces for general defense measures, and on August 10 he sent Ch'en Pao-chen, the Hupeh judicial commissioner, to Nanking to discuss joint action. Chang personally inspected local river defenses and sent the provincial commander Wu Feng-kuei north to Tientsin with three battalions and necessary supplies.[11]

Chang also found time to send advice on the conduct of the war to Peking and to harass Li Hung-chang's headquarters at Tientsin with questions. According to one account, this was the reason for an edict of October 8, 1894, which summoned Chang to Peking for an audience with the emperor; Hupeh governor T'an Chi-hsün was temporarily to take over his duties.[12] According to his foremost biographer, Chang then went into a frenzy of activity, trying to complete arrangements for the transport and supply of the Hu-kuang troops heading north, and to secure imperial assurance of continued expansion and development of all his industrial projects in Hupeh before his departure.[13] As a result, he fell ill and was not able to go to Peking immediately. On November 1, he received an edict again ordering him north, but the court then suddenly changed its mind, informing Chang on November 2 that Liu K'un-i, governor-general at Nanking, was to come instead; Chang was then ordered to Nanking to replace Liu.[14] He left Wuchang on November 5 and arrived in Nanking on the eighth.

The sudden reversal of November 2, ordering Chang to Nanking instead of to Peking, invites speculation as to a power shift in

Peking at this time. On the same day, the Supervisorate of Military Affairs (Tu-pan chün-wu ch'u), with special war planning duties, was established, and several other important personnel changes were decreed. Tz'u-hsi seems to have reentered active politics at about this time; she had a number of audiences in the last days of October, ostensibly concerning her approaching sixtieth birthday celebrations.[15]

If the empress dowager did reassert some control over court policy in early November, 1894, it is possible that Chang's move to Nanking saved him from being shunted off into a meaningless advisory position in Peking at a time when Li Hung-chang was still dominant in the north. At any rate, he was now made the most important official in central China. In addition to all the duties with which he was entrusted as part of the Liang-chiang governor-generalship, he was permitted by a special edict to retain complete control over his modern enterprises back in Hupeh; his own appointees were to remain on the job at the ironworks, the arsenal, and the textile mill.[16] Later in the fall, Chang received authority to bring provincial officials in Chekiang, Fukien, and Taiwan into line with coordinated regional defense measures. He was also given permission to take loans from native merchants for defense expenditures, and his own yamen acted as a purchasing office for arms and munitions bought abroad and sent to the armies in the north.[17]

Chang's ascent in politics did not escape contemporary observers. The rapid fall from power of Li Hung-chang after so many years as China's foremost official and statesman led some foreigners to look to Chang Chih-tung, who had escaped direct involvement in the humiliations of the war, as the rising power of the future.[18] For example, after Chang had sounded out Jardine, Matheson and Co. early in 1895 about a loan for China, William Keswick, Jardine's strategist, decided that Chang and a "provincial faction" would have control over the disposition of any postwar loans for indemnity payments or developing projects. Scorning the example of the Hong Kong and Shanghai Bank, which made its contacts in Peking, Keswick concluded in late April that "so long as Chang Chih-tung's party are so powerful it seems impossible that any big consolidated loan will be arranged in Peking."[19]

Keswick was wrong. There was no "provincial faction," let

alone one dominated by Chang Chih-tung. The political center of gravity was still in Peking, as events between 1895 and 1900 would show. Chang looked important, and he was—even more so after the war than before—but not because he had some sort of power base beyond the reach of the central government. Rather, he was developing the ability and the prestige to move from the position of a provincially based "self-strengthener" to that of a promoter of reform on a broad national resource base.

In Canton, during the 1880's, Chang had already grasped the interconnected nature of modern industrial, military, and educational systems. But then, and in Hupeh during the early 1890's, his position in the political system permitted him to operate only in his own jurisdiction. Cooperation with other areas was almost impossible considering the relative indifference of the court, which would have to play a key role in coordinating regional actions.

During the war, Chang at last had an opportunity to take steps toward a more broadly based, interregional program of national development. He transferred more than half a million taels of Liang-chiang defense funds to the Hanyang Ironworks during the war, and he made an effort to have the Kiangnan Arsenal moved from its vulnerable Shanghai location inland, preferably to Hupeh.[20] From the end of the war until he returned to Hupeh in early 1896, he also pressed for the buildup of a southern navy, new army units, and coordinated defense and supply measures all along the Yangtze. He started several new schools in Nanking, similar to those he had already founded and would continue to establish in Hupeh.[21] He advocated a national postal system and promoted a nationwide railroad system, including the Peking-Hankow line, a line from Peking through Tientsin into Manchuria, and a network of lines in the Yangtze delta which would connect Shanghai, Soochow, Nanking, and Hangchow.[22] All these activities pointed Chang in the direction that many other thoughtful postwar reformers would go.

Unfortunately, many of the projects which Chang began in Nanking were still in the formative stage when he was removed from their direct supervision. At the end of February, 1896, Liu K'un-i took up his former post at Nanking, and Chang returned to Wuchang. There is no evidence that Liu purposely undercut more than one of the endeavors that Chang had begun in the Liang-chiang area, but most deteriorated from neglect.[23] The fate of the modern army units that Chang had formed in Nanking immediately after the war is an indication of the ease with which worthwhile projects declined into stagnation under the traditional fragmented system of provincial administration. These thirteen modern battalions, called the "Self-Strengthening Army" (Tzu-ch'iang chün), consisted of high quality, well-paid, perhaps largely literate, recruits, trained and partly officered by thirty-five Germans. Chang hoped to expand this force from three thousand to ten thousand men, and expended considerable effort to find provincial sources of financing for the larger force. Although Liu was directed to continue to develop the Tzu-ch'iang chün upon his return to Nanking, instead he tried to persuade Chang to take the troops back to Hupeh with him. This Chang could not do, because there was no source of funds for them there. The brigade remained in Liang-chiang, but because of friction between these troops and Liu's old fashioned Hunan forces, Liu soon transferred the brigade to Woosung, where it sat unused.[24]

Although many of his ideas were only partially implemented, Chang had still displayed an ability to plan far reaching reforms during his short Nanking tenure, and this enhanced his political standing. But even more important than his vision and his abilities was the imperial support he had received, and continued to enjoy. In February, 1895, the emperor issued an edict explicitly on behalf of Tz'u-hsi, praising Chang for his past diligence, encouraging him to speak out unhesitatingly on matters of national importance, and confirming his broad powers in the south. Chang thus not only proceeded with confidence on his many regional projects in the Yangtze Valley, but he freely bombarded the court with his rather belligerent opinions on the armistice and treaty with Japan, relations with other foreign powers, an alliance with Russia, and other such topics.[25] He probably overdid it. Sometime in the seventh month (August 20–September 18) of 1895, he received an imperial rebuke; an edict complained about the volume and verbosity of his recent telegraphed memorials, and told him to be more concise in the future.[26]

This apparent partial withdrawal of imperial support may have been reflected in the events of the next few months. Many of Chang's projects continued to be viewed with favor, but not all. His attempt to relocate, or at least reform, the Kiangnan Arsenal was eventually thwarted entirely after he left Nanking.[27] More important, his urgent pleas to keep the Hanyang Ironworks under government management and provide it with the capital it needed were denied. After some complaints about the lack of results after so many years of effort and expenses, a series of edicts in late 1895 and early 1896 absolutely refused any further government funding and ordered Chang to arrange the transfer of the ironworks to private investors. This he did in the spring of 1896, reluctantly and on fairly disadvantageous terms; Sheng Hsüan-huai took over as director of the now private concern in May.[28]

Nevertheless, Chang's position within the central government system remained strong. No provincial official could get everything he wanted from Peking, and occasional inconsistencies in support from the throne were, again, a possible consequence of the duality of power between the emperor and the empress dowager at the center. Chang still saw himself as an obedient part of the central apparatus and directed his postwar efforts for reform through the system of which he was a part. What is more important, he assumed that, in producing policy and action results, there was no alternative to operating within that high level matrix of throne and "national bureaucrats," or "national elite." It was unthinkable for initiatives to come from elsewhere.

Chang and the Provincial Gentry Class

The nature of the relationship between the imperial official and the local elite is amply illustrated by Chang Chih-tung's career before 1895. Chang needed the cooperation of the local gentry to carry out even the most basic functions of administration. He needed them still more to provide the resources for the various local projects he tried to encourage in Canton and Hupeh. Chang usually got from them the cooperation and financial commitments he sought, but only by the most intensive persuasion and browbeating. Moreover, their tendency to evade their tax or investment obligations, and their occasional attempts to undercut him by appealing to friends in other sectors of the bureaucracy, caused Chang to mistrust the provincial gentry. He viewed them more as adversaries than as allies in government.

I have mentioned the difficulties Chang encountered in the 1880's in imposing long-evaded land taxes on the Cantonese gentry, and the reluctance of those with wealth to subscribe to the industrial projects promoted by Chang in Canton. One way in which Chang was able to scrape together the capital to finance his enterprises in Canton was officially to license some *wei-hsing* lottery brokers, then demand that these brokers buy shares in the enterprises, on threat of loss of their licenses.[29] He raised hundreds of thousands of taels in this manner in 1888 and 1889, with more pledged for the future. On the strength of these commitments, he ordered large quantities of equipment from abroad for the cotton mill and the ironworks he was promoting. But after Chang was transferred to Wuchang in 1889, the lottery tycoons simply reneged on their pledged subscriptions to both enterprises. Chang was powerless to compel them to pay up, and the loss of capital was a severe blow to the fledgling industries, especially the ironworks.[30] From this time on Chang would be extremely suspicious of the financial commitments of gentry and merchant groups, even when they seemed to be given freely, as they would be in the enthusiasm of the rights recovery movement after 1900.

After his transfer to Wuchang in 1889, Chang found that the Hupeh gentry class was no less difficult to manage than that of Kwangtung had been. Two of his most precious educational projects of the early 1890's were the Liang-Hu Academy and the Self-Strengthening School (Tzu-ch'iang hsüeh-t'ang), founded in 1890 and 1893, respectively. To raise the money for these institutions, Chang put pressure on the Wuchang commercial community, especially the tea merchants, who had been getting by more lightly than their colleagues dealing in salt and other commodities. Chang found that the tea merchants would be "pleased and happy" to pay a new special levy for the academy, and their money was probably partially behind the Self-Strengthening School as well.[31]

The tea merchants, and others who had felt Chang's powers of persuasion when he needed some funds for one of his projects, were not without recourse. They had ties with the Hupeh gentry class of scholars and landowners, who in turn had contacts throughout the imperial bureaucracy. Strings were pulled in Peking, memorials were generated, and the emperor was informed that Chang was oppressing the tea merchants and ruining tea sales. Chang was forced to reduce the tea levy by one third in 1891, and after more lobbying behind the scenes in 1892, he had to abolish the special tea tax altogether.[32]

Even short of this kind of political power play to bypass Chang, influential locals were not without means of seriously embarrassing him. This was done by way of anonymous public placards. Within several months of his arrival in Wuchang, placards not only attacked various of Chang's development schemes, but also ridiculed his personal appearance and accused him of licentious and immoral behavior. Perhaps most significantly, he was accused of employing people in his *mu-fu* who did not follow "the traditions of Chinese officialdom," and was denounced for not giving local scholars their usual gratuities for essays and petitions.[33] Chang's lack of rapport with the local gentry is, I think, evident in some of these charges against him.

Despite the occasional placarding and the thwarting of his tea tax scheme, there was only one serious political attack mounted against Chang during his first five years in Wuchang. Local Hupeh gentry, through their fellow provincials in Peking, seem to have inspired a personal assault on Chang which took the form of a memorial of impeachment submitted by Hsü Chih-hsiang of the Grand Court of Revision on March 12, 1893.[34] Hsü indicted Chang for inefficiency, bad manners, and corruption, first at Canton and now at Wuchang. He also accused Wang Chih-ch'un, Hupeh treasurer, former Kwangtung judicial commissioner and ally of Chang in both places, of using coercive administrative tactics. Finally, Hsü charged Chao Feng-ch'ang, a member of Chang's staff in Wuchang, with slander.[35]

Li Han-chang at Canton and Liu K'un-i, Liang-chiang governor-general at Nanking, were ordered to investigate these charges. Li cleared Chang and Wang of all charges of misdeeds at Canton. Liu sent agents to investigate matters in Hupeh, after which he, too, exonerated them both. Liu did censure Chao Feng-ch'ang, however, and suggested that he be removed from his duties and sent to his home district. The final edict settling the case reflected these findings and also suggested that in the future Chang should try harder to control his subordinates. Thus, although he was more or less fully acquitted, Chang did have to undergo the minor humiliation of an investigation by his peers and to endure a mild reprimand from the throne. The provincial economic and political interest groups of gentry and merchants were not able to do Chang mortal harm, judging by his experiences in Canton and Wuchang, but they were able to retaliate against his encroachments on their prerogatives, sometimes effectively.

The result of Chang's experiences with the provincial elite class before 1895 was to give him a deeply felt prejudice against it. He had little faith in local gentry and merchant financial resources, and until the end of his life he tried to capitalize major industrial projects through the central government, even preferring a foreign loan to dependence on the whim and fortunes of wealthy locals. He also saw the provincial gentry as the enemy of effective central administration. They tried to thwart his campaigns against corruption and tax evasion and always tended to aggrandize their own power if they could, at the expense of the central government.

The virulence of Chang's opposition to the concept of *min-ch'üan,* or "people's rights" in the late 1890's and after, undoubtedly stemmed partly from his mistrust of the gentry. Chang knew that the local elite groups were an indispensable part of government administration. He saw, correctly, that constitutionalism and representative institutions would serve to give the elite class a more formal, and therefore more secure, place in the political system. But he also suspected that the gentry would use this enhanced power position for their own local interests, not those of the dynasty. This duality of grudging acceptance of the gentry's role and constant suspicion of their ultimate trustworthiness characterized Chang for the remainder of his career.

Chapter 2

The Reform Movement within the Bureaucracy after 1895

The shock of China's humiliating defeat at the hands of the long despised Japanese reverberated throughout the entire official class. Its impact was intensified by the renewed demands put upon China by the Western Powers for economic development rights and other imperialistic privileges after 1895. In many ways, the response of officialdom to this challenge was unanimous. All agreed that China had to make more strenuous efforts than in the past to attain the goals of "rich country, strong army" (*fu-kuo ch'iang-ping*). In order to stand up to the Powers, to retain her self-respect, and indeed to ensure her very existence, China had to go further than ever before in changing her traditional ways.

Before the Sino-Japanese War, institutional reform in general had been the concern of only a few isolated individuals in the government. Political reform ideas were seen even less often, and only on the outer fringes of the bureaucracy.[1] After the war, changes in political structures, even constitutional democracy and parliamentary systems, were discussed openly; eventually, after 1900, significant changes would actually be made. But perhaps more important in the short run was simply the rapid growth of informed discussion and activity within the bureaucratic elite itself after the war. Regardless of the content of the debate over any particular issue, the manner in which people organized themselves and publicized their views in itself constituted a new "politicization" of the elite, and thus an important watershed in modern Chinese history.

The Tide of Enthusiasm for Reform

It was an indication of the times that in the spring of 1895, soon after the humiliating terms imposed upon China by Japan in the Treaty of Shimonoseki became known, candidates for the metropolitan examination organized themselves to sign petitions and hold mass meetings in Peking. They protested the terms of the treaty and advocated continuation of the war, removal of the capital farther inland, and institutional reform to improve the nation's strength. They echoed the sentiments of many in the bureaucracy who wanted to continue resistance, including Chang Chih-tung.[2]

Soon afterward, in the early summer of 1895, K'ang Yu-wei, one of the prime organizers of the spring movement and a talented though controversial Cantonese scholar, began the daily newssheet called for most of its short life the *Chung-wai chi-wen* (News from China and abroad). The paper was printed and distributed by one of the "Peking Gazette" (*Ching-pao*) firms in the capital, and it advocated new departures in internal reforms.[3]

By late August, enough officials in Peking were familiar with the new reform ideas in the air for K'ang and Ch'en Chih to hold a large dinner party at which the Ch'iang-hsüeh hui (Society to Study Strengthening), devoted to promotion of public discussion and publications on reform issues, was established. Within a short time, the society had attracted support from many sectors and counted among its members two grand councillors, four Hanlin compilers, three governors-general, two military commanders, and three foreign missionaries; even the United States and British ministers were involved to some degree.[4]

In 1896, the new currents which had first found their outlet in Peking began to appear elsewhere throughout the country. There were concerned, capable young gentry members, some of them returned veterans of the Peking spring campaign against the treaty with Japan, in or near cosmopolitan places such as Canton and Shanghai. They, and many of their elders, were eager to debate China's future. A responsive chord was touched in more remote areas of the country as well. By 1898, the new newspapers, journals, schools, and study societies all over the country numbered in the dozens.[5]

In January, 1896, the Peking Ch'iang-hsüeh hui, and the organ closely associated with it, the *Chung-wai chi-wen,* were closed down. Contrary to Liang Ch'i-ch'ao's implications, this action does not seem to have been a simple attempt by the government to suppress public discussion of unwelcome issues. Rather, the record of events suggests that the society and the newssheet went under in the crossfire of partisan political infighting between individuals and cliques in the never ending political wars of the court. Without going into detail, it should be noted that some Ch'iang-hsüeh hui members, especially Wen T'ing-shih, had gone out of their way to insult Li Hung-chang, who despite his disgrace was by no means powerless after the war. Li had even been denied membership in the society when he applied. K'ang Yu-wei had also had personal quarrels with more conservative individuals in the society.[6] Before the Peking group was disbanded, a Shanghai branch of the Ch'iang-hsüeh hui had been established, with participants from throughout the lower Yangtze area and its own daily paper, the *Ch'iang-hsüeh pao.*[7] It also had to be dissolved when the parent organization in Peking came under attack.

Yet, after January, 1896, there was very little in the way of central government attempts to prohibit other societies and journals from operation until 1898. It was difficult for the government, perhaps still embarrassed from its inept performance in the war, to criticize those who claimed the shield of patriotism. Discussion of reforms to save the nation and the dynasty, to enrich China, and to defend her from predatory foreigners undoubtedly made many around the court, especially Manchus, uneasy. But they were hardly in a position to cavil, with reform advocates sprinkled liberally through the whole government structure. In Peking, within two months after the Ch'iang-hsüeh hui had been suppressed, the entreaties of several high officials and of the Tsungli yamen resulted in a new organization, the Kuan-shu chü (Officials' Bookstore), to take its place.[8]

An obvious index to the widespread interest in change was the growing popularity of reform writings of various kinds. These included several updated versions of the famous collection on "statecraft" of the early nineteenth century, *Huang-ch'ao ching-shih wen-pien.* Writings of missionaries such as Timothy Richard and

Young J. Allen, and their Chinese journal *Wan-kuo kung-pao* (The Review of the Times), were read by many high officials.[9] An example of an especially diverse collection of reform writings was one for which Chang Chih-tung wrote a preface in the late summer of 1895. This was entitled *P'u-t'ien chung-fen chi* (Loyal rage of the whole nation), and was edited by K'ung Kuang-te (under the pseudonym Lü Yang-sheng), who had been on the staff of the Manchu general at Foochow during the Sino-Japanese War.[10]

A striking characteristic of all these organizing and publishing activities is the extent of acceptance they were accorded within the bureaucracy and those close to it. Many incumbent Chinese officials, as well as the young reformers seeking to influence them, were active in one way or another, and a surprisingly broad spectrum of political opinion was expressed. Items in the larger collections of reform writings, for example, ranged from essays by Tseng Kuo-fan and Feng Kuei-fen in the 1860's to very recent pieces by K'ang Yu-wei. Almost everyone had some favorite complaint or idea to air, although Manchu officials were usually conspicuous by their lack of participation.

Accordingly, it is difficult to speak of specific groups operating within this broad movement in the immediate postward period, during late 1895 and 1896. There were different degrees of agreement between individuals on what kind and how much reform was needed in certain areas, not a division into definable groups which held together on all issues. Everyone could agree on the magic goal of *fu-kuo ch'iang-ping,* and on the need to throw off the foreign yoke. Both those who wanted to revitalize old institutions and those who wanted to create new ones could agree on the obvious failure of self-strengthening; both also tended to have little use for Li Hung-chang, who now symbolized the inadequacies of pre-1895 reforms.

The ideological affinities between seemingly disparate elements on the postwar scene are perhaps most apparent in discussion of foreign affairs. The rather passive approach to foreign policy which had characterized most officials dealing with it in previous decades was now thoroughly discredited, providing an opportunity for both traditional and modern critics to offer their favorite prescriptions as alternatives.[11] Ideas stemming from the *ch'ing-i* tradition of the late

1870's and 1880's, itself heir to a strain of militant conservatism with deep roots in Chinese history and emphasizing unity of the ruler and the people, as well as moral fervor, again became current.[12] The more novel ideas of K'ang Yu-wei expanded the scope of traditional Confucianism to include all of modern civilization and provided for the wholesale restructuring of most Chinese political, social, and economic institutions. This approach drew the allegiance of many young political activists like Liang Ch'i-ch'ao.

There were some interesting ideological similarities between these two critiques of China's predicament after 1895. Despite important differences, both the old *ch'ing-i* militant conservatives and the more modern reformers like K'ang and Liang stressed the need for a fully aroused and internally united China. It was especially important to keep open lines of communication between the throne and loyal officials, though the support of all subjects should be mobilized. Both groups also showed a sense of extreme crisis, manifested in fervent emotional rhetoric. In many ways, therefore, the post-1895 nationalistic reformers drew upon parts of traditional ideology.[13]

There was in fact much more than an ideological link between new reformers and old *ch'ing-i* adherents. Richard Howard and John Schrecker have shown that there were concrete relationships between several members of the militant *ch'ing-liu* group of the 1880's and K'ang Yu-wei, even before 1890.[14] Some of these men were instrumental in the early success and impact of the Ch'iang-hsüeh hui in Peking in late 1895. Thus both in ideology and in personnel, there was a broad foundation for advocacy of reform in the postwar period, one which at first muted the differences between those who wanted to cling to a refurbished tradition and those who wanted to dismantle the old system.

The crucial importance of these developments in the immediate postwar period lies in the fact that a debate had been launched within the scholar-official class that had far deeper implications than did the traditional debates over varieties of Confucianism and practical reforms. These traditional, and quite acceptable, differences of opinion aired among literati and officials never questioned the central values or institutions of the imperial Confucian state itself. It would soon become apparent, however, that some of those in the new debate did question those values and institutions, and this in turn would cause a deep split in the ranks of the scholar-official class, hitherto united on basics.[15] Moreover, by 1898 the debate would spill out of the boundaries that formerly restricted serious policy discussion to the ranks of the bureaucracy and those upper, or national, gentry closely associated with practicing officials.[16]

In effect, then, new conditions of political life were created in China within a fairly short period of time. As study societies and publishing ventures of various kinds became commonly accepted means of raising and discussing issues, they eventually worked to set free forces which would operate entirely outside the traditional political system and even help to destroy it. But for some time their effect remained mainly in and around the bureaucracy itself. Old reformers and new ones, both spurred by a kind of "bureaucratic nationalism," took advantage of the new conditions to become more active politically within the traditional system, not yet seeking to operate outside it.

The Role of Chang Chih-tung

Probably more than anyone else at the time, Chang Chih-tung stood at the center of the postwar reform currents. He was a solid and influential member of the established bureaucracy. Although his activities had begun to take on national significance as his influence spread during the Sino-Japanese War, the projects he promoted in Nanking and after his return to Hupeh in early 1896 were still in the general mold of the provincial "self-strengthening" which had proved inadequate to defend China. On the other hand, Chang had himself been an important member of the original *ch'ing-liu* group of the late 1870's and 1880's. Moreover, he had maintained close ties with several other members and associates of the group who retained their preference for a militant but traditional solution to China's problems. Finally, Chang developed close and sympathetic ties with several of the individuals and organizations following the general leadership of K'ang Yu-wei; some of these came to advocate drastic reform of all Chinese institutions.

Chang kept many links to his old comrades of the *ch'ing-liu* group. The oldest surviving member of the original band was Li Hung-tsao, who was at the very top of the Peking power structure after the war. Li was a grand councillor, president of the Board of Civil Office, an assistant grand secretary, and also a member of the Tsungli yamen until his death in 1897. Li was a member of the Peking Ch'iang-hsüeh hui, and his then number one disciple, Chang Hsiao-ch'ien, was the society's titular president. Li Hung-tsao and Chang Chih-tung remained on good terms over the years, and Chang greatly mourned the old man's passing in 1897.[17] Two other *ch'ing-liu* associates, Ch'en Pao-ch'en and Liang Ting-fen, had remained very close to Chang, both as members of his *mu-fu;* Liang headed various academies under Chang at Canton, Nanking, and Wuchang. The names of Ch'en, Liang, and Huang T'i-fang, yet another original *ch'ing-liu* member, were among the fifteen which Chang submitted in August, 1895, in response to an imperial request for recommendations of talented men for office.[18]

The relationships between Chang Chih-tung and that part of the reform movement dominated by K'ang Yu-wei can be amply documented. In 1886, when thinking of establishing a translation bureau at Canton, Chang asked K'ang Yu-wei and Wen T'ing-shih to plan it; soon thereafter he invited K'ang to teach in two different Canton academies.[19] In the spring of 1895 K'ang reciprocated this indication of respect when in the famous "petition of the degree candidates" he named Chang as one of only two officials of the nation who were competent and reliable.[20] Chang and the other official mentioned, Li Ping-heng, had been most outspoken in their protests against concluding peace with Japan, thus prompting K'ang's admiration.[21] At about this same time, T'an Ssu-t'ung, to be the most radical of the "six martyrs" of 1898, also expressed great hope and faith in Chang Chih-tung in a letter to a friend.[22]

In the summer of 1895, Chang Chih-tung's son Chang Ch'üan was in Peking, having just received his *chin-shih* degree in the spring. Not only was Chang Ch'üan one of the charter members of the Ch'iang-hsüeh hui, but he lent personal financial help to K'ang to defray the costs of printing the *Chung-wai chi-wen.* Chang Chih-tung himself contributed five thousand taels to the Peking society, as did his fellow governors-general Wang Wen-shao of Chihli and

Liu K'un-i of Liang-chiang.[23] Chang was seemingly even closer to the group which participated in the Shanghai branch of the Ch'iang-hsüeh hui, organized at the end of 1895. Out of one list of twenty-four members of the Shanghai branch, Chang had a definitely positive link with at least eleven of them, and he probably had a high regard for several more. He also contributed 1,500 taels to the Shanghai organization.[24]

Thus Chang's relationship with reform groups was extensive. But it was also ambiguous, and the ambiguity was nowhere more apparent than in Chang's connections with K'ang Yu-wei personally in 1895. K'ang left Peking in October, after coming under increasingly heavy political fire in the opening rounds of the controversy over the Ch'iang-hsüeh hui. He apparently went directly to Nanking, arriving on November 1; it is conceivable that he was referred by his friend Chang Ch'üan, Chang Chih-tung's son, for it seems to have been K'ang's major purpose in going to Nanking to consult with Chang, still the temporary governor-general there.[25]

K'ang later said that he remained in Nanking for more than twenty days and discussed the proposed Shanghai branch of the Ch'iang-hsüeh hui with Chang Chih-tung, Liang Ting-fen, and Huang Shao-chi. Moreover, he claimed to have gained Chang's support for the venture, a claim which seems reasonable in view of Chang's financial contribution of 1,500 taels. K'ang's account goes on to assert that a few weeks later, when he was in Shanghai actually engaged in organizing the branch society of the Ch'iang-hsüeh hui, Chang Chih-tung suddenly withdrew his support and urgently advised K'ang not to proceed further with it. K'ang's description of these events strongly implies political expediency and betrayal on Chang's part.[26]

K'ang's account of these events may be basically true, and does seem to be corroborated by a piece of evidence from another source. In the 1895 collection of reform writings entitled *P'u-t'ien chung-fen chi,* there are included a preface (*hsü*), regulations (*chang-ch'eng*), and a postface (*hou-hsü*) to the Shanghai branch of the Ch'iang-hsüeh hui; the preface is written by Chang Chih-tung, the postface by K'ang Yu-wei.[27] It seems likely that K'ang himself wrote up all these organizational documents while visiting Chang in Nanking and gained Chang's agreement to sign his own name to the preface.[28] K'ang often dashed off memorials and essays for other, more strategically placed men to sign. Later, Chang finally made up his mind not to help sponsor K'ang's Shanghai project after all and withdrew his support. In the meantime, however, the *P'u-t'ien chung-fen chi* collection had been published, with Chang's name on the preface to the regulations.

Why would Chang be so inconstant in his support for K'ang? It is possible, of course, that Chang's motives were entirely political in nature, as K'ang implies. Chang could easily have been warned of the changing political winds in Peking by his son, who was still there, and he may have simply wanted to dissociate himself from K'ang before the impending suppression of the Ch'iang-hsüeh hui. Yet this is only part of the story, and perhaps the lesser part. Chang unquestionably had deep philosophical and scholarly differences with K'ang which made it very difficult for the two to cooperate directly.

Chang was, all in all, a fairly orthodox Neo-Confucian when it came to doctrine and ideology. He simply could not abide K'ang's insistence on viewing Confucius as a "reformer" by using the "new text" school's approach to the classics. These doctrinal contortions in effect expanded to infinity the limits to permissible change within the traditional value system. As K'ang himself admitted, Chang tried hard during their Nanking meetings in November, 1895, to persuade him to give up these views.[29] Thus Chang's withdrawal of support from the Shanghai branch of the Ch'iang-hsüeh hui had principles as well as politics behind it, although the two elements are difficult to separate.

In the future, Chang never would recommend K'ang Yu-wei for official employment, although he recommended many other activist reformers, for example Liang Ch'i-ch'ao. K'ang's most famous tract, "Study of Confucius as a Reformer" (*K'ung-tzu kai-chih k'ao*), on which he had worked during most of the 1890's, was not finally published until late 1897, but the basic concepts of his political thought were already becoming well known by the winter of 1895–96. Chang wanted no part of them.

And yet, as I have indicated, Chang was very close to the most vigorous of the postwar reform organizations, in which K'ang Yu-wei played a leading part. Even after his break with K'ang,

Chang stood firmly behind the journal *Shih-wu pao* (The Chinese Progress), which in the summer of 1896 evolved out of the remains of the Shanghai branch of the Ch'iang-hsüeh hui, suppressed early in the year. K'ang was back in Canton by this time, and the reorganization of the society into the *Shih-wu pao* in Shanghai was mainly carried out by Liang Ch'i-ch'ao and Wang K'ang-nien, who became editor and business manager, respectively. The first issue of the new publication, which came out every ten days, appeared in August, 1896.[30] Chang was fairly close to Wang K'ang-nien, having formerly hired him to tutor his grandsons in Canton and later to teach in the Liang-Hu Academy in Wuchang. And Chang was so impressed with the manner in which Liang edited the new paper that he tried to bring him to Hupeh as a member of his own staff in late 1896 or early 1897.[31]

Chang's general ideas on the value and function of newspapers and journals of opinion in Chinese political life at this time were probably very close to those of Liang Ch'i-ch'ao. Both saw the press operating to strengthen the nation by spreading news and ideas among the literate population. Liang thought in 1896 that newspapers should strive to "cause readers to give thought to purging the nation of its humiliations," and he hoped to promote interregional communication and national solidarity through the press. In his famous tract *Ch'üan-hsüeh p'ien* (An exhortation to learn), written in early 1898, Chang said, "The chief value of the newspaper to the people and empire is publicity concerning their own defects."[32]

Chang probably provided considerable direct financial support for the *Shih-wu pao,* and definitely helped it to boost circulation in the Yangtze region. In September, 1896, only about a month after publication began, Chang directed all officials and teachers in Hupeh to read the paper, and he described it in glowing terms. He arranged for a subscription to be given every civil and military yamen, every bureau (*chü*), and every academy and school in the province. Moreover, the provincial government paid the full cost for the total of 288 subscriptions.[33] Chang's example was soon followed by others in late 1896 and 1897, including Governor Liao Shou-feng of Chekiang, Governor Ch'en Pao-chen of Hunan, and Wang Hsien-ch'ien, head of the Yüeh-lu Academy in Hunan; the scale of their subscription support was nowhere near that of Chang, however.[34]

Growing Divisions in the Reform Movement: Chang Chih-tung's Aversion to *Min-ch'üan*

Between 1895 and 1898, as discussion of reform proceeded among the scholar-official class of China, divisions appeared in the ranks of those searching for solutions to the nation's plight. I have mentioned one of those divisions, the theoretical rationale for reform which divided K'ang Yu-wei and Chang Chih-tung. But of greater importance than this was the more explicitly political problem associated with the increasingly popular concept of *min-ch'üan,* or people's rights.

Reformers of all complexions agreed on the necessity of taking steps to increase China's military and industrial capacities and to broaden her sources of knowledge by studying the West more closely. This would, by implication, enhance the power of the central, formal political structure. Many reformers also agreed, as noted, on the need for better communication and solidarity between ruler and subjects, to promote the national unity required to fend off the West. But the problem was how to achieve that communication, solidarity, and unity.

More traditional thinkers, including Chang Chih-tung, would recommend vigorous action from the throne, supported unanimously by leading officials and the entire bureaucratic elite, as the path to unity. The central government could command the united support of the nation by correct policies, correctly implemented.

New thinkers, however, began to promote the concept of *min-ch'üan* as the only way to national unity. Better communication between ruler and subjects, and effective national solidarity, could only be attained through more active participation of the subjects in the affairs of the nation. The idea of participation, in fact, was the key to the popularity of the *min-ch'üan* slogan. The term occurred with growing frequency in reformist publications after 1895, studding the writings of K'ang Yu-wei, Liang Ch'i-ch'ao, and others.

This was not to be mass participation, directly involving the illiterate peasantry or others without a certain social and economic standing. Neither was it to be participation just on the part of those individuals already within the formal bureaucracy as officials.

Rather, this was to be fuller participation in politics by the nation's elite class of gentry, in their capacity as representatives of local society. *Min-ch'üan* quite clearly meant movement toward a representative system of government with the elite class of local gentry leaders attaining some formal status within the political system. The monarchy would remain, but its prerogatives would have to be limited, under some sort of constitutional system, to make way for the new participants in the political process. The goal was not representation for its own sake, or democracy, but a society more firmly united with its government.

Resistance to such political renovation could be expected from many sectors of the government, especially from the imperial house, always jealous of its autocratic powers. Yet the example of Meiji Japan showed that a constitutional system could be imposed upon an absolute monarchy. Moreover, the end result might be an actual enhancing of central government powers by the construction of a more effective "transmission belt" linking the center with local society through the local elite's formal participation in the system.[35]

To Chang Chih-tung, any such political evolution was anathema. While others perceived the possible unifying and centralizing effects of broadened political participation, Chang saw only the tendency toward disintegration. He was an imperial official, and all his instincts and personal experience told him it would be disastrous to incorporate formally the local elite into the central political structure. He was willing to grant the gentry their crucial informal role in the overall functioning of government and administration. But he was convinced that if they were accorded a formal niche, with "rights," they would only use their position to protect their own interests, probably harming the state.

Between 1895 and 1898, Chang became more and more vexed at the infatuation of others with *min-ch'üan,* and his strong feelings on this issue became one of the main points of difference between him and more "radical" reformers in 1898.[36] Chang did not really see the potential centralizing effects of *min-ch'üan,* or of constitutionalism, and was totally preoccupied with its centrifugal tendencies. This can be seen clearly from his treatment of the subject in his *Ch'üan-hsüeh p'ien* of early 1898, which will be considered as a whole in the next chapter. In that section of the work devoted to "Rectification of Political Rights" (*Cheng-ch'üan*), Chang's vigorous attack on *min-ch'üan* shows a remarkable twisting of the basics of Western constitutionalist doctrines to suit his own prejudices. If the concept of *min-ch'üan* is implemented, he warns, authority will crumble: "Every family will be selfish for itself, every village will be selfish for itself, every scholar will want to sit and eat, every farmer will want exemption from his tax, every merchant will want a monopoly. . . . "[37]

Moreover, he obviously believes that an institution such as a parliament is only designed to give people a way to satisfy their own private ends, and associates representative government with erosion of central political authority. The same section of the *Ch'üan-hsüeh p'ien* gives four arguments against China's having a parliament.[38] The first is that Chinese merchants, who would normally comprise part of the legislature, are not public spirited or far sighted. The second is that people are already able to establish commercial enterprises, therefore further "rights" to do so are not needed. Besides, merchants' ethical standards are so low that government authority is needed to restrain their rapaciousness. The third reason is that it would be unwise to remove the government's hand from the educational system and turn it over entirely to the local gentry, as he believes would occur with establishment of a parliament. The fourth reason he gives is that the central government's authority must remain to import needed military equipment and to guarantee foreign loans financing improvement of the military establishment.

The assumption behind Chang's reasoning is that any sort of a parliament in which local gentry and merchant interests were represented would not be a part of the central government but its rival. To Chang, *min-ch'üan* meant destruction of the central government's present powers, and a devolution of authority to an ignorant, incompetent, nonaccountable, and irresponsible local elite. As noted at the end of the first chapter, Chang's extreme and uncharitable suspicions of the power ambitions of the local gentry and merchant class undoubtedly stemmed largely from his own encounters with its representatives in Kwangtung and Hupeh. To him, the particularistic interests of the local elite were to be battled and overcome, not incorporated into the central apparatus itself. To range far ahead of the narration, one might suggest that the practical results of the constitutional system after 1911 corroborated Chang's convictions.

Thus, as the national reform movement began its acceleration in 1898, Chang stood in the more moderate of what had become its two streams. He favored any and all innovations that would enhance central government power. He violently opposed opening up the political system to elements whose local interests, he believed, often outweighed their commitment to national and dynastic interests.

Chapter 3

Chang Chih-tung in the Reforms of 1898

As his differences with K'ang Yu-wei and others in the reform movement grew larger, Chang Chih-tung took the offensive. He made full use of his political and personal leverage to help bend the reform movement toward his own position in two important cases: the Shanghai *Shih-wu pao* and the provincial reform program in Hunan. However, events in Peking in the summer of 1898 were beyond the reach of his influence, as the more radical wing of the reform movement around K'ang Yu-wei made its move for national power.

Control of the *Shih-wu pao*

The Shanghai *Shih-wu pao* was the brightest star in the galaxy of postwar journalism. A direct descendent of K'ang Yu-wei's *Ch'iang-hsüeh pao,* it was edited during its first year of operation by the young and brilliant Liang Ch'i-ch'ao. Combining editorial essays with factual news and translations from the foreign press, the journal provided the first public forum for many young men who would later be important figures in the first decades of the twentieth century. By late 1897, there were over one hundred places in seventy towns or *hsien* where the paper was available, and each issue was selling about twelve thousand copies, more than three times as many as Young J. Allen's popular *Wan-kuo kung-pao.*[1] Yet almost from the start, Chang Chih-tung was able to exert a surprising degree of influence over editorial policy, and by early 1898 the newspaper faithfully echoed his own views. The fact that Chang was a major financial supporter and subscriber undoubtedly facilitated this, but Chang also relied upon his personal relationship with the business manager Wang K'ang-nien to achieve his aims for the paper.

In the fall of 1896, soon after the establishment of the paper, Wang K'ang-nien himself contributed an essay entitled "On the Benefits of China's Adoption of People's Rights" (*Chung-kuo ts'an-yung min-ch'üan chih li-i*).[2] Wang described how national weakness stems from resting state power on only a few officials, whereas strength would come from massing the people together as the foundation of the state, as in the West. Wang predicted that many scholars would be appalled by this thought and call it heresy. He was right. Chang Chih-tung, with his supersensitivity to *min-ch'üan,* was greatly offended by this piece. Chang had his chief lieutenant for educational affairs, Liang Ting-fen, write a letter of complaint to Wang, an old friend of Liang. The implicit threat was clear, and at least partly because of it, Wang never again praised the virtues of *min-ch'üan* in the *Shih-wu pao.*[3]

Chang's influence over editorial policy soon extended beyond the writings of Wang himself. Letters from Liang Ting-fen arrived in the Shanghai editorial office quite regularly during 1896 and 1897. Through this indirect leverage, Chang was able to modify some articles by Liang Ch'i-ch'ao, to keep out K'ang Yu-wei's writings entirely, and to stop a series of pieces by Hsü Ch'in which savagely attacked the old educational system. This sort of censorship and constraint was probably one of the main reasons that Liang Ch'i-ch'ao left the paper in the late summer of 1897 and went to Hunan, where his talents were less hampered. Liang was said to have complained that he was being treated like a servant by the time he left the editorship.[4] After this, Wang K'ang-nien was in undisputed control of the *Shih-wu pao,* and he continued to follow an editorial line approved by Chang Chih-tung until the transformation of the paper in 1898.

An indication of the degree to which the *Shih-wu pao* had come to reflect the views of Chang Chih-tung, as opposed to those of K'ang Yu-wei, was provided in the spring of 1898. When K'ang organized the short-lived Pao-kuo hui (Society to Protect the Nation) in Peking, he sent a membership list to the *Shih-wu pao* for publication. Upon the urging of Liang Ting-fen, Wang K'ang-nien refused to print it; the list was eventually printed by Yen Fu's *Kuo-wen pao*.[5]

It should be emphasized, however, that the paper had by no means become a reactionary organ. It still promoted progress and change, and printed articles by advocates of moderate reform. In the spring of 1898, Wang K'ang-nien and others formed a daily version of the paper, the *Shih-wu jih-pao,* which began publication on May 5. In the first issue, Wang stated that the aims of the paper were still to "change entrenched habits, break through [old ways], and excite and encourage [new thinking]."[6]

In the summer of 1898, during the "100 days" of reform in Peking, Wang K'ang-nien had a confrontation with K'ang Yu-wei over control of the *Shih-wu pao.* On July 17, the censor Sung Po-lu submitted a memorial suggesting the nationalization of the *Shih-wu pao* under the management of Liang Ch'i-ch'ao. K'ang Yu-wei admitted drafting this memorial for Sung, claiming that Wang K'ang-nien had so mismanaged the paper that it had to be saved in this manner.[7] K'ang may also have had a personal grudge over the exclusion of his writings and theories from the paper. At any rate, the matter was turned over to Sun Chia-nai, prestigious former tutor of the emperor and head of the recently established imperial university in Peking. Sun approved Sung's proposal, saying that such a move would provide "a medium for conveying true information to the emperor," under responsible management. On July 26, an imperial edict ordered that the nationalization take place. On August 9, again on the initiative of Sun Chia-nai, K'ang Yu-wei himself was directed to go to Shanghai to manage the paper, ostensibly because Liang Ch'i-ch'ao could not leave his new duties at the translation office of the imperial university.[8]

Wang K'ang-nien refused to submit to this removal of the paper from his control. He immediately undertook a formal reorganization, changing the name of the original paper to the *Ch'ang-yen pao* and that of the daily to the *Chung-wai jih-pao.* He also hired Liang Ting-fen, one of the foremost members of Chang

Chih-tung's *mu-fu,* as editor of the former publication. In the first issue of the *Ch'ang-yen pao,* on August 17, Wang published a justification for his actions. He claimed that the assets of the *Shih-wu pao* had been his from the start. He had hired Liang Ch'i-ch'ao, Mai Meng-hua, Chang Ping-lin, and the other writers and translators as his employees. In rebuttal, Liang Ch'i-ch'ao pointed out that the original assets of the *Shih-wu pao* consisted of the remainder of Chang Chih-tung's contribution to the Shanghai branch of the suppressed Ch'iang-hsüeh hui, proceeds from the sale of its books and office equipment, and gifts from Huang Tsun-hsien and others. Wang had only been business manager.[9]

In this struggle for control of the paper, Chang Chih-tung supported Wang K'ang-nien completely. During August, Sun Chia-nai pressured Liu K'un-i, governor-general at Nanking, to stop Wang's new independent publishing venture, and K'ang Yu-wei telegraphed both Liu and Chang Chih-tung, requesting the same thing. On August 26, Chang sent Sun Chia-nai a telegram defending Wang's position, and saying that official funds could be used to start a new paper under K'ang. Sun replied on September 5, backing off from his previous demands, and no more was heard on the issue. Wang K'ang-nien and Liang Ting-fen continued to put out the *Ch'ang-yen pao* for only ten issues, or until sometime in November, but the *Chung-wai jih-pao* survived until 1907 or 1908.[10]

A postscript to the *Shih-wu pao* story shows the depth of feelings aroused by the whole affair. K'ang Yu-wei later claimed that after the empress dowager's coup in September, 1898, Wang K'ang-nien reported K'ang's local supporters to the Shanghai magistrate, and even led police officers to the Ta-T'ung Book Company and Liang Ch'i-ch'ao's residence in search of them.[11]

Chang Chih-tung was not the master of Wang K'ang-nien, able to impose his own views upon Wang all of the time. Wang would show his independence of Chang in 1899 and 1900, when his daily, the *Chung-wai jih-pao,* took a more favorable stance toward the activities of the K'ang-Liang group of exiles and vehemently protested Tz'u-hsi's moves to get rid of the emperor once and for all. Yet from 1896 to 1898, Chang found Wang receptive to his encouragement of a moderate position on political reform, and the radicals turned to other areas to promote their ideas.

Control of the Hunan Reform Movement

The reform movement in Hunan province from 1896 to 1898 was a remarkable phenomenon. In a conservative, tradition-bound inland province, there occurred a combination of enlightened officialdom, a vigorous local elite, and an infusion of iconoclastic intellectual leadership from outside. The result was a brief period of sparkling experimentation and disputation, followed by suppression of the most extreme advocates of reform.[12] Chang Chih-tung, the nominal supervisor of events in Hunan, normally left matters there to the care of the governor and other provincial officials; he had his hands full in Hupeh. But in 1897 and 1898, Chang kept close track of developments in Hunan and eventually intervened, perhaps decisively, to help secure what he considered a favorable outcome.

The new governor of Hunan after the Sino-Japanese War, Ch'en Pao-chen (not to be confused with Ch'en Pao-ch'en, member of Chang Chih-tung's *mu-fu*), was a progressive and able official. With his son Ch'en San-li assisting him, he promoted such technical projects as mining, a telegraph, electricity for the provincial capital Changsha, and better roads. The educational commissioner, Chiang Piao, was also a reform-minded official. He introduced translations of Western works into the provincial examinations and pushed hard for a general modernization and expansion of the curricula of the old academies. Chiang was mainly responsible for the publication of a new journal, the *Hsiang-hsüeh pao,* which appeared every ten days after April, 1897; it discussed the new academic subjects, as well as other items of current interest. At the start, the journal seemed to try to avoid controversial political issues and polemics.[13]

The Hunanese gentry, shaken by China's humiliating defeat at the hands of the Japanese, proved more responsive to these initiatives than their conservative, orthodox reputation warranted. Members of leading gentry families like Wang Hsien-ch'ien and Hsiung Hsi-ling took the lead in forming companies to undertake shipping ventures, construction projects, even a railroad line. The reform movement was advanced another step when Huang Tsun-hsien, former diplomat and admirer of the Meiji reformers in Japan, became salt commissioner, then acting judicial commissioner, in 1897. Huang organized a modern police force (*pao-wei-chü*) for the capital and led reform organizations such as an antifootbinding society.

Chang Chih-tung viewed the developing situation in Hunan with approval. Governor Ch'en had formerly served with him in Hupeh; Huang Tsun-hsien had been a member of Chang's *mu-fu*, specializing in missionary cases, for some time after 1894, and had helped establish the Shanghai *Shih-wu pao*. The projects of Ch'en and Huang were of the same sort that Chang had been promoting for years, and educational commissioner Chiang Piao's ideas on academic reform were apparently very much like Chang's own. Moreover, Chang could only have been envious of the enthusiastic response evoked by Hunan officialdom among the gentry, given his own history of constant battles with local elites. The nature of that gentry response, including a growing willingness to take the initiative in province-wide affairs, portended the time after the turn of the century when they would no longer necessarily follow the lead of the governor or governor-general, much less the central government in Peking. But for now, at least, their participation was welcomed.

In 1897, Chang became concerned with the tendencies of the new Hunan journal, the *Hsiang-hsüeh pao*. In late summer, he followed Governor Ch'en Pao-chen's lead in giving it his official approval. He ordered several subscriptions for the major provincial offices and the two large academies in Wuhan, and he also directed lower officials down to the district magistrate level to subscribe to the paper and disseminate it in their areas. Yet his praise of the new paper was not unqualified. He registered his concern at the journal's recent discussion of K'ang Yu-wei's theory of "Confucius as a Reformer" (*su-wang kai-chih*); even though the paper's own standpoint was not clear, it seemed to lean in the direction of this "new heresy" (*hsin-ch'i*). One reason he was willing to extend his blessing to the publication was that Chiang Piao himself had telegraphed, saying that the editors' intentions were proper and that the offending words had been mistakenly included.[14]

Those mainly responsible for the *Hsiang-hsüeh pao* until the fall of 1897, especially Chiang Piao, were thus not unmindful of Chang Chih-tung's worries. In the September issue which carried the above statement of support by Chang, the editors appended a comment defending themselves. They claimed to have brought up the concept of Confucius as a reformer only to criticize it as too radical; they did not intend to abuse the classics.[15] On October 1, 1897, T'an Ssu-t'ung, son of the governor of Hupeh, who would soon emerge as one of the most brilliant and fiery of the advocates of radical reform in both Hunan and Peking, wrote to his friend in Shanghai, Wang K'ang-nien. T'an noted the recent complaints by Chang Chih-tung on the contents of the *Hsiang-hsüeh pao* and predicted that Chiang Piao would knuckle under. Indeed, Wang himself knew well that kind of pressure on his own paper, as we have seen. At any rate, no more talk of K'ang Yu-wei's controversial theories appeared in the Hunan journal for a short while that autumn.[16]

With the arrival of several new faces in late 1897, the Hunan reform movement moved to a much more radical level of activity. Earlier in the year, gentry leaders such as Wang Hsien-ch'ien had proposed establishment of a school to teach current affairs (*shih-wu*) to complement their other reform projects. The Shih-wu hsüeh-t'ang (Academy of Current Affairs) was formally opened in September, 1897, under the general management of Hsiung Hsi-ling. The well-known editor of the Shanghai *Shih-wu pao,* Liang Ch'i-ch'ao, was hired as chief lecturer of Chinese studies, and Liang's colleague Li Wei-ko as head of Western studies. When he arrived in Changsha that autumn, Liang also brought along three fellow Cantonese as assistants: Han Wen-chü, Ou Ch'ü-chia, and Yeh Chüeh-mai, all, like Liang himself, intellectual followers of K'ang Yu-wei.[17]

The impact of the new group of Cantonese around the Shih-wu hsüeh-t'ang was compounded when the relatively cautious Chiang Piao was replaced as educational commissioner by the more outspoken Hsü Jen-chu. Under Hsü's supervision and the actual editorship of T'an Ssu-t'ung, the *Hsiang-hsüeh pao* took a distinct turn toward supporting "new text" or "Confucius as a reformer" theories in late 1897 and early 1898. Hsü himself contributed a long series entitled *Yu-hsüan chin-yü,* which was expressly modeled on Chang Chih-tung's *Yu-hsüan-yü,* a handbook on study and composition for students written in the 1870's, when Chang was educational commissioner in Szechuan. The very act of updating this work implied the obsolescence of the original, of course. Far worse, Hsü followed the new text or K'ang-Liang interpretation on some items—not slavishly, but often enough so that some conservatives charged that the series was actually ghostwritten by Liang Ch'i-ch'ao.[18]

Meanwhile, Liang and his assistants at the Shih-wu hsüeh-t'ang were exposing the sons of the Hunan gentry (there were forty in the first class of the academy) to the controversial theories of K'ang Yu-wei, talk of *min-ch'üan,* and drastic criticism of previous Ch'ing scholarship, all with anti-Manchu overtones.[19] Even the liberal Governor Ch'en must have been shocked to see Liang's private proposals to him for the possible independence of Hunan and a form of provincial parliamentary government; Liang produced these in December, 1897, and January, 1898, under the impact of the latest and most serious round of foreign demands on China.[20]

During the winter and early spring, a variety of new organizations appeared, dominated by Hunanese allies of the most radical Cantonese reform advocates. The most important of these were in Changsha itself, where the *Hsiang-pao,* a daily paper, and the Nan-hsüeh hui (Southern Study Society) were established. The *Hsiang-pao* was run mainly by the Hunanese Hsiung Hsi-ling, T'an Ssu-t'ung, and T'ang Ts'ai-ch'ang (the latter two were close friends from Liu-yang), though the Cantonese group also participated. The paper boldly advocated *min-ch'üan* and printed more shocking proposals, for example, one by a young man named I Nai; I Nai proposed to link East and West by combining their cultures, religions, political systems, and even, through intermarriage, the races themselves.[21] The distinguished Hunanese scholar of the new text school, P'i Hsi-jui, was made head of the new Nan-hsüeh hui, which sponsored lectures and discussion sessions on intellectual currents, politics, and science from late February to late May. Lectures, which sometimes drew as many as a thousand people, were also reprinted in the *Hsiang-pao.* Branch societies, under a variety of names, mushroomed all over the province, carried home by locals who were inspired by the exciting intellectual climate of Changsha in early 1898.[22]

The Nan-hsüeh hui was, at least potentially, the most important of all the reform projects. There is evidence that Liang Ch'i-ch'ao, T'an Ssu-t'ung, Huang Tsun-hsien, and perhaps others saw the society as a rudimentary provincial assembly, with enlightened members of the gentry representing all of the territorial subdivisions of the province. The most ambitious reform leaders hoped that the Nan-hsüeh hui would assert itself in conducting, on a province-wide scale, all of the quasi-governmental functions which local gentry leaders had traditionally performed—establishment of schools and industries, public works, tax collection, legal and police administration. In their view, such a development would have provided a working example of representative government, and might have paved the way for a national constitutional system.[23]

The rapid acceleration of reform activities in the spring of 1898 finally provoked the ire of the more conservative members of the Hunanese establishment. T'an Ssu-t'ung was by now openly advocating K'ang Yu-wei's theories in the *Hsiang-pao;* the Nan-hsüeh hui seemed to be brazenly arrogating to itself governmental functions; and some of the province's conservative scholars at last realized the nature of the education their sons were receiving at the Shih-wu hsüeh-t'ang. The reaction was intense; even former supporters among the gentry, for example Wang Hsien-ch'ien, became opponents of the reform leaders. They organized an opposition movement which intimidated and harassed those around the Shih-wu hsüeh-t'ang, the Nan-hsüeh hui, and the two newspapers, and which applied pressure to the Hunanese participants through their home communities. By late spring and early summer, the countermoves of the Hunanese elite seemed to have taken effect; all of the reform activities slowly ground to a halt.[24]

Yet it is uncertain that the opposition of the provincial gentry was in itself sufficient to halt the momentum of the Hunan reform movement. Perhaps it was more important that, as the radical "second stage" of the movement unfolded in early 1898, official sanction and approval was withdrawn, both at the provincial level and above. Governor Ch'en Pao-chen himself was appalled by some of the manifestations of the radicals' enthusiasm, as were the other provincial officials under whose benevolent aegis the reform movement had taken root.[25]

The strongest reaction, however, came from Chang Chih-tung. Chang had followed events in Hunan closely through the pages of its two newspapers, and by May, 1898, he was quite angry about the nature of the articles being published. On May 11, he fired off two telegrams to Hunan. One, to Governor Ch'en, noted that the *Hsiang-hsüeh pao* had been getting much worse in its addiction to the theories of K'ang Yu-wei, but that the new *Hsiang-pao* was absolutely terrible; Chang especially noted the recent article by I Nai. He chided Ch'en for actually hurting the cause of moderate reform by permitting this sort of publication to continue, because it gave the conservatives a good excuse for repression. Along with Chang's message to the governor he sent a copy of his recent treatise on moderate reform, *Ch'üan-hsüeh p'ien,* as an example of literature appropriate for publication.

The other telegram was to Hsü Jen-chu, the educational commissioner. Chang reprimanded Hsü bitterly for the direction which the *Hsiang-hsüeh pao* had taken. He reminded Hsü that the previous year, when Hsü was enroute to his post in Hunan, Chang had warned him of the journal's heretical tendencies, and had secured from him a promise to restrain it. Now he had been forced to cancel the several subscriptions he had taken out, and he wanted no more copies of the offensive paper sent to Hupeh.[26]

Hunan officialdom, probably already sharing many of Chang's criticisms, was quick to conform. Two days later, on May 13, Governor Ch'en replied to Chang, agreeing completely and reporting that he had instructed Hsiung Hsi-ling to confiscate copies of the issue with the I Nai article.[27] Hsü Jen-chu responded by reasserting control over the editorial policy of the *Hsiang-hsüeh pao.* On May 20, in the first issue to appear after Chang's complaint, the paper began publication of his *Ch'üan-hsüeh p'ien,* in serial form. Sections of Chang's treatise extolling the virtues of moderate reform and the sins of the radicals now ran in each issue of the *Hsiang-hsüeh pao* from May 20 until August 8, when the paper ceased publication.[28] This was impressive proof of Chang's ability to influence events when he was sufficiently aroused, as he was in this case.

By mid-June, when the "100 days" of reform were just beginning in Peking, the Hunan reform movement was under control. The combination of pressure from the conservative Hunanese gentry and the crackdown by Chang Chih-tung and provincial officials had taken effect. P'i Hsi-jui left the province and the Nan-hsüeh hui withered; the two papers ceased publication during the summer; the Shih-wu hsüeh-t'ang faded to a shadow of its former vigorous self as Liang Ch'i-ch'ao and the other leaders of its staff drifted toward Peking or Shanghai. In August, Governor Ch'en denounced K'ang Yu-wei's theories and requested that his recently published "Confucius as a Reformer" be burned, though he stopped short of personal criticism of K'ang.[29]

The days of glory were over, and the remains of the reform movement in Hunan had to make accommodation with the continued strength of tradition. Yet the movement was not killed by the events of late spring, only restrained. Most of the top provincial officials who had welcomed and promoted the reform movement in its early stages were still in their jobs. The final blow to the provincial reforms was not dealt until the removal of these officials after the empress dowager's Peking coup d'etat in September, 1898.

Between Radical Reform and Reaction: Chang Chih-tung and the "100 Days"

The preceding discussion has shown how Chang broke with the most insistent advocates of K'ang Yu-wei's theories and *min-ch'üan* by the summer of 1898. Historians in mainland China have pointed to Chang's role in the *Shih-wu pao* and the Hunan reform movement as proof of the superficiality of Chang's reform convictions; he was really only concerned with "consolidating the advantages of his feudal ruling class." Moreover, his *Ch'üan-hsüeh p'ien* is said to have become a "bible" for conservatives and reactionaries, and a potent weapon against K'ang Yu-wei, Liang Ch'i-ch'ao, and other political reformers.[30]

Indeed, the gentry intellectuals who hampered the reform movement in Hunan did recommend Chang's work as an ideal study manual in place of K'ang's "Confucius as a Reformer," and other conservatives would use some of Chang's arguments against overzealous reformers in the future. Furthermore, some of those very close to Chang, for example Liang Ting-fen, showed a remarkably consistent and deeply bitter rancor toward K'ang Yu-wei and his followers right from the start.[31]

Yet this interpretation hardly does justice to the complexities of Chang's role. His personal views were not necessarily always the same as those of Liang Ting-fen or others in his entourage, and there would probably be as many people who would quote from the *Ch'üan-hsüeh p'ien* in the future to support vigorous and far-reaching reform proposals as those who would use it to defend the status quo. It is my contention that Chang, during the crucial year of 1898, continued to occupy what was essentially a middle position, one which preserved the essentials of a worthwhile reform program, while falling short of political constitutionalism. As his position in the reform movement became more and more distant from that of other participants, less through shifts in his own ideas than through the progression of others toward more extreme stances, Chang, by actions and writings, defined his own reform position somewhat more clearly. In the process, Chang also tried, as a realistic practicing official, to avoid the alienation of powerful forces in the provinces and at court.

The outlines of Chang's position can be seen from the manner in which he supported the *Shih-wu pao* and the *Hsiang-hsüeh pao,* but tried to restrain them when they ventured into forbidden subjects. A reform organization more under Chang's direct control was the Chih-hsüeh hui, which began in Wuchang in mid-1897. Its "regulations" (*chang-ch'eng*) reflected Chang's own view of the two great dangers of the times: on the one hand to cling blindly to old ways, and on the other to discard one's roots (*pen*). This society published a new edition of T'ang Chen's *Wei-yen* (Words of warning), which had first appeared in 1890. It seems significant that while T'ang Chen had advocated considerable institutional change, including a sort of parliament, this clearly was meant only for the participation of members of the existing bureaucracy as a device to make better information available to the emperor, not for an introduction of "people's rights."[32]

By early 1898, the Hunan reform movement had gotten out of hand, K'ang Yu-wei's "Confucius as a Reformer" had just been published and was selling well all over the country, and Chang must have felt impelled to take a more direct role in providing an alternative, moderate reform program. This was the background for the writing of his famous *Ch'üan-hsüeh p'ien*. He completed it quickly in late winter, and it first appeared sometime in April, 1898, though the final authorized version was not published until the fifth month (June 19–July 18). The nine essays of the first part of the work (*nei-p'ien*) stressed the selective retention of the Chinese heritage, while the fifteen essays in the second part (*wai-p'ien*) elaborated upon the use of Western ideas and tools to attain national power. Thus the work as a whole was a conscious political restatement of the famous *t'i-yung* dichotomy, and did much to popularize the slogan, "Chinese learning for the essence [*t'i*], Western learning for practical use [*yung*]."[33]

The introduction to this book showed that Chang was specifically refuting K'ang Yu-wei's ideas and the advocates of *min-ch'üan*. However, his purpose was not only to denounce, but to offer an alternative. Chang made it clear that he was as aware as anyone of the foreign threat and said that China should indeed feel fear and shame at the prospect of vassalage—being like India or other colonies. Moreover, the old self-strengthening ideal of tacking Western gadgets onto an unchanged Chinese "essence" was no longer sufficient. Chang acknowledged that not just technology but also some institutions and methods of administration should be borrowed from the West. All in all, the *Ch'üan-hsüeh p'ien* was a masterful political document, designed to tread the ground between radical reform and reaction. It played up to outraged nationalism and went beyond the discredited self-strengthening position, yet fell short of a total renunciation of Chinese tradition or anything smacking of parliamentary government.

Some of Chang's other activities during 1898 also point to his working for a distinct middle-of-the-road position. In February and March, he established the School of Agriculture (Nung-wu hsüeh-t'ang) and the School of Industrial Arts (Kung-i hsüeh-t'ang) in Wuchang; both of these were safely apolitical.[34] During the spring, as Chang gave up on the Hunan newspapers, he sponsored a new journal in Hupeh, edited by Liang Ting-fen; this was the *Cheng-hsüeh pao*. Apparently no copies survive, but the very title meant "rectitude," and in a preface written for the journal Chang again attacked the heretical philosophy of K'ang and Liang.[35] In August, Chang supported Wang K'ang-nien and his transformed *Ch'ang-yen pao* in Shanghai, as noted. And there is evidence that Chang himself actively pursued other journalistic endeavors in Wuchang during 1898, including an official provincial newsletter (*Kuan-pao*) and a journal of commercial affairs (*Shang-wu pao*).[36]

Another indication of Chang's middle position was the sort of men to whom he began to be attracted in late 1897 and 1898—those who were progressive and talented, but whose reform convictions seemed to fall short of *min-ch'üan* or constitutionalism. Chang admired the Chekiang scholar T'ang Shou-ch'ien, who contributed moderate reform articles to the *Shih-wu pao,* and he invited T'ang to give a lecture series in Wuchang in late 1897.[37] Chang also saw the writings of Ch'en Yen in the Shanghai paper and brought him to Wuchang in January, 1898, as a member of his staff, with duties in the areas of journalism and translations. Ch'en was also one of the backers of Chang's antiradical journal, the *Cheng-hsüeh pao,* in the late spring.[38] In 1897, Chang had been impressed with the *Nung-hsüeh pao* (Agronomy Bulletin), put out by Lo Chen-yü and his Shanghai agricultural society, and he recommended the journal to Hupeh officials. In 1898, Chang brought Lo to Wuchang to head the new School of Agriculture, and Lo remained associated with Chang's educational projects for several years.[39]

Chang was thus establishing for himself a general policy position of moderate reform in 1898 and was gathering around him men representative of it. Yet he did not consider adherents of more radical ideas, except K'ang Yu-wei himself, to be beyond the pale of political acceptability. It may be useful to note some of the individuals whom Chang recommended to the throne in the summer of 1898. In response to a call upon provincial officials to recommend candidates for a "special examination in political economy and administration" (*ching-chi t'e-k'o*), Chang in July submitted eighteen names, including that of Liang Ch'i-ch'ao.[40] Chang's willingness to vouch for Liang as late as July suggests that the break between them was not irreparable. Having made Liang feel his power both in Shanghai and in Changsha during the past year, perhaps Chang now had no desire to harass him further, and still hoped to cooperate with Liang, whose abilities he admired.

Others Chang recommended for the special examination included Yang Jui, soon to be martyred in Peking, and Tsou Tai-chün, a Hunanese who had cooperated closely with Liang Ch'i-ch'ao and the Cantonese radicals in various Changsha reform projects in late 1897 and early 1898. Among those Chang recommended on July 19 as having special expertise in foreign affairs was Huang Tsun-hsien, a leading light among the recently chastised Hunan reform officials.[41] As yet, there was obviously no particular danger in being associated with these individuals, even with Liang Ch'i-ch'ao; if there had been, Chang's sensitive political antennae would have picked it up.

It is not my purpose to make a detailed analysis of the 1898 reforms as a whole, but from Chang Chih-tung's perspective at least one feature seems worthy of note. As far as Chang was concerned, in the early summer of 1898 the divisions in the reform movement were those of principles and issues, mainly centered around K'ang's philosophy and *min-ch'üan,* not divisions of personal factionalism. Individuals did not yet carry labels and align themselves permanently with others of similar views on all issues. There persisted enough of a common body of opinion about the kind of reforms China needed, perhaps, for Chang and others still to assume the feasibility of forming a broadly based reform coalition in government which would be acceptable to a large number of officials. Hunan Governor Ch'en Pao-chen, Chang's ally in reform on most issues, saw no incongruity in submitting for recommendation in early August the names of men who by September would seem to run the gamut of the political spectrum. Of his seventeen nominees, two (Yang Jui and Liu Kuang-ti) would be killed by the empress dowager in September for their "radicalism"; two (Ch'en Pao-ch'en, Chang Chih-tung's old *ch'ing-liu* friend and follower, and Ou-yang Lin, former assistant to *ch'ing-liu* patron Li Hung-tsao) had impeccable "conservative" credentials; and two (Wang Ping-en and Yün Tsu-ch'i) were presently members of Chang Chih-tung's *mu-fu*. These men, as well as some of those that Chang himself grouped together in his recommendations of the summer, are undoubtedly much more incompatible in retrospect than they actually were at the time.[42]

In other words, it was probably not the case that already existing factions and power divisions were manifested by the imperial reforms of the "100 days" which began in Peking in mid-June, 1898. Rather, the summer edicts themselves created the factions and divisions; this seems especially true of those measures taken at the end of the summer to build a K'ang Yu-wei clique high in the policy organs of government and to move toward a national advisory assembly of sorts. When the "100 days" began after K'ang Yu-wei's famous June audience with Kuang-hsü, Tz'u-hsi was suspicious, and took steps to keep a close watch on further developments. Yet there seems to be no hard evidence of a plot on her part, or on that of anyone, to suppress and exterminate the "radical" reform leaders, much less Kuang-hsü, right from the start. For most of the summer, many more besides the small group around K'ang Yu-wei welcomed the reform edicts rolling down from the throne. Indeed, the emperor's remarkable receptivity to reform proposals was a great opportunity not for K'ang Yu-wei alone, but for others as well, including Chang Chih-tung, to recommend reforms.

In early July, Chang and Governor Ch'en of Hunan submitted a lengthy joint memorial on educational reforms which was promulgated almost verbatim as an imperial edict. This memorial had been lifted mainly from the description of a new educational system in Chang's *Ch'üan-hsüeh p'ien,* and provided for extensive changes in the form and content of the nation's school and examination systems. Other educational reform measures suggested by Chang were also accepted and issued as law during the summer.[43]

There is evidence that the *Ch'üan-hsüeh p'ien* as a whole had a great attraction for the young emperor. In July, Kuang-hsü happened to complain to Huang Shao-chi, former associate of Chang Chih-tung and now an official in the Hanlin Academy, about the one-sidedness (*p'ien-chien*) of arguments at court. Huang took this opportunity to promote the recent work by Chang, and soon presented a copy to the emperor for his perusal. After reading it, on July 25 Kuang-hsü ordered that forty copies be distributed to governors-general, governors, and educational commissioners around the country, saying that it would help strengthen "true Confucianism" (*ming-chiao*) and put a stop to "all-embracing expressions" (*chih-yen*).[44] On August 22, another edict commanded that three hundred more copies of the work be issued through the Tsungli yamen.[45] The emperor obviously felt that he had an ally in Chang Chih-tung, despite the bias of the *Ch'üan-hsüeh p'ien* against the doctrinal and political ideas of his close adviser K'ang Yu-wei.

A commonly noted reason for the failure of the "100 days" is that the imperial edicts were opposed and ignored by provincial officials. This was not the case with Chang. He was conscientious, not only in implementing the newly promulgated educational reforms, which he himself had largely devised, but also in carrying out other edicts; he planned and established a commercial affairs bureau (*shang-wu chü*) in Hankow and tried to eliminate superfluous provincial posts, a touchy political task.[46] One problem Chang encountered in this last area may throw light on the nature of the provincial "opposition" to the reform decrees. Chang was quite befuddled by a vague decree of early September to streamline and consolidate the provincial bureaucracy and to report the results within a month. In a telegram to Liu K'un-i, Chang requested advice on how best to do this, and certainly evinced no desire to thwart the imperial will.[47] During the summer, the emperor castigated some provincial officials for not carrying out his instructions, and there undoubtedly was real opposition in some quarters. But perhaps the novelty and vagueness of the demands made on these men were partly responsible for what appeared from the throne to be conscious evasion of orders. At any rate, the crucial events of the summer took place in Peking.

What of those events in Peking which finally precipitated the empress dowager's coup of September 21? A closer look at some of those usually considered to be the main characters in the drama may reveal less cohesion on the part of either "reformers" or "reactionaries" than is usually asserted.[48] Many of the reformers, for example, were followers of K'ang Yu-wei and his general theories, but as Hao Chang has noted, they ranged from some more moderate than K'ang himself to T'an Ssu-t'ung, whose intellectual radicalism and wholesale abandonment of the Confucian tradition was quite beyond that of K'ang or indeed of anything that could still be called reformism.[49] Moreover, the opposition to reform of, for example, the Hunanese gentry was by no means of a piece with that of Manchu officials in Peking.[50] One can even discern great differences in viewpoint among the "six martyrs" executed by Tz'u-hsi on September 28, from T'an Ssu-t'ung on the "left" to Yang Jui and Liu Kuang-ti on the "right," with Yang Shen-hsiu, K'ang Kuang-jen, and Lin Hsü somewhere in the middle.[51] All this is only suggestive of what might prove to be a very complex picture of Peking political alignments as the fateful September days approached.

As I have speculated, the reform items which finally roused the empress dowager to action may have been those which seemed to insert a K'ang Yu-wei faction high in the government and which broadened the participatory base of the entire government structure. In August, the emperor had taken the unprecedented step of permitting not only all officials, but all subjects, to communicate directly with him by memorial. By early September, it was apparent that Kuang-hsü was intent upon convening an assembly of officials at the Mou-ch'in court; this was to be a rudimentary representative deliberatory body, the first step toward sharing imperial authority. On September 4, Kuang-hsü rashly dismissed all the top officials of the Board of Rites in a pique of rage at their recalcitrance. The very next day, he appointed T'an Ssu-t'ung, Yang Jui, Lin Hsü, and Liu Kuang-ti to be secretaries of the Grand Council, with special responsibilities for reforms. From their crucial position within the highest state policy organ, these four, who appeared to many as a team of K'ang Yu-wei's cohorts and lackeys, could have effectively eroded the position of K'ang's enemies, who now staked all on a return to power by the empress dowager. The key nature of the appointment of these four to the Grand Council secretariat is shown by the fact that all four were among the six who perished in the coup.

Chang Chih-tung had many friends and associates in Peking during the late summer and he undoubtedly followed events there as closely as he was able. Chang was the patron of Yang Jui, a Szechuanese whom Chang had befriended when he was stationed there in the 1870's and had treated as a son ever since. He also knew Yang Shen-hsiu, having hired him to teach at one of his schools in Shansi in the early 1880's. Ch'en Yen, close friend of Lin Hsü and member of Chang's own *mu-fu,* was now in Peking. Ch'ien Hsün and Cheng Hsiao-hsü, both having been highly recommended by Chang during the summer and both also probable members of his *mu-fu* at this time, had been summoned for imperial audiences. Ch'en Pao-ch'en, Chang's old *ch'ing-liu* friend whom he had been recommending for office since 1895, was also called to

Peking in late summer. Though Ch'en held back in Hupeh, somewhat fearful of the uncertainties awaiting him in the capital, Chang strongly urged him to go.[52]

Chang himself possibly could have been a compromise candidate for leader of a coalition reform program in the capital. There seemed to be important figures at all points of the political spectrum who thought highly of him. On the reform side, T'an Ssu-t'ung and K'ang Yu-wei, both former admirers of Chang in 1895, were now estranged, but Liu Kuang-ti had expressed great admiration for Chang as recently as September, 1897.[53] Most important, the emperor himself would have welcomed Chang, judging by his reaction to Chang's writings. At the other end of the political scale, it is noteworthy to recall that Chang had previously been summoned to Peking in the spring of 1898, largely at the instigation of the ultraconservative grand secretary Hsü T'ung. Chang had actually reached Shanghai, enroute to the capital in May, when he had to return to Hupeh to deal with an antiforeign fracas at Sha-shih, west of Wuhan. Even though his call to Peking may have been more related to the desperate diplomatic situation of the time than to the reform movement, the point that he was acceptable to some archconservatives remains valid.[54]

As the critical days of September proceeded, other key officials turned to Chang, perhaps as an alternative to the reaction which was gathering strength around the empress dowager. After Yüan Shih-k'ai's audiences with the emperor on September 16 and 17, it was rumored that Yüan intended to ask for an edict bringing Chang to Peking and into the central organs of government.[55] And on September 22, Governor Ch'en of Hunan, as yet unaware of the previous day's coup, memorialized that Chang Chih-tung would be the ideal man to help direct the reforms which had been undertaken, and that he should be called to Peking.[56]

Neither Yüan nor Ch'en was unaware of Chang's long and excellent relationship with Tz'u-hsi, of course. Indeed, one possible solution to the rising tension in Peking was to have a man of Chang's stature and wide appeal move in to take over the leadership of the reform movement at the capital. Chang likely would have been acceptable to both Kuang-hsü and Tz'u-hsi, and his own respectable reform credentials would have been sufficient to mollify all but the most uncompromising of the radicals. At some point earlier in the summer, the addition of Chang to the reform mix in Peking might have staved off disaster. By mid-September, it was too late.

Chang himself, mindful of the possible dangers involved, had no desire to go to Peking at this crucial juncture. On September 18 he telegraphed Ch'ien Hsün to do what he could there to prevent the imperial summons rumored to be in the works. Before it came, the coup occurred. Those in the south did not hear of it at once, but on September 25, after several days of contradictory and confusing reports from the capital, Chang received definite word that several men were under arrest, including his protégé Yang Jui, and that K'ang Yu-wei had fled on a British ship.[57]

Chang immediately did all that he could to save Yang. In a flurry of telegrams to various people, he insisted that Yang Jui was not an adherent of K'ang's theories, and in fact disapproved of them. Chang, moreover, claimed that Yang had recently been appointed as a secretary to the Grand Council not through K'ang's favor but because of Governor Ch'en Pao-chen's recommendation. Later, Chang reproached Hsü T'ung for not trying to save Yang.[58] Chang undoubtedly grieved a great deal over the loss of Yang. Even the unforgiving Liang Ting-fen, who was happy to see K'ang Yu-wei and Liang Ch'i-ch'ao in exile with a price on their heads, only being sorry that they still had them on their shoulders, very much regretted that Yang Jui and Liu Kuang-ti had perished.[59]

Chang had little time to mourn lost friends just now, however. He had to worry for his own political health during the coming weeks, as the postcoup political situation slowly settled into a new equilibrium. As I will describe in the next chapter, his own local reform program was somewhat curtailed, though by no means halted, in the aftermath of the resumption of power by Tz'u-hsi.

An overall descriptive and analytical history of the 1898 reforms remains to be written. One of the interesting features of the summer drama was the pattern of the relationship between the central authorities in Peking and the local gentry class at home in the provinces. The throne, in close association with a few maverick members of the gentry class (Hao Chang considers them the first representatives of the modern Chinese intelligentsia, viewed as a separate class), initiated broad reforms. These reforms actually would have brought representatives of the gentry class (as class representatives per se, not as individual officials) into the national political structure. Yet those whose position would have been thus enhanced, the provincial gentry and merchant groups who dominated the local economy and society, did not respond to this initiative from the center. On the contrary, they more often than not opposed the reforms, especially the culturally symbolic ones such as abolition of the eight-legged essay. They did not really see the interesting power possibilities for themselves in political reforms that would permit them to have representation in a provincial or national assembly of some kind, and to deal with a monarch whose theoretical authority, for the first time in recorded history, might be less than total.

Change was on the way, however. The Hunanese movement had evoked some, if an insufficient, response from within the elite. After 1900, even the most conservative gentry members there would take part in more independent economic, educational, and political activities. All over the country, the same sense of nationalism and crisis that drove the radicals of 1898 to constitutionalism as a means of national strengthening would soon seep through the whole gentry class. Already by 1900, there would be evidence of the provincial elite groups, especially in urban areas, asserting themselves in the protest over the attempted deposition of Kuang-hsü. By 1905, the central government would again move toward constitutionalism, partially in an attempt to provide an outlet for the energies of the rapidly mobilizing provincial elite.

Chang Chih-tung, of course, had long seen the possible disadvantages to the center in any mobilization of the gentry and merchant groups, without seeing the potential advantage of the greater national unity, and thus the more effective real state power, that might result from a political system built on a new rationale of participation and legitimization by "the people."[60] Hence, his deep aversion to the concept of *min-ch'üan*. The results of the events of 1898 permitted Chang, and the center with which he identified, to delay yet a little longer in coming to grips with the need more effectively to incorporate the provincial elite into national affairs, but the time for delay was running short.

Chapter 4

Reaction, Reform, and the Emergence of New Political Forces, 1898–1900

It is usually thought that the September, 1898, coup by the forces of the empress dowager ushered in a period of reaction which culminated in the Boxer debacle of 1900. One reason for this view is the obviously rising bellicosity in foreign affairs during this period, and the ignorant xenophobia of many of those influential in bringing on the Boxer tragedy. It is easy to ascribe to domestic affairs the same obscurantism, but that gives an incorrect impression of internal politics during these years. In general, the 1898–1900 period seems to be one of continuation, adjustment, and further development of the opposing forces which had grown out of the pre-1898 reform movement.

On the one hand were the radical reformers led by K'ang and Liang, in exile and removed from normal channels of influence and power. Their group, now known as the Pao-huang hui (Protect the Emperor Society), would spend these two years in experimentation with new allies, such as the students in Japan, the forces of Sun Yat-sen, and secret societies back in China. On the other side were moderate reformers like Chang Chih-tung and Liu K'un-i. To the extent that they were willing to speak frankly of the need for much significant reform, they were suspect among the reactionaries around the court and were vulnerable to occasional attacks from the most conservative political elements. But the Empress Dowager Tz'u-hsi was by no means the prisoner of the extreme conservatives, and though progress was slower than Chang would have liked, he was able to proceed with many reform projects of importance during this time.

The Ambiguity of the 1898–1900 Period

The most important feature of the September coup and accompanying purge was the resumption of direct rule by the empress dowager. The summary execution of the "six martyrs" on September 28 showed that she was in no mood to make generous allowances for what she had come to view as a threat to her (and the dynasty's) political position. Besides the six who died, in the next few weeks some thirty men were variously arrested, imprisoned, dismissed from office, or banished to the frontier, and for a time there were rumors that the purge would extend to hundreds more.[1] But the purge went no further, and its overall effect certainly was not to root out reform sentiment from within the government, but only to make its proponents more cautious.

After the destruction or removal from office of some of those thought to be associated with K'ang Yu-wei, the most important measures of the first weeks after the coup reaffirmed the rights of those who had felt threatened during the summer and halted the extension of political participation to the lower reaches of the bureaucracy and the gentry class. Some, though not all, sinecures were reestablished, and the councils of officials and gentry which were to advise the throne were abolished. The opening of the *yen-lu,* or right to memorialize the throne, which had been given to all lower officials and common citizens in the late summer, was rescinded, as were the various reforms of the examination system.[2] Many of the summer edicts were allowed to stand, however, especially those providing for more effective administration of industrial and commercial affairs, the structural expansion of the school system, and military reforms.[3]

It should be noted that some important elements of journalistic opinion were receptive to Tz'u-hsi's resumption of direct rule and did not equate it with total reaction. Wang K'ang-nien's Shanghai daily, the *Chung-wai jih-pao,* which had commented favorably on most of Kuang-hsü's reform edicts, welcomed her return. At the same time it made clear that it did not expect a reversal of reforms but a stronger and more united China.[4] In December, 1898, the conservative Shanghai *Shen-pao* claimed that Tz'u-hsi had retained almost all important reforms of the summer and was doing a better job of attaining *fu-kuo ch'iang-ping* (rich country, strong army) than K'ang Yu-wei ever could have done.[5] This latter theme was elaborated by Chang Chih-tung's intimate Liang Ting-fen, who had long been a vicious critic of K'ang Yu-wei and his ideas. Not surprisingly, in the fall of 1898 Liang exulted in the exile of K'ang and his followers. However, in the essays and articles he wrote that fall, Liang did not condemn K'ang for his reform ideas, but for being a power-made usurper who did not even understand the reform doctrines he peddled. Liang claimed that the perverse and false reform ideas of K'ang would only have led to disorder (*luan*), whereas a correct reading and use of Western concepts would in fact help China attain wealth and power.[6]

The reform consensus which emerged after the defeat by Japan can be seen as continuing in some respects, despite the cataclysmic events of the "100 days" and the September coup of 1898. A specific index is the great popularity of Chang Chih-tung's personal reform platform, *Ch'üan-hsüeh p'ien,* which he had written in the spring of 1898. During the summer, the emperor had ordered a total of over three hundred copies of the tract given to top officials; this spurred reprints and heavy sales all over the country. But the conservatives who opposed the Hunan reform movement also praised the *Ch'üan-hsüeh p'ien,* and in November, 1898, the *Shen-pao* published a laudatory review of the work, calling it an "indispensable" book which bridged the gap between conservatives and reformers.[7] Opponents and critics of K'ang Yu-wei were of course quick to appreciate Chang Chih-tung's attacks on K'ang's theories and defense of Chinese values. But the work as a whole can scarcely be called a conservative apology, and in fact devotes most of its space to justifying needed institutional changes in all spheres of Chinese life, excepting only politics. Thus its continued popularity and acceptance indicate how far issue-conscious Chinese had come since 1895 in accepting the need for widespread national reforms.

Nevertheless, the political atmosphere between later 1898 and 1900 was not entirely conducive to progressive innovation. At Peking, the most hidebound Manchu and Chinese figures were dominant around the court, and those parts of the Kuang-hsü Emperor's reforms which they dismantled were precisely the most significant ones, those which had tried to open up the political structure. The purges in the bureaucracy which resulted from Tz'u-hsi's coup actually were not very extensive, by the account noted above, involving only some thirty men, but this may have been partly due to foreign pressure rather than to the natural restraint of the court. In fact, it is fairly clear that British and Japanese pressure was decisive in having Chang Yin-huan's sentence reduced from death to exile, and in having Huang Tsun-hsien released in Shanghai.[8] Moreover, when edicts, rumors, and ambiguous doctors' diagnoses had apparently cleared the path for Kuang-hsü's physical as well as political demise by early October, the very direct warnings by the British and Japanese ministers were instrumental in suppressing further moves against him.[9] And though it is unlikely that any foreign nations would have taken action to intervene in Chinese politics even had the purge been extended further through the bureaucracy, short of the emperor, officials such as Sheng Hsüan-huai and Liu K'un-i were able effectively to use the threat and fear of foreign intervention to dissuade the court from casting its net farther among reform-minded officials.[10]

The continuing dangers of reformist politics were shown by the fate of Tseng-ho, the Manchu appointed governor of Hupeh in November, 1898. In January, 1899, he requested that the edicts rescinding many of the "100 days' " decrees be canceled and that the summer measures be allowed to come back into effect. He was immediately denounced, dismissed from office, and denied future employment.[11] The empress dowager again seems to have entertained hopes of doing away with the emperor in the winter of 1898–99, and finally took what appeared to be a decisive step toward that end in January, 1900, with the establishment of P'u-chün, Prince Tuan's son, as heir apparent to the T'ung-chih Emperor.[12]

Thus the throne's attitude toward reform was inconsistent during this time. Although some of those at court would have liked nothing better than to roll back each and every reform of the "100 days," the empress dowager did not go so far, and even encouraged certain kinds of innovations. But, on the other hand, if one went too far in the direction of reform, it was easy to incur charges of being sympathetic to K'ang Yu-wei and Liang Ch'i-ch'ao, and officials like Chang Chih-tung were keenly aware of this.

The Position of Chang Chih-tung

After the empress dowager's September coup, Chang Chih-tung's position was undoubtedly in some danger. The last chapter has discussed Chang's very extensive connections with many major figures in both the Hunan and Peking reform programs, and had the purge been extended further through officialdom, it is possible that Chang would have been a victim. On September 28, the Hupeh judicial commissioner Ch'ü T'ing-shao, then in Peking, underwent sharp and detailed questioning from Tz'u-hsi concerning the situation in Hupeh. And the Japanese consul general in Shanghai, a well-informed and astute observer of Chinese politics, reported later in 1898 that immediately after the coup in September it was widely believed that Chang would be removed from his post, or at least degraded in rank.[13]

It is likely that the purge came its closest to Chang in early October. At that time, several of those who had directed the Hunan reform movement from the start were cashiered: Governor Ch'en Pao-chen, his son Ch'en San-li, former educational commissioner Chiang Piao, and the gentry leader Hsiung Hsi-ling. Through orders to Chang, the remnants of the Hunan reform apparatus were also destroyed.[14] It has been asserted that Chang, along with Liu K'un-i, intervened to save Governor Ch'en and his son San-li from a worse fate, perhaps death, but it is unlikely that Chang felt free enough to make any overt moves on their behalf, with his own position in question.[15] In fact, he seems to have washed his hands of anything having to do with the Hunan reforms. When some former students of Changsha's Shih-wu hsüeh-t'ang, including T'ang Ts'ai-ch'ang, applied for admission to Chang's Liang-hu Academy in Wuchang, they were turned away.[16]

One reason for Chang's political survival at this time was probably his long and close relationship with the empress dowager. He likely welcomed her return to the political arena, although he did not approve of the extensive rollback of the summer's reforms and he evinced no enthusiasm for her seeming determination to do away with the emperor.[17] On the other hand, Chang did not protest the moves against Kuang-hsü and counsel against extension of the purge, as did Sheng Hsüan-huai, Liu

K'un-i, and others.[18] Moreover, ostensibly for foreign policy reasons, he deprecated British interference in any attempted deposal of the emperor, saying it might throw the court "into the arms of Russia."[19] His hands-off attitude may have been due partly to the delicate nature of his own political position at the time, and perhaps as well to the fact that he was relatively indifferent to what happened to Kuang-hsü since his own career had not been tied closely to the young emperor.

In the winter of 1898–99, Kuang-hsü's fate was again in question, and the court made a discreet inquiry as to Liu K'un-i's reaction. One account has Liu suggesting to Chang Chih-tung that the two of them send a joint protest; the message was prepared, but Chang removed his name from it at the last minute and Liu had to register his protest alone.[20] Again in early 1900, Chang was absent from the group of several officials who vigorously opposed the apparent attempt to depose the emperor at that time.

From the fall of 1898 through the spring of 1900, the Ch'ing government used every device at its disposal to capture, assassinate, or prevent sanctuary to the former leaders of the radical reform movement and their followers in exile abroad. K'ang Yu-wei, Liang Ch'i-ch'ao, and their associates were pursued much more eagerly than were Sun Yat-sen and his band of revolutionaries during this time, although Sun was already well known. The former, being literati and former officials, were seen as a more serious threat, a government in exile of sorts, than were Sun and his lower-class cohorts.[21]

Chang Chih-tung was in the forefront of this fight against the reformer-exiles. He was tireless in his efforts to have them thrown out of Japan, and it was even rumored that the supervisor of the students sent to Japan by Chang in the fall of 1898 had secret orders to assassinate K'ang and Liang if he could.[22] However, Chang was not simply currying favor with the court by his efforts; he had two very specific reasons for working against the exiles in Japan. The first was that their presence in Japan was an obstacle to his plans for very close cooperation with the Japanese in his own Hupeh reform program, which he was continuing to carry out. The second was because they were rivals for the same reform constituency to which Chang himself looked for support, and they had begun actively to contest him for this constituency by attacking Chang personally in their publications.

Chang had long been an advocate of study abroad, and by 1898 he had concluded that Japan offered the best hope for training large numbers of Chinese students in new skills at a reasonable cost. He discussed the matter of sending Chinese students to Japan with two Japanese military representatives early in the year, and later in 1898 sent one of his lieutenants on a mission to inspect Japanese schools. He responded eagerly to a plan put forward by the Tsungli yamen to send students to Japan, hoping to send two hundred, and he was disappointed when financial straits limited to twenty the number he could actually send. He also had plans to utilize Japanese instructors in several of the new schools he was organizing in the Wuhan area.[23]

During the "100 days," there had been three edicts strongly urging the Tsungli yamen, provincial officials, and private gentry families, respectively, to send students abroad, especially to Japan.[24] After the coup, there was no more mention of this for some time. Moreover, Japan had offered asylum to K'ang, Liang, and several of their followers and had permitted them to publicize their cause through meetings and publications. Chang was now fearful that continuation of his plans to cooperate closely with Japan would bring suspicion upon him from the court conservatives, and he was afraid to bring up the subject of sending more students.

Chang therefore took a public stance of pressuring the Japanese government to throw out the K'ang-Liang group because they were traitors and bandits, and privately told the Japanese that his hopes of cooperation with them were stymied until they took some action against the exiles. On November 30, 1898, Chang argued this very forcefully with the Shanghai consul general Odagiri, who was visiting Wuchang. He then sent a personal representative to follow Odagiri back to Shanghai to press him further, while he himself badgered Segawa, the consul stationed in Hankow, for action. Segawa sent a telegram to Tokyo on Chang's behalf on December 2, noting particularly that all local projects involving Japanese advisers depended upon Japanese cooperation in moving against the K'ang-Liang group. Segawa also relayed Chang's request that the Japanese foreign ministry take the initiative with the

Tsungli yamen in bringing up the subject of sending more Chinese students to Japan; Segawa noted Chang's fears of denunciation were he to take the initiative himself.[25]

The new Japanese government, which replaced the one which had invited K'ang Yu-wei to Japan only five days after K'ang's arrival in October, was responsive to Chang's requests. It had no particular desire to alienate the Ch'ing government, and many Japanese military men wanted very much to promote the kind of cooperation which Chang Chih-tung seemed to be offering.[26] Thus Foreign Minister Aoki responded sympathetically to Chang by a telegram to Consul Segawa on December 6. He agreed to work through the Peking government to get more Chinese students to Japan and promised to do everything possible to get K'ang Yu-wei to leave. Chang now sent another envoy to pester Odagiri in Shanghai about the implementation of this commitment. Odagiri speculated that perhaps the Japanese government could pay K'ang's passage to North America, and estimated it might still take two months to persuade K'ang to leave. This was enough for Chang, however. On December 19, he sent a memorial to the Tsungli yamen, describing his efforts to secure K'ang's ouster, and reported a rumor that K'ang in fact had already left Japan. He took the greater credit for this achievement himself and also assured the government that no one in his Liang-hu jurisidiction was in the slightest impressed by the heretical doctrines of K'ang.[27] Chang was premature in his claims, for K'ang did not leave Japan until March 22, 1899. But the Japanese gave him nine thousand dollars to finance his trip, and it appears that he was under some coercion to leave.[28]

Chang now revived his program of cooperation with Japan during 1899. He hired a small Japanese military mission to teach at his new Noncommissioned Officers' School and sent several officers and senior enlisted men to Japan to study military organization and to observe field maneuvers.[29] The Peking government reaffirmed its approval of sending students abroad during the summer of 1899. Hsia Chieh-fu, an official of the Board of Works, was designated the first supervisor of Chinese students in Japan, and an edict promised employment in schools and government offices upon successful completion of study abroad. Chang responded quickly, sending at least twenty-seven more students to Japan in October, 1899.[30]

As K'ang Yu-wei's departure from Japan became imminent, Chang still pressed for the ouster of Liang Ch'i-ch'ao, Wang Chao, and other important figures who remained there. He occasionally contacted Consul General Odagiri in Shanghai on this matter and invariably mentioned it to Japanese visitors whom he saw in Wuchang.[31] Yet what really aroused Chang's ire was a direct attack upon him by the exiles early in 1899.

In December, 1898, Liang Ch'i-ch'ao began his long and influential career as journalist in exile when he founded the *Ch'ing-i pao* (The China Discussion) in Yokohama. Liang's style, as well as the substance of his writings, soon won the paper a wide readership among Chinese abroad and at home as well. In the fifth issue, February 2, 1899, there was an article denouncing Chang Chih-tung. It recounted the manner in which he had helped various reformers before Tz'u-hsi's coup and accused him of being cowardly in not joining Liu K'un-i in protest against the plan to do away with Kuang-hsü afterward. It also accused him of toadying to Jung-lu and the obnoxious conservatives around the court.[32]

Chang did not welcome public reminders of his past associations with the purged reformers. His own position was still such that he wanted to avoid arousing questions in the minds of the ultraconservatives in Peking. Thus, after the attack on him, he tried to have the *Ch'ing-i pao* closed down, or at least to prevent its circulation in China. In late February and March, he complained about the paper to both Consul Segawa and Consul General Odagiri, and he memorialized the Tsungli yamen, requesting it to put pressure on the Japanese foreign ministry to shut down the newspaper and deport the rest of the reformer-exiles.[33] Just at this time K'ang Yu-wei did leave Japan, and this fact, plus the apparent absence of any further attacks on Chang for the next few months in the *Ch'ing-i pao,* probably mollified him to some extent.

This was only the first skirmish in what would eventually (in 1900) develop into a full-scale verbal battle between the *Ch'ing-i pao* and Chang Chih-tung. At a more profound level, the clash between Chang and the exiled reformers signified their rivalry over the legacy of the 1895–98 reform effort. In Chang's eyes, K'ang and Liang were mortal enemies, because they could claim to be the rightful owners of this legacy. They provided potent competition for the bureaucratic reform constituency which had surfaced during those years, a constituency that Chang wanted to keep identified with a moderate dynastic reform program. For the remainder of 1899, however, Liang Ch'i-ch'ao went about the business of adjusting himself to his new role of publicist and teacher in exile with his newspaper and his Tokyo Ta-t'ung school, and Chang Chih-tung continued his reform program on a local level in Hupeh.[34]

Despite the atmosphere of the times within the bureaucracy, and the danger that critics might point to such activities as evidence of unreliability, Chang proceeded not only with his plans for cooperation with the Japanese, as described above, but with his local reform program in general. He revived a commercial newspaper (*Shang-wu pao*) which had been halted in 1898: it began publication again in the late spring of 1899. He drew up new provincial army regulations and devised new sources of revenue so as to be able to increase the size of the most modern sector of the military forces; these troops were praised by foreign observers already in 1900. And he spent much time on what was very dear to his heart, his new educational institutions such as the Agricultural School and the School of Industrial Arts, as well as the reform of the traditional academies (*shu-yüan*). In particular, he made extensive changes in the administration of the three major academies and modernized the curricula considerably, even introducing physical education.[35]

The Controversy over the Establishment of the New Heir Apparent

At this point I would like to introduce the notion of a changing and expanding social-economic-political constituency for reform, appearing for the first time in early 1900. In the 1895–98 period, there had been an impressive growth of study and discussion societies, as well as of the new journalism. But there was as yet no organized political action outside of what might be called the "bureaucratic community"—officeholders and their peers among the national elite of literati or gentry. In early 1900, however, for the first time a discernible extrabureaucratic public opinion made its appearance.

The occasion was the announcement, on January 24, 1900, that P'u-chün, Prince Tuan's son, was to be heir apparent to the T'ung-chih Emperor. Many observers at the time, and scholars since, concluded that this was a hesitant first step toward deposing Kuang-hsü, a kind of trial balloon that would allow the court, before proceeding further, to gauge both foreign reaction and the reaction of Liu K'un-i, who had protested apparent moves against Kuang-hsü in 1898 and 1899.[36]

This action did not arouse any significant foreign opposition. Neither the public decree nor previous discreet private inquiries by Li Hung-chang brought forward any foreign defenders of the sovereign.[37] The only possible remaining obstacle foreseen by the court was the venerable Liu K'un-i, who had been consistent in his counsel against deposing the emperor. Accordingly, Jung-lu had already arranged for Liu to be called to Peking to an audience in late December, 1899; the omens were clear enough, and all that Liu managed to do in the way of protest was to delay his trip to the capital until the following March.[38]

The edict of January 24, 1900, thus did not arouse opposition where it was expected, but it touched off a great wave of protest in quarters where none had ever existed before. In response to the edict and its implications, large numbers of lower officials, urban gentry groups, merchants, students, and overseas Chinese registered their opposition. Groups of people in Tientsin, Hangchow, Wuchang, and Shanghai turned in complaints to officials to be forwarded to Peking. Lower officials petitioned higher ones to join them in protest. Most Chinese newspapers were against the court's action, and groups of overseas Chinese telegraphed not only the Tsungli yamen, but also the British, American, and Japanese ministers in Peking, requesting foreign pressure to save Kuang-hsü.[39] Probably the most striking manifestation of protest was a mass telegram sent from Shanghai to Peking on January 26 and signed by 1,231 individuals, prominent among them Ching Yüan-shan, Shanghai director of the Imperial Telegraph Administration, other officials, private merchants, gentry, and students.[40] Whether due to this reaction, which I am inclined to credit, or to some other factor, the moves against Kuang-hsü, if that is what they were, proceeded no further.

These events symbolized a key stage in the evolution of China's political process. Previous to this time, individual high officials sometimes protested specific government policies or actions by memorial or by privately pulling strings in Peking. The formation of factions (*tang*) within the bureaucracy had been effectively discouraged since early in the dynasty. Only examination candidates gathered for the exams had petitioned the government as an "outside" group before, the most recent time being in the spring of 1895, when they had been led by K'ang Yu-wei. But now people and groups at the fringes of the traditional political structure, or outside it altogether, were beginning to play a role in the expression of what might be called a nonbureaucratic public opinion.

The effectiveness of these protests in this instance may be debated. They stressed the danger of foreign intervention, and the fear of intervention remained a lively one for the court; perhaps it was decisive in preventing the culmination of the alleged plot against Kuang-hsü. But the new role of nonbureaucratic public opinion was now firmly established, and in future years the scope and tempo of this activity would grow: protests over Russia's refusal to leave Manchuria in 1903; the boycotts against the United States in 1905 and Japan in 1908; movements to recover railway and mining rights; and finally the constitutional movement at the end of the dynasty.

The relevance of this new political development for our purposes is that its chief immediate beneficiary was Chang Chih-tung's rival, the *pao-huang* movement led by K'ang and Liang. Since 1898 the reformers' newspapers had consistently defended the emperor and attacked the empress dowager and her court allies. Now other, more moderate newspapers and newly activated groups within China and abroad joined the exiles in protest. A good example was Wang K'ang-nien and his Shanghai daily, the *Chung-wai jih-pao*.

Wang K'ang-nien in his publications remained a stalwart spokesman for the moderate reform position of Chang Chih-tung through most of 1898, and his paper even welcomed the resumption of power by Tz'u-hsi. But Wang became increasingly impatient at the lack of reform initiative at the top of the Peking government, and by the late summer of 1899 he began to advocate returning active power to the emperor. By the end of 1899, Wang was backing the activities and programs of the reform exiles in Japan, defending them against continued attacks by the conservative *Shen-pao* and deploring the court's elaborate efforts to have K'ang and Liang captured or assassinated. In late January, 1900, the *Chung-wai jih-pao* unreservedly backed the mass Shanghai telegraph petition, and an editorial even hinted that violence would be justified to protect the emperor's person.[41] At the same time that Wang K'ang-nien moved closer to the exiled reformers in policy, he mended his personal feud with Liang Ch'i-ch'ao, which had reached such a bitter level in 1898 over the issue of who would control the *Shih-wu pao*.[42]

If the reformers in exile were gaining new allies among elements of an emerging public opinion by early 1900, Chang Chih-tung was taking a corresponding loss. By this time Chang was probably also hoping for vigorous leadership in reform from Peking and deploring the dominance at court of men for whom he had little respect. He was especially unhappy with the increasingly belligerent tone in foreign relations and with the court policy of fostering poorly trained local militia as a means of defense, both of which policies would lead to the Boxer debacle a few months later.[43] Yet he did not equate a national reform program with Kuang-hsü's survival, and saw no reason for jeopardizing his own political position by protesting to the court on what perhaps to him was a peripheral issue. He may not even have believed that there existed a real plot against Kuang-hsü. Thus, as before, he was quiet on the subject of the emperor's fate. He was undoubtedly surprised at the widespread public outcry of late January and February, 1900, and unpleasantly so when he realized that many of those protesting classified him along with the obscurantists around the court.

A year earlier, in 1899, Chang had been eager to avoid charges in the reform press that he had been an early ally of the radicals of 1898. Now he showed himself eager to refute charges in the same press that he was reactionary, allied with the most conservative princes and ministers. Soon after the infamous January 24 edict, the *Ch'ing-i pao* claimed that Chang Chih-tung had been consulted in advance about the alleged plot against Kuang-hsü, and that he had approved it happily.[44] By mid-February, a story current in many circles purported to describe events in Hupeh after the January 24 edict, a story which was devastating in its portrayal of Chang Chih-tung and which is worth recounting in some detail.[45]

Supposedly, upon receipt of the news from Peking great numbers of local officials, gentry, and merchants gathered in Wuchang, all determined to protest. Their leaders included the provincial judicial commissioner Ts'en Ch'un-ming and the taotai Cheng Hsiao-hsü.[46] They wrote a vigorous protest document and took it to the top provincial officials for approval. Governor Yü Yin-lin was pleased to sign it, but Chang Chih-tung tried to squelch it. Ts'en Ch'un-ming was so enraged that he cursed Chang, but Chang merely laughed, told the group not to get so excited, and to think it over again before acting. The group left his yamen in a huff, and the next day over fifty officials and merchants left Hankow for Shanghai, intending to go all the way to Peking to deliver their protest even at great risk (*p'in-ming*). The story concluded with comments by the editor deriding the position which Chang took on the issue.

This made great propaganda, with its picture of Chang as at best indifferent to and at worst conniving in the emperor's demise, but it was undoubtedly greatly distorted. There is no hard evidence of such a group of people starting out for Peking to protest, let alone arriving there.[47] Moreover, Governor Yü was not the sort to acquiesce in this kind of politically colored activity. Yet the assertion of widespread concern among leaders of official and nonofficial Hupeh public opinion is certainly credible, and something vaguely similar to the description of the confrontation in Chang's office may well have taken place, given Chang's inclinations on the issue.

Chang was stung by this kind of story appearing in print, and he reacted in a typically vigorous manner. On February 10, 1900, he sent a telegram to Ch'ien Hsün, a trusted member of his *mu-fu* who was then supervisor of Hupeh students in Japan. He ordered Ch'ien to go directly to the Japanese foreign ministry to complain about the newspapers in Chinese treaty ports which were technically registered in Japanese names and which were disseminating the propaganda of the K'ang-Liang group. He was very angry and specifically mentioned the charges that he had been consulted in advance over the move to depose Kuang-hsü as the kind of nonsense that had to be stopped. Significantly, Chang mentioned Yen Fu's Tientsin *Kuo-wen pao* and Wang K'ang-nien's *Chung-wai jih-pao* among the papers that he demanded be curbed.[48] In addition, Chang appealed to the foreign consuls in Hankow, requesting them to move their governments to suppress seditious Chinese newspapers which were springing up under foreign protection in the treaty port concession areas.[49]

Chang also took more direct action. On March 7, 1900, he directed customs officials in his jurisdiction to confiscate all copies of the *Ch'ing-i pao* and other seditious newspapers, and to be very thorough in checking the background of any persons who wanted to start new publications.[50] The court in Peking was also eager to put a stop to the considerable publicity given to the exiles by the campaign to save the emperor. On February 14, 1900, there was issued an edict renewing the offer of a reward for the capture or proof of the death of K'ang and Liang, and directing coastal officials to be especially strict about publications carrying their propaganda. On February 23, the Chihli governor-general received an order to close down Yen Fu's *Kuo-wen pao* in Tientsin.[51] In the end, however, little headway could be made in these efforts to prevent dissemination of unwelcome reading matter. Too many newspapers and bookstores were under the legal ownership of foreigners, and the fact was that, without foreign cooperation, their permanent suppression was almost impossible.[52] Indeed, the circulation of the worst offender, the *Ch'ing-i pao,* probably continued to increase.

Thus in early 1900 the Ch'ing government was coming into increasing disrepute with a fledgling Chinese public opinion forming outside the bureaucracy and centered in the treaty ports. Chang Chih-tung, as a loyal servant of the central government, could not help but be tarnished along with it, and among the new reform constituency he lost ground to the K'ang-Liang party. In March, 1900, sensing victory, Liang Ch'i-ch'ao wrote a confident editorial for the *Ch'ing-i pao* in the form of a long letter to Chang Chih-tung.[53] Liang again castigated Chang for supposedly being loyal to the emperor but actually conniving in his deposition, while all "responsible people" easily saw through the ruse of establishing a new heir apparent and righteously protested.

During the next few months, over the fateful Boxer summer, times would get much worse for both the central government in Peking and for Chang Chih-tung, its defender in central China. For a flickering moment there was even a possibility that the reformers-in-exile might return to lead a new government. Yet, in the end, the actions of the reformers themselves during 1900 would lose them much of the support that they had won in late 1899 and early 1900. Since the collapse of the "100 days," Chang Chih-tung and other spokesmen for the dynasty had called K'ang, Liang, and their followers bandits and rebels, like the followers of traditional secret societies. This was an attempt to hide the fact that the K'ang-Liang group was feared precisely because they were not traditional rebels, but heretics from within the ruling class itself; not carriers of social chaos like the Taipings, but credible rivals for power inside the existing political framework.

During 1899 and 1900, however, the exiles in Japan, led by Liang Ch'i-ch'ao, drifted ever closer to advocating and then fomenting the sort of political revolution and social upheaval that the dynasty had always claimed they represented. The contacts between the *pao-huang* "reform" group and Sun Yat-sen's more openly revolutionary movement were closer during these years than ever before or after.[54] After K'ang Yu-wei left Japan in the spring of 1899, Liang Ch'i-ch'ao began to assert his independence of his master, and his own inclinations, manifested clearly in the *Ch'ing-i pao* and his Ta-t'ung school, led to a more and more radical stance. Both Liang and the group of young Hunanese students who would eventually participate in the Tzu-li hui uprising in Hankow in August, 1900, edged closer to armed force and actual overthrow of the government, though they still pledged loyalty to the Kuang-hsü Emperor.[55]

In the spring of 1900, when Liang Ch'i-ch'ao was in Hawaii competing for adherents in Sun Yat-sen's own bailiwick, he crossed the hazy line between reform and revolution by allying himself and the reform cause with secret societies, even joining the Triads himself. In the correspondence of the first half of 1900 between Liang in Hawaii, K'ang Yu-wei in Singapore, and T'ang Ts'ai-ch'ang and others in Shanghai and Macao, the picture of a conspiratorial revolutionary group emerges clearly.[56] K'ang Yu-wei, raising funds in Southeast Asia, was reluctant to dabble in pure revolution, but Liang's insistence carried him along. The results of their endeavor constituted a direct challenge not only to the dynasty but to Chang Chih-tung personally in the summer of 1900, and also left K'ang and Liang open to a counterattack by Chang.

Chapter 5

The Boxer Debacle and the Tzu-li hui Uprising of 1900

Nineteen hundred was a crucial year in modern Chinese history. In the aftermath of the cataclysmic events of the Boxer summer, considerable realignment of individuals and groups took place on the political scene. The grip of the court reactionaries was shaken, though at tremendous cost in humiliation and indemnities imposed by the Boxer protocol. The empress dowager herself remained in overall control, but the court would now take the initiative in promulgating a comprehensive national reform program, helped and prodded by Chang Chih-tung, Liu K'un-i, Yüan Shih-k'ai, and others. This achievement took until well into 1901, and will be dealt with in the next chapter.

More immediately, the central government, and Chang Chih-tung as its representative, survived a potentially formidable threat in central China in the summer of 1900. This was the alliance between the exiled reformers around K'ang and Liang and the traditional local secret societies, culminating in the abortive August, 1900, uprising of T'ang Ts'ai-ch'ang and the Tzu-li hui (Independence Society). By taking advantage of the disillusionment of a large segment of moderate public opinion with the extremist tactics of the reformer-rebels, Chang was able to help isolate the reform group in Japan. By the end of 1900, the considerable support they had won in late 1899 and early 1900 was largely gone, and the major competitors to bureaucratic reformers like Chang Chih-tung were on the defensive.

Foreign Intervention and Local Unrest

The position of Chang Chih-tung and other officials of central China became exceedingly precarious during the summer of 1900. Opposed to the rising xenophobic Boxer movement in the north, and appalled to see the court's appeasement of, then alliance with, the Boxers, they were in despair over the ultimate folly of the June 21 declaration of war against the Powers and the attack on the Peking legations. Chang himself, confronted with the order to implement the declaration of war of June 21, instead ignored it. Joined by the other top officials of central and south China, he chose to interpret the imperial edict so as to allow him to keep the peace within his jurisdiction and confine hostilities to the north.[1]

For this strategy to have a chance of success, it had to be reciprocated by the Powers. The foreign governments were receptive. In fact the foreign community at Shanghai, led by the British consul general Warren, was eager to carry out a preemptive occupation of parts of the lower Yangtze in conjunction with the governors-general, so as to help keep the peace. A British proposal for this was first made to Liu K'un-i and Chang Chih-tung about June 16. The governors-general, especially Chang, discouraged such a move, knowing that it would provoke a violent reaction from the bellicose and antiforeign Imperial Commissioner of Naval Forces, Li Ping-heng, stationed near Shanghai.[2] Instead, the Yangtze officials, represented by Sheng Hsüan-huai in Shanghai, tried to negotiate an agreement with the foreign consuls whereby the Powers would look to the defense of the foreign settlement there, but the peace of the entire interior of the Yangtze Valley would be guaranteed by the governors-general at Nanking and Wuchang. The Chinese officials presented a draft agreement of nine articles effecting this arrangement to the consuls on June 26, and the Chinese minister in London, acting on the instructions of Chang Chih-tung and Liu K'un-i, offered the same document to Lord Salisbury, the British foreign secretary.[3]

The Chinese, especially the governors-general Chang and Liu, who had ultimate responsibility in the Yangtze Valley, were looking for a concrete agreement, manifested in a written guarantee of the foreign governments' commitments. A tangible document could be expected to carry some weight with the court when the time came, as it well might, when they would be held accountable for their action in defying the imperial declaration of war. If they had been independent regional satraps, effectively beyond imperial sanction, such a formal guarantee would have been irrelevant; on the contrary, they were acutely aware of the retribution that might be in store for them for their acts.

Unfortunately, the foreign powers, led by the British, were reluctant to put anything in writing; they were all in favor of actually implementing such an agreement, but they were fearful of the possible effects of any formal commitment on established treaty rights. Thus British Consul General Warren in Shanghai was evasive about fully honoring such a deal, and Salisbury in London refused to put anything in writing.[4] It was fairly clear, however, that the foreign governments intended to cooperate fully with the governors-general, according to their proposed agreement, at least for the immediate future. In fact, it is possible that the McKinley administration issued the second "Open Door note" on July 3 as a direct signal to the governors-general that it intended to honor the agreement.[5]

This was all well and good, but it left Chang and Liu still at the mercy of an abrupt change in British (and other foreign governments') policy, yet without concrete proof to offer the court that they disobeyed its orders in good faith and for the good of the dynasty itself. Nevertheless, and to their credit, though they had little feasible alternative, they fully lived up to the "agreement" with the Powers. Locally Chang was vigorous in publicizing the agreement as though it were a formal treaty, in disciplining his subordinate officials to protect foreign lives and property, and in suppressing Boxers and other rebels in his jurisdiction.[6] Moreover, he continued to urge the court, especially Grand Councillor Jung-lu, to end the siege of the legations and to make peace, and he maintained contact with Chinese diplomats abroad; he even corresponded with Ito Hirobumi, elder statesman of the Japanese government in Tokyo, on how best to bring the hostilities to an end.[7]

Yet Chang remained very concerned about the vulnerability of his position. In response to a direct order, in mid-July he sent altogether about five thousand troops from Hunan and Hupeh to the north as reinforcements for the imperial forces, though these were perhaps not the best troops at his disposal.[8] At the end of July, Chang grew very uneasy as Warren, representing an increasingly frantic and panicked Shanghai foreign community, seemed on the verge of some rash action in the lower Yangtze. Warren even intimidated Liu K'un-i into accepting British naval action outside Shanghai proper.[9] This endangered the always precarious local peace. At the same time, in the last few days of July, the most militant reactionaries in Peking reversed a small trend toward moderation at the court and engineered the execution of two high ranking anti-Boxer ministers. Three more foes of the Boxer supporters died two weeks later.[10] The possible fate of Chang Chih-tung and Liu K'un-i was writ large, with the executioner's sword.

The Yangtze officials, with their work endangered by the British and now reminded of their domestic political vulnerability by events in Peking, reacted in self-defense. Sheng Hsüan-huai prudently applied for British protection, if it should be necessary. Chang and Liu chose partially to protect themselves by now publicly declaring themselves to be unconditionally loyal to the person and position of the empress dowager, and demanding that the British government guarantee her safety and authority. This was probably done less in serious hopes of gaining British acquiescence on this point, which was not forthcoming, than in repair of their political position in regard to the court.[11]

A more serious test of British willingness to support the "Yangtze compact," and if necessary to support Chang personally, was Chang's private request in late July for a "loan" of half a million taels to "pay his troops," a loan Chang was pointedly unwilling to secure adequately. When the British government agreed to this in early August, it was in effect purchasing Chang's continued willingness to endanger himself politically for the sake of peace and protection of foreign interests in the Yangtze Valley.[12] Chang would retain a very close relationship with the British over the coming months of uncertainty in the aftermath of the truce and the working out of the peace settlement, as will be recounted in the next chapter.

Thus, during the summer of 1900 Chang had to keep close watch on his relations with elements beyond his reach and largely out of his control; fast work was necessary to shore up his position vis-à-vis throne, court, fellow provincial officials, and foreign governments. And meanwhile, there was the constant danger that his own province of Hupeh would explode in rebellion and social chaos beneath his very feet.

Local unrest and social disorder was an increasingly large problem in many provinces during the last years of the nineteenth century, and Hupeh was no exception.[13] The activities of secret societies, the incidence of general banditry, and violent attacks on missionaries and other foreigners all seemed to be on the rise even before Chang Chih-tung arrived in Wuchang in 1889, and they occupied a fair amount of his administrative energies all through the 1890's.[14] Indeed, every year of the decade was marred by some form of secret society (usually Ko-lao hui) disruption or missionary incident, often by both.

The more spectacular of these outbursts, since they often occasioned outraged foreign reaction and attendant diplomatic complications, were the antiforeign incidents. The riots and unrest all along the lower Yangtze Valley during spring and summer 1891, for example, brought on both a national diplomatic crisis for the court and a local headache for Chang Chih-tung. Secret societies, in particular the Ko-lao hui, seem to have made a conscious attempt to foment antiforeign violence in order to embarrass the national government and to embroil it in bitter conflict with the Western powers.[15] Chang, who was usually unsympathetic to the complaints of missionaries and consuls concerning violence encountered by the former in their attempts to proselytize, reacted more vigorously when there was evidence of organized secret society antidynastic agitation behind such violence. In the aftermath of the 1891 riots, Chang conducted a rigorous search for Ko-lao hui adherents. He acquired new river gunboats for more effective patrolling, and he imposed a stringent system of interrogation of suspicious transients.[16] One reason he may have been willing to act quickly in such cases is that sometimes he personally, as an imperial official, was denounced in the placards and propaganda disseminated by the societies.[17]

The pattern of unrest of the 1890's created in most foreigners in the Yangtze Valley a morbid preoccupation with incidents and rumors of antiforeign violence. This in turn created apprehension on their part that Chang and other high provincial officials might have neither the power nor the will to hold the forces of violence in check. The result was constant consular pressure on Chang to deal sternly with all perpetrators of violence against Westerners and to exercise constant vigilance against such disorders.[18] In the late 1890's, in the atmosphere of the "race for concessions," such pressure often became associated with territorial demands and constituted a real danger to the integrity of the Chinese state.[19] This pressure was unwelcome from Chang's point of view for still another reason. While he had every desire to thwart and crush secret society plots, he had considerable sympathy for the anti-Christian and antiforeign resentment to which the societies catered. Moreover, many respectable and orthodox gentry, men whose position and power Chang had to respect, and whose status and connections put them beyond his ability easily to coerce, also engaged in antiforeign pamphleteering, directed especially against missionaries. Some leading members of the Hunan gentry class devoted considerable time and energy to the sporadic production of imaginatively scurrilous anti-Christian tracts during most of the 1890's, and these had at least some role in fomenting violence.[20]

Indeed, the prospects for unrest somewhere in the province were never distant all through the 1890's. Besides secret society activity and literati pamphleteering, the rapid growth of the Hankow tea trade in the 1880's had created a seasonally transient class of warehouse and dock workers numbering close to 100,000, which frequently caused a security problem.[21] The correspondingly rapid growth of the foreign concession area in Hankow, including a spacious bund, provided a convenient focus for the curious to gather, and crowds of Chinese often congregated there, especially when examinations were being held across the river in Wuchang, as they frequently were. The concession handled its own security, with a police force of Chinese which already numbered forty by 1890, under a Western chief of police. The result was frequent tension between the crowds and the Chinese concession police, who were abused as foreign lackeys by the crowds and who were resented for their arrogance and quick resort to the nightstick.[22] The Chinese troops who were usually depended on to keep the peace in the

Wuhan cities became themselves heavily infiltrated by the Ko-lao hui in the 1890's, and it proved to be almost impossible to disband military units, as after the Sino-Japanese War in 1895, without provoking violence.[23] It is not surprising that establishment of modern municipal police forces soon became attractive to many urban reformers. This was one of the institutions which Chang Chih-tung tried to save out of the wreckage of the Hunan reforms of 1898, and one which he himself implemented in Wuchang after 1900.[24]

Outside the cities, Chang's authority was also weakened by the potential for disorder and, often, by circumstances unrelated to the ever present threat of missionary incidents. For example, by the 1890's there had been a rapid growth of river extortion rackets, which preyed on Chinese commercial and passenger steamers and which undoubtedly were connected to secret societies.[25] Moreover, as gangs of railroad coolies working on the Peking-Hankow railroad pushed into the countryside in the early 1890's, there were occasional clashes with local residents.[26] And of course the Ko-lao hui was capable of mounting insurrections outside the Wuhan cities, as well as fomenting disorder within them. An especially large and destructive Ko-lao hui revolt from November, 1898, through February, 1899, covered a wide area of the province and required strenuous effort to suppress.[27]

Chang was opposed to an 1898 reform of the military examinations providing that real firearms be used on the basis that the resulting wider dissemination of weapons would mean more revolts. And he was consistently opposed to the court's encouragement of the formation of local militia between 1898 and 1900, believing this to be an open invitation to riots and missionary incidents.[28]

As chaos spread across north China in the early months of 1900, the danger of unrest, and especially of secret society revolts in the Yangtze Valley, became more acute. Only a few Boxer bands seem to have made their way into Hupeh province, though their placards were often seen, but there were plenty of native Hupeh troublemakers to tax the authorities. In the late spring, several *hsien* experienced disorder ranging from riots and church burnings through outright revolt. The Peking-Hankow railroad and the foreign engineers working on it also came under occasional attack. Chang gradually built up the regular army forces camped along the railway to protect it, until eventually four battalions were so assigned, under the authority of one of his top lieutenants.[29]

After the court's declaration of war on the Powers and his own precarious agreement with the foreign governments to preserve the peace in central China, it was even more imperative that he keep local unrest under control. Against this background of delicately balanced factors, then, there occurred the Tzu-li hui uprising, centered in Hankow, across the river from Chang's very own yamen.

The Nature of the Tzu-li hui Uprising

The history of the Tzu-li hui (Independence Society) uprising of August, 1900, has been treated in some detail in recent years.[30] The rebellion was planned by T'ang Ts'ai-ch'ang and other veterans of the old Hunan reform movement and was directly supported from abroad by Liang Ch'i-ch'ao and K'ang Yu-wei. It was designed to take advantage of the confusion of the Boxer Rebellion in the north to overthrow the central government's authority in the Yangtze area, in hopes that a new government could be founded in central and south China, eventually to take over full national authority. The Kuang-hsü Emperor would lead this new government, but until he could be installed, authority would reside in a "National Assembly" (Kuo-hui) based in Shanghai and other major cities. The revolt, delayed for various reasons, mainly the lack of funds from abroad, was uncoordinated, its headquarters in Hankow were prematurely raided on orders from Chang Chih-tung, and its leaders were captured and killed.

For my purpose, which is to relate the Tzu-li hui plot to Chang Chih-tung, the interesting factors are not the facts and personalities of the revolt, but its contradictory political and social elements. It is undoubtedly correct, as Lewis has especially emphasized, that the Tzu-li hui, in "doctrine and objectives was derived directly from the Hunan reform movement."[31] Yet, as noted at the end of the last chapter, the legacy of that reform movement was ambiguous, and the chief reform spokesman, Liang Ch'i-ch'ao, was becoming quite revolutionary during 1899 and early 1900. He, and even more so the young student veterans of the Hunan movement, retained only a vague loyalty to Kuang-hsü personally, as a symbol of their 1898 hopes. Their rhetoric became more anti-Manchu, they were willing to consider cooperation with Sun Yat-sen's revolutionaries, and they became increasingly committed to violent overthrow of the central government.

T'ang Ts'ai-ch'ang and the other young men who made their way from Japan back to China at the end of 1899 to begin practical planning for an insurrection were undoubtedly romantic idealists. They probably saw themselves as Chinese equivalents of the Japanese *shishi,* men of courage and determination who engineered the overthrow of the Tokugawa government and the Meiji Restoration in the 1860's. Like these heroes, T'ang and his group would "restore" the Kuang-hsü Emperor and embark on a whole new national course. Liang and K'ang may also have been somewhat enraptured by this flattering analogy.[32]

When planning revolution, however, even the stature of a *shishi* is insufficient without allies. And just as Sun Yat-sen had done long ago, the reformer-rebels looked for those allies among the traditional secret societies. Using the contacts first made for him by Pi Yung-nien, an agent of Sun Yat-sen, and with one of the leaders of his group, Lin Kuei, also having such contacts, T'ang Ts'ai-ch'ang began to cultivate the societies of central China, especially the Ko-lao hui, as the foundation of a projected insurrection. Lin Kuei went to Hankow in the early spring of 1900 to conduct local relations with the societies; T'ang Ts'ai-ch'ang remained in Shanghai until the summer, then transferred general coordinating activities to Hankow.

Meanwhile, Liang Ch'i-ch'ao in Hawaii and K'ang Yu-wei in Singapore lent their considerable talents to fund raising among overseas Chinese to support the venture, and Liang in particular expended great energy trying to maintain communication and coordination among the various participants, who were now spread out all over the Pacific basin. Both Liang and K'ang were resigned to the necessity of violent overthrow to gain their political aims, though perhaps somewhat reluctant about it.[33] Thus were intellectual reformers wedded to the muscle of old-fashioned secret society rebels.

Despite this reality, reformist rhetoric continued to dominate the public stance of Liang, K'ang, and their agents. Their program of restoration of the emperor and revival of the "100 days" reforms was winning many adherents, especially after the furor created by the establishment of a new heir apparent in January, 1900. The manifesto of the main Shanghai organization begun by T'ang Ts'ai-ch'ang in the late winter or early spring of 1900, the Cheng-ch'i hui (Uprightness Society), was quite moderate in tone.[34] The change of the society's name later in the spring to use the term *tzu-li,* independence, gave a more accurate indication of its goal of a new government, but none as to the precise means of achieving it.

The next, and most important, part of the conspirators' plan was the creation of an organization that could provide a credible framework of a new government when the revolt, now projected for the late summer, occurred. This task was the major occupation of T'ang in Shanghai in the late spring and early summer.[35] Already on July 2, K'ang Yu-wei in a circular letter claimed that his followers were forming a preliminary national assembly in Shanghai.[36]

The summer of 1900, of course, brought much disillusionment with the Peking government on the part of China's best-informed official and nonofficial elite; this was especially so in the urban areas, foremost among them Shanghai. There T'ang Ts'ai-ch'ang took good advantage of this mood, and did in fact summon a National Assembly (Kuo-hui) as the potential nucleus of a new government, albeit one still to be under a "restored" emperor. The two meetings held on July 26 and July 30 attracted many respectable people; Yung Wing (Jung Hung) and Yen Fu (whose Tientsin newspaper had just been closed down by the government) were elected chief officers, though T'ang himself undoubtedly kept control through his position as secretary.[37]

The Kuo-hui was an excellent front organization. It drew the support of solid citizens like Wang K'ang-nien, who helped to publicize the meetings in advance and praised the organization in his newspaper, the *Chung-wai jih-pao,* besides participating himself.[38]

Yung Wing and Yen Fu were well known in the foreign community, and the Kuo-hui manifesto written by Yung and communicated to the foreign diplomats in Shanghai appealed strongly to the preferences of Westerners in the kind of constitutional government it promised for the future. In an August report, the British consul general in Shanghai commented favorably on the "Chinese National Association," as he called it, and noted that "the Association has the sympathy of several expectant officials of good families and standing, besides several Hanlins and gentry from nearly all the provinces of China."[39]

Beyond the manifesto written by Yung Wing, which was probably directed mainly at foreigners in the first place, the platform of the Kuo-hui was uncertain. Its participants were divided on such questions as the extent of imperial authority that would exist under a new constitutional system, and what political changes would actually occur. There was discussion of the use of violence, but no firm decision was made on whether to kill top provincial officials like Chang Chih-tung or to try to use them in the new structure.[40] On this last point, the views of Wang K'ang-nien may be of interest, since he probably represented a certain element of moderate opinion at the time. A two-part editorial in his paper praised the Kuo-hui for offering an alternative to the bankrupt Peking government and claimed that those officials engaged in the Yangtze peace agreement really had no choice but to follow the lead of the Kuo-hui. They should declare their provincial independence and come together in some new form of national authority, with the Kuo-hui as the highest organ.[41]

Thus Wang K'ang-nien, for one, looked for the peaceful adherence of the existing provincial governments in central-south China, not their violent overthrow. Much less did he anticipate an alliance with secret societies, and there seems to have been no discussion of such an alliance in the Kuo-hui meetings. Yet this was precisely what T'ang Ts'ai-ch'ang and his cohorts were about. To them, the Kuo-hui and its organizational predecessors, while perhaps an eventual working government, were for the present only public window dressing, a means to attract support and especially funds, which were then invested in the Ko-lao hui leaders of the Yangtze Valley. Society leaders were heavily subsidized by T'ang, and the recruitment of armed followers (called the Tzu-li chün or Ch'in-wang chün) was done entirely through secret society channels. Over twenty thousand *fu-yu p'iao* tickets, a version of a recruitment device commonly used by the societies, were printed and distributed. The insurrection itself was laid out along secret society lines, with esoteric code words and other paraphernalia; K'ang Yu-wei, Liang Ch'i-ch'ao, and T'ang Ts'ai-ch'ang were listed as *lung-t'ou* (dragon's heads), a standard society designation for leaders.

The reformer-conspirators, having put all their resources into this venture, ended up riding a tiger. The seal of the Kuo-hui was used on documents proclaiming a new government, and preparations were made to set up branch Kuo-hui offices in major cities after the revolt. Placards calling for law and order and the protection of missionaries and foreign property were prepared, to neutralize the fears of foreign governments. There is some evidence that lists of local officials and gentry were compiled, at least for Hupeh, in anticipation of calling upon them to support the new government.[42] Yet all this was done while the secret societies, mortal enemies of officials, gentry class, and foreigners alike, were being cultivated, and in the unusually tense atmosphere of the precarious peace being maintained in the Yangtze Valley at the time. Ch'in Li-shan, one of the major organizers and leader of the contingent at Ta-t'ung in Anhui, even approached a Boxer chieftain about an alliance during the summer, although he was rebuffed.[43]

Moreover, as their funds ran low, it became clear that the control of T'ang, Lin Kuei, and the others over the secret societies and their real leaders was very tenuous. As the first date for the revolt, August 9, was moved back, some units just dropped out. Ch'in Li-shan's group at Ta-t'ung, Anhui, revolted on its own on the ninth; it was suppressed quickly but had time to post its placards and thus give some warning to the authorities of the extent and nature of the projected uprising. The revolt headquarters and leaders in Hankow were captured with little difficulty on August 21, though sporadic violence connected with the planned uprising occurred at several places in the last part of August.

The Position of Chang Chih-tung vis-à-vis the Uprising

The attitude of the Tzu-li hui leaders toward Chang Chih-tung was ambiguous. The more moderate parts of the movement, including supporters of the Kuo-hui like Wang K'ang-nien, were hopeful that Chang and Liu K'un-i would "defect" peacefully to the new government. This also seems to have been the hope of K'ang Yu-wei, who reportedly vetoed a proposed plan to assassinate Chang and insisted that instead he be compelled by force to join the movement. Liang Ch'i-ch'ao also wrote two letters to Chang during the summer of 1900, though there is no evidence that Chang received them.[44]

Those actually responsible for dealing with Chang in Hankow were somewhat less sanguine in their hopes for cooperation with him. Lin Kuei, the chief liaison man with the secret societies, was the proponent of the plan to assassinate Chang, which K'ang vetoed. T'ang Ts'ai-ch'ang himself was at first apparently not serious about possible cooperation with Chang, but he became more hopeful as the situation in the north deteriorated over the summer, and he even took the dangerous step of indirectly sounding out Chang's views through a Japanese intermediary. Shen Chin, a former clerk in Chang's office and now leader of the rebel forces at Hsin-t'i, was also enthusiastic about dealing with Chang, and hoped that he could be won over if presented with the fait accompli of a successful revolt.[45]

In considering the situation in early August, 1900, with all its confusion and uncertainties, it was not entirely unrealistic of the leaders of the revolt to hope for some sort of positive, or at least neutral, reaction from Chang Chih-tung. For example, if the allied powers' drive on Peking had resulted in the death of the emperor and empress dowager, leaving a political vacuum, some action in concert with the Tzu-li hui and the Kuo-hui might have held some attraction for him. But the successful flight of the court on August 15 and the edict of August 19 empowering Li Hung-chang to sue for peace allayed fears of a total collapse at the center, and would have sharply reduced the appeal of such a desperate move on Chang's part.[46]

In fact, however, the real possibilities of Chang's allying with the Tzu-li hui must have been close to zero, given their intimate relationship with the secret societies. His failure immediately to move against the conspirators, even after T'ang had contacted him indirectly and the premature uprising in Anhui had taken place on August 9, has been taken by later writers as proof of his uncertainty and his serious consideration of joining the movement.[47] On the contrary, his hesitation may have actually stemmed from two other factors. One was a reluctance to suppress physically the group in Hankow, whom he probably had difficulty taking seriously as revolutionaries. The other was his need for time to make precautionary troop movements and to prepare the foreign consuls, so as to ensure effective action with no danger of foreign intervention if suppression proved necessary.

Chang had a fairly good idea of the nature and activities of T'ang Ts'ai-ch'ang's group, not only from T'ang's contacting him but from his own spy network. He was not without sympathy for these idealistic sons of the gentry class, and the last thing he wanted to do was to exterminate them. Chang remembered T'ang from the latter's days at the Liang-hu Academy, where he was an outstanding student, and now he tried to persuade T'ang to drop his schemes and leave the city. As late as August 17, Chang reportedly sent one of his subordinates to visit T'ang at his hideout and urge him to flee.[48]

Yet, when the conspirators proceeded nevertheless, Chang had no other choice than to capture them and execute the leaders. Knowledge of the projected revolt, and its relationship with the secret societies, was simply too widely spread for Chang to be able to ignore it, especially given his own shaky domestic political position at that time. Chang was reportedly under some pressure from more conservative officials, including Governor Yü Yin-lin, to take decisive action, and the determination of the conspirators to press on with their plot left him no other choice.[49]

He was prepared for suppression, for since the first few days of August, and especially after the Ta-t'ung uprising of August 9, he had intensified his vigilance against unrest. He shifted some troops around, authorized increased recruitment to augment local forces in several places, issued stringent orders to local commanders warning of probable revolts, and kept in close contact on defensive measures with Liu K'un-i in Nanking and Yü Lien-san, the governor of Hunan. On August 18, when he apparently decided finally for suppression, he issued public proclamations threatening summary execution for "Boxer" conspiracies and warned Governor Yü in Hunan of impending violence by groups in Hankow with secret society connections, against whom he was preparing to move.[50]

At the same time that Chang made preparations to crush the conspiracy, he took precautions to avoid any chance of foreign sympathy for or assistance to the rebels. To accomplish this end, he was able to turn to his own advantage the local British sensitivity to unrest, now at its height. He merely had to intimate to the British consul general the extent to which the conspirators were involved with secret societies, and to warn that these would of course take advantage of the confusion of a revolt to attack foreigners and their property. Consul General Fraser in Hankow was so convinced of the anarchic antiforeign nature of the planned uprising that he instructed the concession police to aid the Chinese forces in capturing the rebel headquarters on the evening of August 21. Upon discovery there of handbills printed in English, promising to treat foreigners and their property with respect, Fraser considered these to be something of an oddity, and did not take them seriously at all. Fraser's report of August 23, less than forty-eight hours after the capture of the leaders, already took Chang Chih-tung's version entirely: the revolt was an alliance between the followers of K'ang Yu-wei and the Ko-lao hui and also had connections with Sun Yat-sen. This in fact was largely the truth, except for the allegations of direct connections with Sun, and Chang had no trouble in persuading the British and other foreigners to believe it, panicked as they were at the mere thought of secret society antiforeign violence.[51]

Just as Chang had been reluctant to capture T'ang and the other student leaders, and had hoped until near the end that he could dissuade them from their reckless act, so it was with much regret that he ordered the execution of over twenty of them in the immediate aftermath of the raid on their headquarters. Almost all accounts note Chang's unhappiness over the necessity to inflict such a tragic end on T'ang and his fellow student rebels, though there were certainly no regrets over the destruction of some real secret society leaders among those captured. Consul General Fraser reported that Chang "was personally very loth to execute many of the conspirators, but he had to yield to popular feeling and the wishes of the Governor and his subordinates."[52] Chang's biographer Hsü T'ung-hsin agrees, saying that Chang could not bring himself to conduct a thorough trackdown of all participants, and he was especially reluctant to see T'ang Ts'ai-ch'ang's younger brother, Ts'ai-chung, captured and killed in Hunan. He released another arrested person when the man's younger brother spoke on his behalf.[53]

One of the most remarkable accounts of this aspect of the revolt deals only indirectly with Chang, but may well reflect some of his feelings.[54] Chang picked one of his most trusted subordinates, Cheng Hsiao-hsü, to interrogate T'ang Ts'ai-ch'ang after his capture. Cheng permitted T'ang to sit facing him, instead of kneeling in the standard fashion of a criminal interrogation, and he showed great patience in the face of T'ang's effrontery and insults, more than once having to stay the hands of the eager attendants who wanted to put the prisoner in his place. Finally, in a long, impassioned speech T'ang accused Cheng and Chang Chih-tung of being former comrades (*t'ung-chih*) in reform who were now unwilling to see that the real rebels, Tz'u-hsi and her cohorts, had to be overthrown before they ruined the country. Cheng finally cut short T'ang, who had dumbfounded the guards with his oratory, and he declined to carry on the interview. Upon leaving, he said to T'ang, "You are perfectly right. I was originally your comrade in reform, and if you are guilty, then I cannot avoid suspicion as well. Thus I have no standing [*tzu-ko*] to interrogate you, and I will report this to the governor-general." Others in Chang's entourage may have felt the same way. Chi I-hui, one of the student leaders, was helped to escape back to Japan by the family of Yao Hsi-kuang, who in 1898 had been entrusted by Chang with heading a special mission to inspect Japanese educational facilities.[55]

It has been alleged, even by the best of recent scholarship, that the reason for Chang's reluctance to suppress the Hankow headquarters of the Tzu-li hui was the fact that most of the leaders were his students whom he had chosen and sent to Japan for study.[56] This is clearly incorrect, as a brief analysis of those individuals will show. T'ang Ts'ai-ch'ang himself had indeed been a student of Chang many years before, at the Liang-hu Academy, but as noted, T'ang had been refused readmittance to that institution in the fall of 1898, as were all former students of the Shih-wu hsüeh-t'ang. This would include, besides T'ang, Lin Kuei, Ch'in Li-shan, Li Ping-huan, T'ien Pang-hsüan, and Ts'ai Chung-hao, all major figures in the revolt who had made their way to Japan on their own in late 1898 and early 1899.[57] Of the ten students led back to China by T'ang in late 1899 to organize the revolt, only one, Fu Tz'u-hsiang, was an official student of Chang Chih-tung.[58] Of the six major unit leaders of the armed forces of the rebellion, one, Shen Chin, had formerly worked as a clerk in Chang's office, but had never been a student in Japan.

Of the fifteen students in Japan whom Feng Tzu-yu describes as participants,[59] the following are relevant: Fu Tz'u-hsiang, noted above; Shen Hsiang-yün, probably a Hupeh government student, who did participate actively and escaped; Wu Lu-chen, definitely a Hupeh government student, who returned to Japan after the Kuo-hui meetings of late July, long before the abortive revolt;[60] Chi I-hui, who was from Hupeh but a member of the group of students sent to Japan in 1896 by the Tsungli yamen, and had no relation to Chang; Liu Keng-yün and Wu Tsu-yin, both Hupeh government students, neither of whom ever left Japan;[61] and T'ang Ts'ai-ch'ang himself. Of those captured and killed, only Fu Tz'u-hsiang had any relationship with Chang Chih-tung at the time.

Thus it was not because of their personal relationship with him that Chang was reluctant to deal harshly with these young men. It was that they were members of China's emerging modern student class, with which Chang was so much concerned in his own educational and other reform programs and upon which depended China's future, as Chang was acutely aware. They were also the sons of the traditional gentry class, and many fathers and uncles from now on would be anguished to see members of the following generation devote themselves to the violent overthrow of the old political order. Chang had no choice but to condone repression of the movement in which they were involved, for they had committed the ultimate and unforgivable crime by tampering with the social dynamite of the secret societies. Yet Chang did not blame the students personally. Rather, he felt that these impressionable young men had been led astray by the alluring but false doctrines being peddled by K'ang Yu-wei and Liang Ch'i-ch'ao, and now he spared no effort to try to discredit K'ang and Liang in their eyes.

The Aftermath of the Uprising

The planners of the uprising had hoped to restrain their secret society allies from excesses of violence so as to reassure and gain the support of upper-class Chinese and foreign governments alike afterward. Placards to this effect were posted during the premature Ta-t'ung uprising, as noted.[62] During the fall of 1900, K'ang Yu-wei would stoutly deny the destructiveness of the revolt, and point to these placards as his proof. Yet the reality of the abortive revolt in Hankow and other places belied this claim. On the nights of August 19 and 21, several large fires were set in the Wuhan cities, destroying many homes and shops; these were almost certainly the work of the allies of T'ang Ts'ai-ch'ang.[63]

Despite the capture of the revolt headquarters in Hankow, several scheduled uprisings related to the Tzu-li hui plot did occur on August 22 and 23. The one at Hsin-t'i, led by Shen Chin, was very destructive of property. The Wuhan metropolitan area and the province as a whole teetered on the brink of large-scale rebellion for some time afterward. Many people who could afford it, including officials' families, left the Wuhan cities, and the steamers down the Yangtze toward Shanghai were crowded.[64] Chang Chih-tung continued sending the most urgent demands to local garrisons to remain vigilant for rebels, especially those with the telltale *fu-yu* tickets, until well into September.[65] British Consul General Fraser also noted in early September the great instability along the whole Yangtze Valley in the face of the tremendous power of the secret societies.[66] As late as November, when word was received of Sun Yat-sen's revolt in the far south, at Waichow in Kwangtung province, Chang quickly wired Liu K'un-i in Nanking expressing his concern over the possibility of new uprisings on the Yangtze.[67]

In this extremely volatile atmosphere, severe measures were

used to stamp out any sparks that might set off a general explosion in the city or perhaps the province as a whole. As Fraser observed of Chang on September 3, "the widespread ramifications of the recent plot . . . have apparently made the Viceroy very uneasy, as he stands now between the northern Boxer party, which he has defied, and this new combination of . . . the Reformers and . . . the Ko-lao-hui."[68] Once his hand had been forced and those captured at revolt headquarters had been disposed of, the continuing precariousness of the situation induced Chang to condone a widespread and brutal repression.

During the following weeks, large numbers of troops were stationed at key points in the Wuhan cities, and several dozen, perhaps hundreds of people were executed, sometimes on rather flimsy evidence. Rewards were offered for turning in rebels, and this led to abuses and some false accusations. The purge extended to Hunan, where Governor Yü Lien-san was enthusiastic in its implementation, and to the lower Yangtze provinces as well. The total of those who perished in the whole Yangtze Valley as a direct result of the abortive revolt and the repression it evoked probably reached several hundred.[69] Chang Chih-tung also closed down the *Han-pao,* a Hankow newspaper in existence since the early 1890's, because its editor was in some way implicated in the Tzu-li hui revolt.[70]

In all, this purge in the early fall of 1900 was much greater than that which followed the reaction to the Hunan reform movement and the Peking "100 days" in 1898. Many perished or underwent harsh treatment on only the slightest suspicion. Foreigners, ever mindful of the conspirators' flirtation with the dreaded secret societies, applauded the vigorous measures of repression.[71] Moderate Chinese opinion, however, was unhappy with the indiscriminate and arbitrary nature of the witch hunt being conducted in the Yangtze Valley. Wang K'ang-nien's Shanghai *Chung-wai jih-pao* commented unfavorably upon the wholesale repression and implication of many innocent people, and such men as Chang Chien and the Hunan scholar Wang K'ai-yün noted in their private papers at this time how much they regretted the loss of bright young men like T'ang Ts'ai-ch'ang and the seeming overreaction of the authorities.[72]

The prime justification for the extent and severity of the repression, of course, was that the conspirators had committed the worst of crimes in allying with the secret societies. In their official reports on the incident to the throne, this was the constant and unrelenting theme of Chang and the other officials involved. Chang's memorial of September 23, 1900, submitted jointly with Hupeh Governor Yü Yin-lin, was the longest and most detailed of these reports.[73]

In a carefully constructed and persuasive argument, Chang showed how K'ang Yu-wei and his followers set up the Kuo-hui as a front organization in the foreign concession at Shanghai, but tied it directly to the Ko-lao hui of the Yangtze Valley through the *fu-yu p'iao* and a military arm called the Tzu-li chün. As proof, Chang made an impressive recitation of the incriminating evidence which had been discovered at the Hankow headquarters of the group, which was to be a "branch" Kuo-hui. This included not only weapons and ammunition, but stacks of *fu-yu p'iao,* seals, proclamations, and other documents with the Kuo-hui name, leaving no doubt that the aim of the group was to set up a new national government, doing away with the dynasty. The extent of the plot was apparent from captured membership lists, expense accounts for travel to various cities by organizers, and letters from units in other provinces. Finally, there was the incontrovertible proof of intimacy with the Ko-lao hui in the listing of K'ang, Liang, and T'ang themselves as *lung-t'ou* in some of the captured documents.

Chang then proceeded past this indictment, for which considerable proof existed, to allege a close and well-coordinated conspiracy between K'ang, Sun Yat-sen, and the Ta-tao hui (Long Knives' Society), and to claim that Sun had already gone to Shantung to foment revolt there. Sun was in fact nowhere near Shantung, and without plans to go there, but Chang must have believed this to be true, for at the same time he wired Yüan Shih-k'ai, Shantung governor, that the forces of Sun and K'ang were going to ally with the Boxers there.[74] To conclude his report, Chang pointed out with some satisfaction how he obtained the support of the foreign consuls and the concession police in the capture of the rebels. He also claimed that several of the consuls had informed him since then that whereas formerly they thought rather highly of K'ang and Liang, they now despised them for the bandits they had shown themselves to be.

Conviction of a working alliance between the forces of K'ang Yu-wei's *pao-huang* group and Sun Yat-sen's revolutionaries persisted through the fall of 1900 on the part of many people, despite the fact that the two groups were in fact rivals for financial support and recruits. Hunan Governor Yü Lien-san devoted a special memorial to the subject on October 14, and on October 31, after Sun's Waichow revolt in Kwangtung, Chang Chih-tung again asserted a linkage between the two groups.[75] This was more than simple exaggeration of the evils of the K'ang-Liang group for the benefit of the throne. There seems to have been a genuine conviction here, based on circumstantial evidence, that the two groups were in some sort of cooperation. Chinese officials were not the only ones to believe this; British diplomatic officials operated on this premise for a time as well.[76]

Chang's Attempts to Discredit the Exiled Reformers

Despite his success in forestalling the projected Tzu-li hui uprising and in crushing its adherents, Chang was still faced with the unpalatable fact that they had gained a significant amount of support among moderate Chinese in Shanghai, overseas Chinese, and students in Japan. His reaction to this challenge had several components.

As he had done the year before, Chang appealed to the Japanese government for help. He was particularly upset that a Japanese citizen captured at the revolt headquarters had been spirited away by the Japanese consul and had avoided punishment, and he renewed his request that the propaganda activities of the K'ang-Liang group in Japan be curtailed. Chang also asked Minister Lo Feng-lu in London to request the British government to be more strict in prohibiting the actions of the group in British territories such as Hong Kong and Singapore. He was not very successful in these endeavors. His failure to secure the punishment of the Japanese culprit led to a brief retaliation in the form of the surveillance of Japanese businessmen and the firing of some Japanese teachers along the Yangtze, but it was beyond his power to gain satisfaction from the foreign governments on this score.[77]

Chang soon unveiled a different strategy. This was both to

publicize the heinous nature of the revolt and to approach directly those who had been involved with it in one fashion or another, short of the planning and leadership level. On October 3, he issued a shortened and modified version of his memorial on the revolt in the form of a public proclamation, which was posted and distributed all over central China.[78] This adaptation covered the same major points as his memorial, but especially emphasized the gap between the rhetoric and public posture of the Tzu-li hui and its reality of burning, pillaging, and deceiving the common people. It pictured K'ang and his followers as being totally in the grip of the violent and anarchic secret societies. It was the arguments in this proclamation that K'ang Yu-wei would feel it necessary to attempt to refute in the next few weeks.

In telegrams to Minister Lo in London in early November, Chang suggested trying to separate K'ang from his main source of financial support, the Singapore millionaire Ch'iu Shu-yüan, by pointing out to the latter the trickery and deception of the Tzu-li hui plotters, who had squandered his money on secret society chieftains.[79] He also wrote a small tract directed at the Shanghai supporters of the Kuo-hui, most of whom, he felt, did not know what they were getting themselves into at the time by their participation in that organization, and who now rather regretted their association with it. In a telegram to the Shanghai taotai, to whom he sent five hundred copies of the tract in pamphlet form for distribution, he noted his concern over the large number of respectable people (*wen-jen*) associated with the Kuo-hui, and said he was reluctant to pursue an exhaustive investigation against them. Rather, he hoped simply to discourage them from participation in any such ventures in the future.[80]

In the tract itself, Chang made a pointed appeal to these Chinese moderates, recognizing their reputations and scholarly abilities. He said that he understood and shared their concern for the future of the nation, and believed that the armed insurrection fomented by the Tzu-li hui was not representative of the desires of most of them. Chang agreed that the politics of the nation were rotten, but said that there was hope of improvement; and in any case, if the secret societies were to bring about anarchy, the Powers would partition China and all would be lost. By taking this line, Chang permitted himself to avoid a close investigation of the Kuo-hui, which would have involved some important people and unfavorable publicity.

Considerable success was had in splitting off from the *pao-huang* leaders those unhappy with their secret society tactics. In Singapore, Ch'iu Shu-yüan became disenchanted with K'ang Yu-wei, and accused him of deception and using his young followers as pawns. Ch'iu started corresponding with T'ao Mo, governor-general at Canton, and then with Chang Chih-tung, expressing this change of heart. After Ch'iu contributed to some welfare and relief projects, Chang praised his character and generosity to the throne, which responded with an award of honorary rank and office for Ch'iu. In China itself, several individuals, including Wang K'ang-nien, appalled at the repression and tragedy which had been the result of playing with revolution in the Tzu-li hui plot, washed their hands of all those trying to overthrow the government, whether reformist or revolutionary. Wang's writings showed considerable disillusionment with his Kuo-hui experience and a tendency toward a "plague on both your houses" attitude.[81]

Despite his attention to the matters described above, Chang's major concern in the aftermath of the revolt was probably the problem of the radicalization of Chinese students in Japan. One of his own students had been captured and executed, and the rest of those from Hupeh and other provinces were surely in danger of following the same path as those who led the Tzu-li hui. It is a tribute to his faith in the necessity for modern education, as well as to his faith in the common sense of the students he had sent to Japan, that he was neither vindictive toward them nor regretful that he had been such an enthusiastic advocate of sending them to Japan in the first place.

Chang first contacted those responsible for supervising and disciplining the students in Japan. In early October, 1900, he urged the Hupeh supervisor of students, Ch'ien Hsün, to be very careful in his dealings with the students, yet to be firm in admonishing those toying with radical ideas not thus to harm their reputations and future careers and bring concern to their families. He stressed to Ch'ien the importance, in discussing the revolt, of emphasizing both the plotters' links with the secret societies and the documents proclaiming independence, for this latter could not easily be reconciled with "protecting the emperor." He also requested Minister Li Sheng-to to use the prestige of his office to try to influence the students.[82]

Soon, however, Chang decided to address himself directly to the students in Japan. He may have been moved to action partly by the *Ch'ing-i pao*'s renewal, in late September, of its vicious attacks on his integrity because of his role in the suppression of the revolt, and his concern that the students in Japan might believe these calumnies.[83] At approximately the same time that he was composing his tract for the Shanghai merchants and gentry who had been involved with the Kuo-hui, he also wrote one directed specifically at the overseas students. In early November, he sent the text of both tracts to Minister Li in Tokyo and asked him to reproduce and distribute them to all the Chinese students. This was done, and the resulting manifesto, under the combined title, "A Warning Against the Shanghai Kuo-hui and a Proclamation to Students Abroad," was widely disseminated and evoked considerable comment and debate.[84]

The manifesto, in Chang's typically long-winded manner, first chided a few of the students for their ungratefulness to the government, which sent them abroad and supported them. It then dwelt for a time upon the perfidy of the doctrines of K'ang Yu-wei and the Kuo-hui, who would have them believe that rebellion is loyalty and would incite Chinese against their own race. But the main thrust of the argument appealed quite openly to the students' self-interest. Chang acknowledged that many students were interested in the doctrines of K'ang and Liang, and had associated with them in some way, as yet unaware of their deviousness and evil intentions. But now, after the rebellion and its suppression, they should know better. If they would engage in no more bad activities, the authorities would not implicate them through rigorous investigation, for that would just extend the bloodshed needlessly. Even those who had participated actively in subversive projects, and were now on "wanted" lists, could still absolve themselves of guilt by visiting officials and pledging good behavior in the future. Chang concluded by warning that there were limits to which his leniency could go, and that in the future he would be more strict.

Just as he had done in his appeal to the Shanghai supporters of the Kuo-hui, Chang tried not to force the students into further alienation from the dynasty by pursuing those who had associated with the plotters and branding them as outcasts. Rather, he let the implication of the tragic end of the Tzu-li hui sink in of its own considerable weight. Most of the students in Japan were of upper-class families and hoped to return to good jobs in China after their studies were completed. In offering amnesty as he did, Chang did not threaten those future hopes of status and held out as much incentive as possible for the students to remain apolitical and quiescent.

It is important to note that in regard to his own Hupeh government-supported students, Chang was true to his word. After considering cancellation of the credentials and stipends of the three students reportedly most deeply involved in radical activities, he gave them another chance. Upon their eventual graduation and return, he evaluated them very closely and then rewarded them with positions. One of these was Wu Lu-chen, to be a major figure in early Hupeh revolutionary activity and eventually in the 1911 Revolution.[85]

Some indication of the impact that Chang's manifesto had upon Chinese student circles in Japan is given by the reaction to it on the part of the surviving leaders of the Tzu-li hui. Shen Hsiang-yün, Ch'in Li-shan, and the others who had escaped and made their way back to Japan were reportedly quite upset by the manifesto, and Shen was chosen to compose a reply to it.[86] This document, "A Reply to Chang Chih-tung," which was quite long and showed some care in preparation, was in its turn distributed among Chinese students in Japan and back in China as well. The main points of its rebuttal of Chang's manifesto are worth noting.[87]

Shen claimed that the major flaw in Chang's argument was that he "doesn't know what the nation (*kuo-chia*) is, and doesn't perceive any difference between the nation and the dynasty (*ch'ao-t'ing*)." Coming back to this theme often, he faulted many Chinese for viewing the nation as the private property of the dynasty and the affairs of the nation as the private business of the government. He also criticized Chang's gross misunderstanding of terms and entities like national assemblies (*kuo-hui*) and democratic rights (*min-chu chih ch'üan*), and of how these function in Western political systems to strengthen the nation. Here he justifiably criticized the naive view of such concepts which Chang had displayed in his *Ch'üan-hsüeh p'ien*. Finally, Shen attacked the rather cynical view of human motivation upon which Chang had based his appeal to the students. Shen accused Chang of not being able to imagine any other way of serving the country than being an official, and of assuming that people would follow their material interest in whatever they do.

Chang eagerly took up the challenge of Shen's reply. Feng Tzu-yu, the chief chronicler of the pre-1911 revolutionary movement, says that when Chang saw Shen's rebuttal of his manifesto to the students, he trembled and sweat like rain, fearing the reaction of righteous public opinion (*ch'ing-i*), and was unable to compose an adequate reply to it.[88] This is nonsense, in light of what he did with Shen's essay. He had copies of the piece made and distributed to all the students of the three major academies of the Wuhan cities, and instructed them each to write an essay refuting Shen's arguments. Feng Tzu-yu claims that some students begged off the assignment because they agreed with Shen, but apparently most wrote. One essay of several thousand words, emphasizing how revolution (*ko-ming*) was actually tantamount to destruction (*wang*), especially pleased Chang. He had thousands of copies made and sent them all over Japan to the Chinese students there.[89] Thus he had the confidence to debate the Tzu-li hui survivors, and had the last word as well.

The Isolation of the K'ang-Liang Reform Group

Charlton Lewis has concluded that "the severity with which the Tzu-li hui was suppressed made a mockery of its reformist objectives, and after 1900 dissident literati were left with no alternative but revolution."[90] Yet by no means all of those associated with the revolt went on to advocate and practice revolution. Rather, the various elements which had participated split off in different directions. The abortive revolt, with its tragic and bloody aftermath, caused much bitterness on the part of many connected with it. The net result, apparent during the following months, was a dropping off of former supporters at both political ends of the *pao-huang* group, as radicals drifted off, eventually into more thoroughly revolutionary positions, and as moderates withdrew to acquiescence in, if not cooperation with, dynastic authority.

Some of those among T'ang Ts'ai-ch'ang's colleagues who escaped blamed the debacle entirely on the insufficiency of financial support provided from abroad by K'ang and Liang. Ch'in Li-shan even went to Singapore to confront K'ang with his accusations and may have helped influence the wealthy Ch'iu Shu-yüan to withdraw his financial backing from K'ang. Ch'in and others who were impressed by the apparent ineptness of K'ang's support, such as Chang Chi and Chang Ping-lin, soon became thoroughgoing revolutionaries. The secret society leaders of the Yangtze Valley also blamed K'ang for the failure of the revolt and even tried to assassinate him a few years later.[91]

K'ang and Liang themselves went the opposite way from these former student allies. They swore off violent insurrection, K'ang forever, Liang at least until he would again be tempted to dabble in revolution in 1911.[92] Much grieved over the loss of his student comrades and protégés and unhappy over the recriminations directed at him and K'ang by the survivors, Liang's militancy was modified considerably.[93]

Having lost supporters on the radical side, the exiled reform leaders also lost them on the side of moderation. As I have shown, once the full evidence and implications of the complicity with the secret societies became known, men like Ch'iu Shu-yüan and Wang K'ang-nien, enthusiastic supporters of the Kuo-hui concept but unwilling to sanction full-scale armed insurrection, also turned on K'ang and Liang. As one old supporter of the 1898 reformers noted in his diary at the time, it would have been much better to wait for popular violence from the lower reaches of society to manifest itself of its own accord, and then to appear as advocates of law and order, with special "militia" which could bend the situation to the desired end of independence and declaration of a new government. To be allies of the societies, and thus initiators of social violence, was the fatal move that alienated moderate opinion beyond repair.[94]

Thus the *pao-huang* reform group, which looked so formidable in early 1900, was isolated and weak by the end of the year. Chang Chih-tung consciously attempted to increase the pressure upon them, and to intensify their loss of credibility, by his actions vis-à-vis moderate public opinion in China and the students in Japan. After all, for the most part their loss was his gain. At the time, they provided the only viable alternative to the existing national leadership, within which, in the aftermath of the Boxer Rebellion, Chang might expect to play an enhanced role. As if to confirm their own perception of the passing of the mantle of chief reform leader from themselves to Chang Chih-tung, K'ang and Liang publicly vilified Chang at every opportunity in the fall of 1900.

From late September through mid-December, Liang's *Ch'ing-i pao* devoted a considerable amount of space to attacks on Chang. The subjects ranged from his specific role in the suppression of the Tzu-li hui to old charges about his relations with the martyrs of 1898 or his supposed complicity in the various plots to depose the emperor. The articles also invariably included some general comments on his personal integrity. Of the nine issues of the paper from September 24 through December 12, 1900, no less than five of them had long front page editorial articles devoted to Chang, all or most of these by Liang Ch'i-ch'ao.[95] These were notable for their lack of coherent content, being largely emotional denunciations. One article under the title of a response to Chang's manifesto to the students hardly dealt at all with the contents of that document.[96] Another, concerning the repression in Hupeh province, was rather ineffectual in its attempts to discredit the argument that Chang was forced against his inclinations to crush the conspiracy and condone the repression, because the reckless determination of the plotters left him no other choice.[97]

K'ang Yu-wei himself also contributed two articles to the *Ch'ing-i pao* at this time attacking Chang Chih-tung. One of these, entitled "A Letter to Chang Chih-tung," was devoted entirely to discrediting Chang personally.[98] K'ang first developed the "blood on your hands" thesis in regard to the reform martyrs of 1898 and trotted out the old accusations about the deposition of Kuang-hsü. Then he moved on to the most recent events, claiming that many of those involved with the Tzu-li hui had connections with Chang, and that the students Chang was supporting in Japan had deserted him for K'ang's *pao-huang* group. However, the evidence K'ang was able to muster to reinforce these claims was meager indeed: besides Fu Tz'u-hsiang, K'ang noted the nephew of one of Chang's associates and the older brother of the husband of one of his nieces as participants. This was hardly a devastating incrimination of Chang.

The second article by K'ang, "A Refutation of the False Proclamation by the Members of the Empress Dowager's Faction, Chang Chih-tung and Yü Yin-lin," had more substance.[99] After first making the by now standard rundown of Chang's alleged perfidies toward reformers and the emperor, he moved on to his major purpose. This was to respond to the public proclamation on the Tzu-li hui revolt which Chang and Governor Yü had issued in early October and which had been posted all over the Yangtze Valley. The vigor of K'ang's argument plainly shows the discomfiture he suffered under the onus of conspirator and ally of the secret societies with which he had been saddled.

K'ang claimed that Chang Chih-tung had entirely fabricated the story of the reform party's cooperation with secret societies in order to sully K'ang's followers in the eyes of foreigners. He waxed indignant over the accusation of an alliance with the Ta-tao hui, which may indeed have been nonexistent, but he did not even mention the Ko-lao hui, with which there certainly was an alliance. Another item in the proclamation which exercised K'ang was the description of T'ang Ts'ai-ch'ang and the other leaders as advocates of looting, destruction, and killing as means to their ends. To counter this, K'ang repeatedly pointed out the moderate nature of the placards which had been posted by Ch'in Li-shan at the Ta-t'ung uprising. He insisted vehemently that the aims of the group were pure, only to restore the emperor and not to overthrow society, and claimed that the great majority of Tzu-li hui adherents were of official or wealthy gentry background, if not themselves degree holders. This last claim is clearly false and shows K'ang's desperation to get out from under the consequences of consorting with the societies.

In the October proclamation, Chang had made good use of the ambiguity of the emperor's status under the "independent" government which would be set up under the Kuo-hui to claim that the real aim of the plot was not at all to restore the emperor, but to overthrow the dynasty. Here he could point to the captured seals and documents with good effect, greatly compromising the reformers' chief drawing card, "protection" of the emperor. K'ang could only fume at this accusation, saying that he would be a cad to take the emperor's power after devoting his career in exile to the emperor's restoration. K'ang concluded with a final description of Chang Chih-tung as fearful of the potential power of the *pao-huang* group, vulnerable and desperate. In reality, however, this last tirade against Chang could well have been turned around against K'ang himself.

As the antigovernment alliance around the exiled reformers broke down, the government had a breathing space of sorts, free from significant opposition to its claims of authority. On the whole, the students in Japan remained loyal to the dynasty and manageable. The few becoming radical would not begin to get their revolutionary bearings until 1903. Moderate public opinion within China, disillusioned with the desperate tactics to which the "reform" leaders had resorted in the Tzu-li hui revolt, was perhaps now more receptive to initiatives for reform which might come from within the government itself. Chang Chih-tung on the one hand effectively used the nature of the Tzu-li hui uprising as a stick with which to beat K'ang and Liang. On the other, he hoped that now, with the shock of the Boxer fiasco, the court could at last be jolted onto the path of a national reform program. He was prepared to do what he could to accomplish that, and to provide guidelines and directions for the reform program as well. The task of designing such a program, and Chang Chih-tung's key role in it from 1900 to 1905, is the subject of the next chapter.

Chapter 6

The Dynastic Reform Program after 1900

The setback suffered by the *pao-huang* reform group provided an opportunity for the dynasty to reestablish its credentials as an effective political mechanism and even as a proponent of change. There was of course no guarantee that the central government would be able to take advantage of this opportunity. Its ability to do so was in no small measure due to the political acumen and hard work of Chang Chih-tung.

In order to protect himself, to satisfy the Powers, and to pave the way for an effective reform program, Chang worked for the removal of the worst of the court reactionaries in 1900 and 1901, then pressed for a commitment to a new course on the part of the central government. In the process, he forged a temporary but remarkably effective working relationship with the representatives of the British government in China. Chang emerged in mid-1901 as the foremost spokesman for a comprehensive reform movement, and by the end of the year saw the beginning of the adoption of his proposals. He worked diligently in implementing major reforms in his own jurisdiction between 1901 and 1903, although he was often uncertain of his political standing at court during this time. Then, still dissatisfied with the lack of a broad national reform structure, especially in the field of education, he went to Peking in 1903 to lobby vigorously for most of a year before obtaining approval of his programs. Back in Hupeh, his own views advanced to the point where, by mid-1905, he was willing to consider what was once anathema to him, a constitutional political system.

Political Infighting, 1900–1901

As the court fled westward into Shansi after the fall of Peking in August, 1900, it was accompanied by many of the high-ranking princes and ministers who had helped to bring on the Boxer debacle. Among them were Prince Tuan, Kang-i, and Tung Fu-hsiang, the Moslem commander whose troops had besieged the legations and now, fifteen thousand strong, were the only military force near the fleeing court. As the imperial party moved farther into the hinterland, there was some danger that these reactionaries might dominate court policy. In that case, besides continuing the war, they might well try to take revenge upon Chang and other officials who had acted independently (and treasonously, in their view) in the summer of 1900. Thus one of Chang's first concerns in the early fall was to protect himself against retaliation by this group at the court.

Some who were concerned about the absence of progressive opinion at the court suggested that Chang Chih-tung and Sheng Hsüan-huai, among others, might take high office there. Chang was appalled at the thought of being called to the court at this time, even as a grand councillor, and on September 14 he literally begged Li Hung-chang not to ask for his appointment, claiming that his health was too poor.[1] Chang's instincts were probably sound; it would have been dangerous for him to be defenseless in the midst of his enemies in the fall of 1900, despite the ameliorative effect his presence might have had on the empress dowager.

Even where they were, in their own bailiwicks, Chang and Liu K'un-i were not entirely free from retaliatory action. On September 12, two conservative Manchus were appointed as governors of Kiangsu and Kiangsi, directly under Liu, and Manchus were appointed as lieutenant governors of all three provinces under him.[2] Chang himself wanted to attract as little of the court's critical attention as possible for awhile, and even felt constrained to call home his grandson, who was studying in Japan, "in order to avoid talk."[3] As late as December, 1900, and January, 1901, some court officials were presenting memorials to the empress dowager which demanded that Chang and Liu K'un-i be punished for toadying to foreigners and disobeying imperial orders.[4]

In these circumstances, Chang was eager to maintain the close relationship which he had forged with the foreign diplomats, especially the British, during the tribulations of the summer of 1900. This relationship, to which Chang would resort several times over the next two years, both to protect himself and to generate pressure on Peking to move in desirable directions, stood in stark contrast to Chang's former reputation of aloofness from foreigners. In Canton in the 1880's, his attitude toward the consuls was distant and arrogant. In Wuchang in the early 1890's, Chang was "simply unapproachable" by the British consul; only with great difficulty could he be induced to receive official visits, which he never repaid, and in 1893 most of the consuls had still never laid eyes on him, though he had been in Wuhan for four years.[5] Chang's relationships with foreigners improved after 1895. By 1898, he was employing over two dozen foreigners in his various Wuhan educational and industrial enterprises.[6] And early in 1900, as noted previously, Chang requested the cooperation of the foreign consuls in preventing the sympathizers of Liang Ch'i-ch'ao from establishing seditious newspapers under foreign protection.[7]

An important factor facilitating the improvement of Chang's relationship with foreigners, especially with the British, was the high caliber of personnel linking them by 1900. Liang Tun-yen, a capable and trusted member of Chang's *mu-fu* who sometimes acted as Hankow customs taotai, usually represented Chang's views to the consuls. Liang was rather more pro-British than some of Chang's "foreign experts" had been in the past, and moreover was fluent in English and keen of mind.[8] Everard H. Fraser, who took over the consul general's post at Hankow late in 1899, was a calm and reasonable professional, and he quickly developed a close working relationship with both Chang and Liang Tun-yen. This was vastly enhanced by the cooperation between the British and the Yangtze governors-general Chang and Liu K'un-i to keep the peace during the Boxer unrest. By August, 1900, the British were not only willing to loan Chang money to pay his troops, but Fraser was happy to accept with equanimity Chang's action against the Tzu-li hui conspirators, as recounted in chapter 5. Fraser's attitude toward Chang was one of political respect ("the whole civilized world owes a debt of gratitude to the two loyal and friendly viceroys of this region'') combined with high personal regard (''He strikes me as an honest man—the only mandarin who ever so struck me'').[9]

The British diplomats in China were very sensitive to any political threats to Chang Chih-tung and Liu K'un-i in the fall of 1900, and Chang was able to make good use of this concern on their part. In October, when Chang's fears of retaliation by Manchu court conservatives were at their height and there were rumors of an impending summons to Sian for him and Liu, Chang had an interview with Consul General Fraser in Hankow. He confided that he and Liu would probably be removed from their posts and perhaps summoned to the court in the northwest. He requested British help in averting this.[10] The British diplomatic machinery immediately went into action. On the same day the request was forwarded through Shanghai back to Salisbury in London, and Salisbury immediately gave to MacDonald, the chief British negotiator in Peking, permission to warn the Chinese government against removing the two governors-general.[11] This was only the first of several occasions when Chang would solicit British aid in pursuit of his domestic political goals.

It was in the interests of Chang's own political health that the court reactionaries be removed, but it was also in the best interests of the country. As long as they remained influential, the Western nations would not begin serious negotiations, and there was always the danger that renewed warfare would break out. Chester Tan has noted how Chang ''was always cautious, sometimes to the extent of timidity,'' in directly supporting Li Hung-chang in the latter's advice to the throne to punish severely the Boxer culprits at court, so as to satisfy the Western representatives of the government's seriousness in negotiating a permanent peace settlement.[12] Chang does seem to have been less than courageous in his willingness to let Li Hung-chang stand alone in suggesting unpalatable facts of life to the throne, but Li was undoubtedly in a better position to risk the wrath of Tz'u-hsi, considering his crucial and indispensable role as plenipotentiary.

Chang, moreover, was not idle in working for the same end, albeit indirectly. As Jung-lu was heading toward Sian in early November to join the court and the Grand Council, Chang urged him to be firm in advising punishment of the pro-Boxer officials, especially Tung Fu-hsiang. He let foreign representatives know that he favored meeting their demands for punishment of the guilty parties.[13] He also had a November interview in Hankow with Wu Yung, the magistrate then in very high favor with the empress dowager, in which he strongly complained of the continued influence of the conservatives at the court.[14] In December, Chang telegraphed similar observations to Lu Ch'uan-lin, his brother-in-law and a member of the Grand Council, and to Ts'en Ch'un-hsüan, newly appointed moderate governor of Shensi province; both Lu and Ts'en were at the court in Sian.[15] Later, in the fall of 1901, as the court was heading back to Peking, Chang did not hesitate to pass on to Fraser the names of several allegedly pro-Boxer court officials who had thus far escaped the attention of the Powers and whom Chang wanted purged, although in at least some of these cases their criticism of Chang personally was also a reason for his desiring their demotion.[16]

By the end of 1900, the removal and punishment of the most powerful Boxer "war criminals" was no longer a major issue, this having largely been achieved. China's diplomatic fate, however, still hung in the balance. All during the fall of 1900, Chang had been involved in consultations with Li Hung-chang in Peking, with other Chinese officials, and with foreign diplomats over the terms of the peace settlement between China and the Powers; Chang and Liu K'un-i had been directed to participate in these deliberations from the end of August. Chang had several interviews with Fraser during the fall in which he tried to persuade him of the desirability of restraining the punitive expeditions being carried out by the occupying foreign troops in north China, and of avoiding draconian terms in the final diplomatic settlement.[17] Chang's interest and energy continued to be directed toward these negotiations during the first months of 1901, especially in regard to the one-sided agreements on Manchuria which Russia tried to force upon the Chinese. In the debates over which items of the Allied joint note and the various Russian proposals to accept and which to contest, Chang found himself increasingly at odds with Li Hung-chang. Li, who associated with the Russians, advocated more concessions than the throne was happy to give while Chang, continuing to utilize his close relationship with the British, reinforced the empress dowager's tendency toward recalcitrance by counseling to hold out for better terms.[18]

Even while these matters took up some of Chang's time, however, and while China's diplomatic fate was still being worked out at the conference table in Peking, Chang more and more devoted himself to influencing the future course of domestic policy. With the grip of the worst reactionaries broken through the purge demanded by the Powers, and with Li Hung-chang's energies already overtaxed with diplomatic tasks in Peking, Chang pushed with vigor into the forefront of a domestic reform lobby. In early 1901 he communicated often with his relative Lu Ch'uan-lin, now president of the Board of Revenue as well as a grand councillor, and with other officials in Sian.[19] The fact that Lu was a trusted and important contact for Chang at court is shown by the vigor with which Chang, in the spring of 1901, defended him against charges of complicity in Boxer crimes and by Chang's request to the British to help protect Lu's position, as well.[20] He also sent one of the oldest and most trusted members of his *mu-fu,* Liang Ting-fen, on a journey to Sian, undoubtedly to help present Chang's case for reform to those around the court.[21]

Ever since August, 1900, the throne had been moving only haltingly toward commitment to a significant new national reform program. A decree of December 1 ordered all ministers and top provincial officials to prepare memorials within two months on a wide range of topics: national politics, the bureaucracy, schools and examinations, and military and financial matters. On January 29, 1901, a more definite pledge to enact institutional reform (*pien-fa*) was handed down by the throne, though it was noted that this was not to be a repetition of the wild reforms of K'ang Yu-wei.[22]

Some of the more conservative elements at court undoubtedly saw such pronouncements as useful public relations vis-à-vis the Powers, and no more. These edicts may have been issued in that spirit at first, for not long after the elegant reform edict of January 29, a secretary of the Grand Council secretly informed Wang Chih-ch'un, the governor of Anhui, that the reform proposals solicited by the throne should not overly emphasize "Western methods."

When Chang heard of this seeming imperial prevarication, he was irate; in late February and again in March he protested angrily to his closest communicant at court, Lu Ch'uan-lin, asking the true intention of Tz'u-hsi. On March 31 he tried to mobilize the united efforts of fourteen other major provincial officials to request a significant national reform program, undoubtedly as a way to pressure the court further into a firm commitment.[23]

Finally, on April 21, 1901, the empress dowager took a major step by establishing a special office to receive and deliberate upon recommendations for reform. This was the Office for the Management of Political Affairs (Tu-pan cheng-wu ch'u); two of the eight members were Chang and Liu K'un-i, directed to participate from the distance of their posts.[24] This office was strikingly similar, in the breadth of its responsibilities and functions, to the Bureau of Institutions (Chih-tu chü), one of the key elements in K'ang Yu-wei's 1898 plans which never came to fruition.[25] The establishment of the Tu-pan cheng-wu ch'u can be taken as a symbol, on the throne's part, of the kind of receptivity to serious reform proposals for which Chang and other progressive officials had been hoping. Chang and Liu now continued their joint deliberations on the memorials which they would present in July, and others like Yüan Shih-k'ai also prepared suggestions for new policies.

Even as he was concerned to push the court to meaningful reform in the spring of 1901, Chang was determined not to be hampered in his local efforts by the imposition of an uncooperative governor, and he quickly resorted to his British connection in order to avoid such an eventuality. In early March, Yü Yin-lin, former Hupeh governor who had been transferred to Honan in October, 1900, was reappointed to Hupeh. Chang immediately sent Liang Tun-yen to Consul General Fraser. Liang described Yü as a "bigoted reactionary who previously was doing his best to hamper and thwart the Viceroy, whom [Yü] did not scruple to call a traitor to China."[26] This of course ensured British opposition to Yü's appointment, which was withdrawn. When Hsi-liang, an associate of the pro-Boxer Li Ping-heng, was sent in Yü's stead, Chang again in April requested British pressure for his withdrawal. Finally, Chang was able to secure the appointment of Tuan-fang, the capable acting governor of Shensi, whom Chang himself suggested for the

Hupeh post.[27] At the same time that Chang, through the British, was exercising veto power over the Hupeh governorship, he was also attempting to retain in his post the governor of Hunan, Yü Lien-san, again by appeals to Satow through Fraser.[28] Indeed, Chang's link with the British had become a potent weapon, of which he had come to make liberal use during these months when the court, in exile, was highly susceptible to foreign pressures and demands.

Toward a National Reform Program, 1901–3

In July, 1901, Chang Chih-tung and Liu K'un-i finally submitted the reform memorials upon which they had labored so long; they were mainly the work of Chang, with Liu concurring. The memorials were four in number: the first three were quite long and substantive; the fourth was merely a request to make the necessary loans and other financial arrangements to implement the recommended measures. The first memorial, in four articles, concerned the school and examination systems. The second, in twelve articles, dealt with improvements in existing Chinese institutions and administrative practices. The third, in eleven articles, suggested ways in which Western methods (*hsi-fa*) could be adopted to China's advantage.[29] On the whole, these constituted a comprehensive and well-argued summary of China's need for changes in most areas touched by government administration.

These memorials also introduced a significant new rationale for national reform which had not been apparent in previous calls for change. In Chang's *Ch'üan-hsüeh p'ien* of 1898, as in the writings of K'ang Yu-wei, Liang Ch'i-ch'ao, and others at that time, the major justification for change was the need to strengthen China and stave off foreign aggression. Now, in mid-1901, this reason for reform was still valid, but Chang joined to it a warning that there was danger of popular disaffection in the absence of effective government action. To the need for resistance against imperialism was added the need to restore the Chinese people's faith in their own government, that faith by implication having been eroded in recent years. In the second memorial, Chang noted:

> Popular feelings are not the same as thirty years ago. The people admire the wealth of foreign countries and despise the poverty of the Middle Kingdom. . . . All has resulted in a disunited and disillusioned national morale. Insurgents are slowly emerging, and they take this opportunity to spread subversive doctrines. . . . We must first entirely wipe out the various defects mentioned above before we may expect a permanent unification of the popular mind. Then we may speak of . . . opposing humiliation and resisting aggression.[30]

Chang's recent experience with the Tzu-li hui revolt is evident here, I think. In the third memorial, on adopting Western methods, Chang requested imperial approval of the proposals so as to impress the Western nations with China's determination to become strong. But again, he noted:

> This also will let the scholars and the people know that the Court has the intention of renovating our system. The reactionary people will then modify their blunders, and those who are expecting better government will offer their loyalty. And the heresies that offend the emperor and stimulate uprisings will not arise.[31]

In other words, reform-minded patriots and their hopes should be satisfied, not suppressed.

Chang clearly was concerned here with the kind of public opinion which first emerged as an independent factor in politics in the reaction against the alleged plan to depose Kuang-hsü in early 1900. It had surfaced again in the support which the Kuo-hui front organization had received among Shanghai reformers in the summer of 1900, and once more only recently, in the spring of 1901, this time as a factor which worked in favor of court policies. As the extent of Russian demands for rights in Manchuria became known, there was much expression of nationalistic public opinion in favor of rejecting the proposed Russian agreement. Scholars, merchants, and gentry held protest meetings and signed petitions in several places. Many provincial officials forwarded these sentiments to the court in Sian in late March, and this reinforced the empress dowager's resolve to reject the agreement, a move that paid off when Russia backed down for the time being.[32]

While Chang was quite aware of the need to take into account this sort of public opinion coming into being outside the bureaucracy, and to play for its support, he was as yet unwilling to accord it a formal place in the political system. Among the wide-ranging reform proposals of the July memorials, there were none affecting the basic structure of the state. The measures of real political reform which were recommended (outside the changes in the examination system) dealt with minor items such as administrative streamlining, efficiency, and the elimination of corruption and abuses. Chang sensed the need to placate the increasingly active gentry-merchant public opinion groups, and he increasingly predicated his own reform programs upon the cooperation of the local gentry class. But he could not yet bring himself to overcome his old instinctive reluctance to allocate to this class a formal and independent portion of political power.[33]

The impressive proposals of Chang and Liu were well received at court. Jung-lu reportedly said, "The empress dowager approved of them; I observed that the proposed methods were good, although there is no one capable of implementing them."[34] These, joined by requests for reform from other officials as well, had their effect in a series of imperial decrees and actions in late 1901 which showed some sincerity of commitment on the part of the throne.[35] Several of the most important features of the Chang-Liu memorial on education were adopted in September and October: all military exams and the use of the eight-legged essay were abolished; the content and format of the civil examinations were altered to include more useful subjects; the outlines of a hierarchical national school system were decreed as in the memorial, from the district through the province; and the first dent was made in the old system of degree quotas by promising *chü-jen* and *chin-shih* degrees to those who successfully completed programs of study abroad and passed a special examination upon their return. In December came the first direct linking of the new hierarchy of domestic schools with the degree quotas, though on an irregular and individual basis; the major step of assigning definite and ever-increasing portions of all degree quotas to new school graduates, as requested by the memorial, was not yet taken.[36]

Other edicts in the summer and fall of 1901 addressed themselves to administrative and military reforms, some of these suggested by Chang and Liu in their July memorials and some proposed by other officials.[37] On October 2, an edict specifically mentioned the second and third of the July memorials submitted by Chang and Liu, those dealing with administrative reform and adoption of Western methods, as guidelines for all officials to follow.[38]

Thus in late 1901, Chang had some reason to hope that the empress dowager and the court were well launched on a national reform program. Yet he also discerned evidence that antireform groups, in particular those who might be personally hostile to him, were still influential at court. As the court slowly made its way back from exile in as much dignity as possible, there were a host of uncertainties troubling Chang: who was dominant in the Grand Council, Jung-lu or Prince Ch'ing; what would be the influence of the newly appointed Chihli governor-general, Yüan Shih-k'ai, after the death of Li Hung-chang in November; what were the real intentions of the empress dowager; and what was Chang's own political standing at the center? In particular, was his position at the center solid enough to hope for an important role for himself there if he should be appointed to the Grand Council, or should he remain in his regional post and work from it as a more limited, but more secure, base?

On this crucial question of his political position, there was contradictory evidence. Perhaps hoping to put in a word for himself, on September 13, 1901, Chang requested permission to come to Kaifeng, in Honan province, in order to meet the imperial retinue when it passed through that city and to have an audience with the empress dowager. He noted that he had not had an audience since 1884, and stated his confidence in the ability of Hupeh Governor Tuan-fang to fill his post during his short absence.[39] His request was abruptly turned down by Tz'u-hsi. This may have indicated to Chang that he was being undermined at court. Within a few weeks, as noted above, he denounced to Fraser several officials as Boxer sympathizers, hoping to remove them from court through British pressure. At the same time, he was hesitant to rely too heavily on the British, knowing that this would harm his position even more. So even as he identified his enemies to Fraser, he insisted strongly (and probably unrealistically) that he not be traced as the source of the information. Through the last weeks of the year, and into 1902, Chang watched closely for results from his information leak, and he was disappointed when Satow, beginning to meet resistance to further interference in appointments as the court regained its confidence, was not able to secure the desired demotions.[40]

On the other hand, there also was evidence that Chang's position at court was fairly secure. On November 24, 1901, Chang had the courage to meddle in a very delicate court political issue, though he did so indirectly. He telegraphed Lu Ch'uan-lin at the court, suggesting that Prince Tuan's son P'u-chün, whose appointment as heir apparent in January, 1900, symbolized to many the start of the Boxer fiasco, should now be removed from that post. This was promptly done, on November 30. Another encouraging event occurred on December 8, when the empress dowager for the first time publicly acknowledged the actions taken by Chang, Liu K'un-i, and Yüan Shih-k'ai to prevent the spread of hostilities during the summer of 1900 (no mention was made of the fact that they had to disobey her orders to do so), and rewarded them.[41]

Nevertheless, during December, 1901, Chang seemed to fear that there might occur a major move to reduce his power, either by removal to Peking or by transfer, after the court reached the capital. Accordingly, he sent Liang Tun-yen on several missions to Fraser and requested that Satow casually reveal to the court his (Satow's) hope that Chang would remain in his Wuchang post.[42] Yet he expressed to Fraser no more alarms about his position after late December. The court reached Peking on January 7, 1902, and in the next few days the empress dowager, in receiving the foreign diplomats and even their wives, showed unprecedented graciousness. On January 10, Chang recommended to the throne twelve capable men, among them Tseng-ho, the Manchu governor of Hupeh who had been ignominously cashiered in January, 1899, when he had suggested reviving the reforms of the "100 days"; this alone would seem to indicate that Chang had some confidence in his own position at the time.[43]

Suddenly, an edict of January 20, 1902, ordered first Liu K'un-i, then Chang Chih-tung to come to the capital in the spring for imperial audiences. News of this edict was informally given by Yüan Shih-k'ai to Satow on January 21. Satow naturally suspected that this was the eventuality against which Chang had requested

British protection only the month before, and he protested vehemently to Yüan; the summons was duly retracted on January 24. Meanwhile, in response to Satow's inquiries through Fraser as to whether he wanted formal representations on this point, Chang blandly professed to see no danger in the summons and declined the offer of intercession on his behalf. This behavior seemed quixotic to Satow and Fraser, and they began to tire of Chang's inconstancy, but Chang probably managed to gain his security in Wuchang without being publicly associated with the exertion of foreign pressure on the court.[44]

Again in late May, 1902, Chang warned Fraser that moves were afoot to send him to Shanghai to take over from Sheng Hsüan-huai the negotiations of the new commercial treaty stipulated by the Boxer Protocol, and that the intention was eventually to "shelve him in Peking." Once more Satow wearily rose to defense of Chang's permanence of tenure in Wuchang, though the dangers to Chang in this case may have been more imaginary than real.[45]

Even as he continued to show great uncertainty as to his position in the vagaries of court politics, Chang pressed forward on behalf of the major reform program to which he had become committed. In the summer of 1902, he wrote a preface for a collection of reform writings which even included several pieces by K'ang Yu-wei and Liang Ch'i-ch'ao.[46] Moreover, he worked hard to expand his reform projects in Hupeh. His main concern, as I will describe presently, was implementation of the educational system he had proposed the previous year and which had been partially sanctioned by the edicts of late 1901. But he also developed plans for military reorganization and training and set up a police bureau for the city of Wuchang.[47] The police bureau was quickly emulated by Yüan Shih-k'ai in the north and was approved by the throne, although the police bureau set up in Changsha by the Hunan reformers early in 1898 was one of the institutions which were specifically denounced by the empress dowager in October, 1898.[48]

All during the latter part of 1901 and most of 1902, Chang labored to construct a school system in Hupeh as close as possible to that which he had recommended in the July, 1901, memorial on education. He set up a Hupeh Provincial Office of School Affairs (Hu-pei ch'üan-sheng hsüeh-wu-ch'u) to coordinate and supervise the emerging system, and he sent two educational inspection missions to Japan in the fall and winter of 1901–2. By October, 1902, when Chang was about to leave his Wuchang post temporarily, he was able to report considerable achievements in building a provincial educational structure. He had transformed some of the schools and academies already in existence, or had appropriated their facilities, as well as setting up some new institutions. The memorial of July, 1901, had projected a six-level educational structure for each province: kindergartens, lower and higher primary schools (ages eight through seventeen), all three at the district or department level; middle schools, at the prefectural level; various kinds of high schools and a university, in the provincial capital. Chang had set up schools approximating the top four of these six tiers when he left in late 1902.[49]

The provincial educational system Chang was trying to construct for Hupeh was predicated upon two important ingredients. One was the liberal use of members of his own *mu-fu,* and of his students returned from study in Japan, as teachers and administrators. The other was the cooperation of the gentry class of the province in setting up lower primary schools at the district level to feed into the provincial system. In the former area, he was quite successful. Counting only those individuals specifically named in Chang's October, 1902, memorial on the Hupeh system, there were at least nine members or former members of his private secretariat holding important positions of educational administration.[50] Two students whom Chang had sent to Japan for study, Hu Chün and Ch'en I, had returned to become co-principals of the Wuchang Normal School, working under Liang Ting-fen's supervision, and at least five others were working as teachers in the various civil and military schools in Wuchang.[51]

Chang was disappointed, however, in his hopes for the enthusiastic cooperation of the provincial and local gentry in his new school system. The July, 1901, memorial had assigned the gentry class a major role in setting up and supporting the lower three of the six levels of the system in each district. Again in his October, 1902, report on progress thus far in Hupeh, he noted that the immensity of the educational task had required him to leave the establishment of lower primary schools to the private initiative of the gentry. His system started with the higher primary schools, and even here the five he set up were intended only as models for the districts and departments to emulate.[52]

Beginning with his October, 1902, report, Chang began to express impatience with the gentry's performance in providing adequate modern lower primary schools. He realized that in order to staff the needed primary schools at the district level, an increased number of normal school graduates would be needed. Accordingly, he began to put more stress on expansion of normal schools than he had in his original memorial of July, 1901.[53] For example, in early 1903, while serving as temporary governor-general at Nanking, he set up the San-chiang Normal School, which he hoped would eventually have a thousand students and provide teachers for lower level schools in all three provinces of Liang-chiang. After returning to his regular Wuchang post in early 1904, he similarly tried to boost the capacity of the major normal school there from its original 120 to 1,000. He did his best to induce local government offices also to promote primary education and teacher training, and he berated them in early 1905 for their lack of achievement in these areas.[54]

Yet results outside the provincial capital were dismal. Part of the reason was simply a lack of resources. Chang had trouble adequately supporting his major educational institutions in Wuchang; local governments were far less able to amass the resources for school building, even had they wanted to. The only effective way to get the new school system rolling in the countryside was to enlist the help of the gentry class, which had the necessary money and administrative experience. Chang tried to do this in Hupeh in 1901 and 1902, but the traditional elite did not respond to the call to cooperate in erecting the new system. They continued, instead, to invest their money and their sons in preparations for the traditional examinations. Thus, by early 1903 Chang had come to the conclusion that the old examination system would have to be rooted out in its entirety before the crucial resources of the gentry would be diverted to the new educational structure in which he so firmly believed. Acting on this conclusion, he now turned to the difficult task of obtaining from the court the abolition of the exams and the promulgation of a complete national educational structure.

Politics and Educational Policy in Peking, 1903

A combination of factors drew Chang toward Peking in early 1903, although he remained very anxious about his position vis-à-vis the court and accordingly maintained intimate relationships with the British diplomats he had come to trust. In September, 1902, Chang expressed to Fraser his dissatisfaction with the private intelligence he had been receiving lately from Peking, and asked if Satow would be willing to keep him informed of political developments around the court.[55] When Liu K'un-i died in office on October 6, 1902, and Chang was ordered to Nanking temporarily to fill in as acting (*shu*) governor-general there, for a few days he discussed with Fraser and Satow the possibility of using British influence to remain at Wuchang, but to secure for himself appointment as Commissioner of Trade for the Southern Ports (Nan-yang ta-ch'en), a position always concurrent with the Nanking governor-generalship.[56] Then, after deciding to accept the Nanking post without quibbling, Chang requested Satow to make a special trip to Nanking to see him on his way back to England for leave in late November. Chang also asked that Fraser not be given leave at the same time, though he was due for it, so that he would remain available to Chang as a conduit to the British government.[57]

After taking up the Nanking post on November 9, Chang seems to have considered the desirability of its becoming his permanent appointment. But on December 5 these hopes, if indeed they were serious ones, disappeared when Wei Kuang-tao, governor-general of Yunnan and Kweichow, was given the substantive position. Chang thought poorly of Wei, and considered Wei's appointment over himself something of an insult, especially when during the weeks to come it was not made clear that Chang would return to Wuchang after Wei arrived and his temporary duties at Nanking ended. By early February, 1903, still awaiting Wei's arrival, Chang was sufficiently disgruntled to request the imperial audience which he had long avoided, convinced now that his best chance of shoring up his political position and redressing the wrongs inflicted upon him lay in direct contact with the throne. On February 5, he submitted his memorial requesting an audience.[58] At the same time, he had misgivings over the possible consequences of such direct action, fearing that he might be shunted off into a permanent sinecure in Peking, and he expressed hope that if such turned out to be the case, the British diplomats could extricate him from the capital and secure his return to Wuchang.[59] This fear was greatly enhanced by the death of Jung-lu in April, on the eve of Chang's departure for the capital. Now he assumed that the Grand Council would be under the control of Prince Ch'ing, whom he greatly despised and mistrusted.[60]

While the exigencies of his own political position drew him toward Peking, so too did his desire to speed up the national reform program already begun tentatively by the court, especially in the area of educational administration. Chang's political disgruntlement during his short tenure at Nanking did not prevent him from addressing himself, with his usual reforming zeal, to the affairs of the three provinces. While in Nanking, he tinkered with the military system, with lower Yangtze railroad development, and with the reform of the Kiangnan Arsenal, in addition to keeping close track of events back in Hupeh through frequent communication with Governor Tuan-fang, standing in for him there.[61] But he paid particular attention to educational matters, and it seems that during this stay in Nanking Chang's resolve to fight for more drastic measures to achieve a modern national educational system crystallized.

Perhaps Chang's discovery that the Liang-chiang jurisdiction lagged even further behind his own Hu-kuang area in educational progress strengthened his determination to speed up the rate of change. He turned to Yüan Shih-k'ai, the only other major official who had also tried to foster a new school system in his area, as an ally. They agreed that the old examination system had to be scrapped completely in order to spur the gentry into supporting the new schools, and in early March they submitted a joint memorial proposing this drastic step. In it, they bluntly said, "we have not yet heard of any of the gentry class who are urging the building of new schools," and the only way to make them do so was total abolition of the old exams.[62]

This straightforward recommendation met with the resistance of the entrenched educational bureaucracy in Peking. When she first acknowledged the memorial on March 13, the empress dowager referred it to the Board of Rites and the Office for the Management of Political Affairs for deliberation. Many denounced the proposal. One censor, P'an Ch'ing-lan, impeached Chang and Yüan, and it was said that the prestigious Wang Wen-shao also was bitterly opposed to abolition of the exams.[63] By the time the new Nanking incumbent, Wei Kuang-tao, finally arrived and relieved Chang on March 20, the joint memorial of Chang and Yüan had in effect been shelved in Peking, and it was apparent that vigorous lobbying would be required to win its acceptance. During a stay of about a month in Wuchang, from late March to late April, preparing for his trip to the capital, Chang conferred with Yüan Shih-k'ai by telegram concerning tactics to outflank the opposition. In a telegram to Yüan on April 8, Chang pinpointed the opposition in the fear of academic bureaucrats in the Hanlin Academy that their positions and livelihoods would be hurt without the traditional examinations, for which they served as administrators and graders. He also first hit upon the strategy that would eventually be successful in circumventing this opposition: incorporation of the old-fashioned scholars in the new system by providing positions and functions for them, even if these were only symbolic.[64] When he left Wuchang for Peking on April 25, in addition to his hopes of strengthening his own political position, Chang was determined to do his best to sway the court to adopt his education reforms. Yet he could hardly have foreseen that this trip to the capital, after an absence of nearly twenty years, would involve him in a high-level policy struggle which would occupy the remainder of the year.[65]

Chang arrived in Peking on May 16, 1903. On May 18, he had the first of many audiences with the throne which he would have during the coming weeks. In these audiences, Chang apparently got along very well with Tz'u-hsi, who bestowed many minor personal kindnesses and reward tokens upon him.[66] This must have done much to allay his fears as to his standing at court.[67] However, the society of the great imperial city, much changed since Chang had last frequented its circuits, did not receive him so kindly. He had few people to talk to. Most of his old friends and associates were dead or retired to their provincial homes. The old conservatives still around were bitter, and the younger reformers in government tended to be impatient with Chang. The charm and elegance of Peking had thus faded somewhat for Chang; he was melancholy much of the time, and wrote many poems. One poignant line read, "Why should the people of Peking pay any attention to a decrepit old man?"[68] Yet during the summer of 1903 he proved that he was still an able and influential politician.

At one of his first audiences with the empress dowager in May, they discussed the undesirable tendencies toward radical politics on the part of students abroad, and she commissioned Chang to devise a way to manage them more effectively.[69] After consultation with the Japanese minister in Peking, and through him with the Tokyo government, Chang wrote a comprehensive set of rules governing the study and conduct of students in Japan, the main place of concern to the government. These regulations, memorialized by Chang in person in October and immediately approved by Tz'u-hsi, will be discussed in some detail in the next chapter. At the time, however, this project was not Chang's primary concern. Most of his energies were directed toward securing domestic reform measures: abolition of the traditional exams and establishment of a standardized national educational system under central government supervision. The opposition to these measures had already shown itself to be potent, and at first Chang was not even in a position to influence policy directly. He had to lobby informally, collaring court officials in person and arguing with them, meanwhile working for appointment to a special policymaking post where he could bring his ideas to fruition.

Some insight into the politics of the time can be gained from a telegram of June 15, 1903, which Chang sent to his close adviser Liang Ting-fen, back in Wuchang. Chang said that he had been talking forcefully with as many high officials as possible, arguing that in order to create needed expertise, the government had to reward people adequately, that is, to give the coveted civil service degrees to the graduates of the modern schools. At this time, he said, he was just planning ways to expand greatly the national school system and had "high expectations." However, it is apparent that he was meeting stiff resistance from conservative precincts. In April and May, there had been considerable student unrest over Russia's refusal to pull her troops out of Manchuria on schedule, and expressions of student impatience with government policy had occurred in Tokyo, Shanghai, and other places, including the Imperial University in Peking. In his telegram to Liang, Chang claimed that student activities had put his plans in peril, for many high officials, appalled and mortified by student behavior, were fighting all reforms. Chang argued as best he could, pointing out that one doesn't throw away good food just because of a little difficulty in swallowing it. But he feared that any further outbreaks of student unruliness would give the reactionaries just the chance they needed to press their case with the throne, and he conceded that the conduct of his own Hupeh students caused even him no little trepidation. He hoped that the students could be made to understand the importance of not giving a pretext to those who wanted to destroy the whole modern school system.[70]

Despite Chang's fears that he would not be able to get his views accepted, he seemed to have won a preliminary victory by the end of June. Chang Po-hsi, the general superintendent of educational affairs in Peking, requested that Chang Chih-tung be assigned the special task of consulting with him and his chief assistant, Jung-ch'ing, on reforms to be made in the national school system. On June 27, this request was approved, and Chang was given an office and a staff to begin turning his theories and convictions into concrete form.[71] Along with this strategic appointment came further evidence of Chang's favor with the throne, for at about the same time he was given the prestigious post of chief examiner for the *ching-chi t'e-k'o,* the special examination in political economy and administration which had been widely touted since the latter part of 1902 and which was scheduled for July. It was this special examination, however, in connection with unrelated events in Shanghai, that would provide the reactionaries with a chance to rally their forces and attack the new educational policies.[72]

There had already been considerable grumbling among conservatives about the special examination, which was geared to modern and Western educational content and designed to offer a way into the bureaucracy for those specializing in new skills. *Chü-jen* and even *chin-shih* degrees were to be given to the best performers in the exam. The empress dowager's appointment of Chang as head examiner showed her commitment to using the exam as a means of discovering and employing men trained in the new style schools or abroad. Chang must have been pleased, for he himself was putting great store by the exam as a way of finding appropriate employment for many individuals whose training he had sponsored, or whose talents he admired. Some of these he had been able to employ in his own secretariat or his new educational institutions in Hupeh, but those positions were limited in number, and he wanted to see his protégés advance to positions of higher prestige and influence. In the absence of a transfer of the civil service degrees from the old exams to the new school system, for which he was working, the *ching-chi t'e-k'o* was one of the few means by which these men could gain the status and power of formal government office. Accordingly, Chang recommended sixteen men as candidates for the special exam in October, 1902, at least ten of whom were instructors in his Hupeh schools; and in January, 1903, while stationed in Nanking, he recommended thirty more men from that area.[73]

Unfortunately, the academic exercise of the special exam became grossly politicized in July. The first round of the exam was administered on July 10; Chang, as chief examiner, reported the results to the throne on July 13, and they were announced on July 14. Forty-eight first-class and seventy-nine second-class ratings were given, which constituted a very high percentage of passes. The two top positions, personally selected by Chang, went to Liang Shih-i and Yang Tu, the latter having been one of the first students Chang sent to Japan for study in 1898.[74] At this point there arose a chorus of complaints from the Peking bureaucracy. Some thought that far too many had been passed. Others pointed out the coincidence that the last character in Liang Shih-i's given name, *i*, was the same character that occurred in K'ang Yu-wei's original given name (Tsu-i), giving him the "head of Liang" (the same surname as Liang Ch'i-ch'ao) and the "tail of K'ang."

That this sort of nonsense could have seriously affected the empress dowager is incredible. What gave effect to the blusterings of the reactionaries was the fact that the *Su-pao* case broke in Shanghai just at the time of the first round of the special examination. The clearly subversive propaganda being disseminated by this newspaper since the late spring of 1903 had led to the arrest of several of those associated with it by the International Settlement police in late June and early July, and to its closing on July 7.[75] In

Peking, it was rumored that several of the successful candidates in the special exam had sympathy for the Shanghai revolutionaries (this was probably true), and a general pall was cast over the entire examination. Chang Chih-tung was demoted to assistant examiner for the second round of the examination, which was held on July 21, and he fought vainly against the conservative tide. The announcement of the final results on July 27 revealed that only twenty-seven had passed. Moreover, Liang Shih-i and Yang Tu, in the top two positions after the first round, were dropped altogether, and not one "winner" was given the *chin-shih* degree or a job in the Hanlin Academy; all rewards were very minor—appointment as expectant prefect or the like.

Chang was tremendously disappointed, for not only had his original choices for the top two places been eliminated, but so had all of those he had recommended. Not one whom he or Yüan Shih-k'ai, his ally in the attempt to abolish the examination system, had recommended finally passed. This had obvious implications far beyond the special exam itself. All of Chang's hopes for broad educational reform were now in serious danger, for his opponents had the ear of the empress dowager, at least for the time being. Chang wired his chagrin to Liang Ting-fen on July 29, concluding his report on his defeat by saying, "The opposition is just too numerous and too clever; I'm very depressed."[76]

Things thus looked bleak in the late summer of 1903, but Chang persevered, and by the end of the year changing circumstances and the emergence of some unexpected new allies won him a fairly conclusive victory. For one thing, significant changes took place in the composition of the Office for the Management of Political Affairs, the body whose duty it was to advise the throne on major policy issues: Jung-lu had died in April, and K'un-kang retired in August; Chang himself and Yüan Shih-k'ai were promoted from "consulting" to full membership; and all three of the new members named in November, Chang Po-hsi, Sun Chia-nai, and Jung-ch'ing, were experts in educational affairs and open to persuasion by a well-argued case.[77] Moreover, it is likely that Chang's strategy of preserving some sort of place within the new educational structure for holders of traditional sinecures eased the fear of forced retirement on the part of many. Yet the most important factor may well have been the very apprehension about student disaffection which, when first aroused in the spring, worked against educational reform. Those whose first reaction was to punish the unruly students by abolishing entirely the new schools and study abroad began to see the political wisdom of co-opting them instead.

By September, 1903, reports of unhappy and unmanageable students were coming regularly into Peking from all over the country. With the reports came requests from the officials involved for more firm central direction of the educational system. Few bureaucrats perceived the depth of alienation from the dynasty which some students, especially those in Japan, were experiencing by this time. Nevertheless, government officials saw the need for the skills which the modern students were acquiring, and many officials in Peking began to appreciate the fact that at least one reason for disaffection on the part of the modern student class was its being largely locked out of the normal channels to official status and power, which were still dominated by traditional degree holders. Creation of a broad and regular opening to official careers for graduates of the new schools would, Chang Chih-tung and others now hoped, enlist their skills in the service of the government. On September 7, P'an Ch'ing-lan, the same censor who had bitterly denounced Chang Chih-tung and Yüan Shih-k'ai for their suggestion early in the year that the old examinations be abolished, now himself asked for the first step leading to the same end: that official status (*ch'u-shen*) be given to the graduates of the new schools.[78]

The first major indication that the educational reformers were winning out despite their summer defeat came on September 21, when twelve of the eighteen provincial directors of education were suddenly replaced.[79] These high level administrators of the old examination system had been its most staunch defenders. Finally, late in 1903 or in the first days of 1904, Chang Chih-tung and Chang Po-hsi jointly submitted a package of five memorials constituting a comprehensive national educational program, whose major elements were acknowledged and accepted by the empress dowager on January 13, 1904.[80] The most important element in this package was the proposal to implement the basic plan first suggested by Chang and Liu K'un-i in 1901: to abolish the old examination system in a series of three steps, beginning with the 1906 exams, with ever larger portions of the degree quotas being assigned to the graduates of the new schools.

This document was a political masterpiece.[81] Its very title, "A Memorial Requesting the Gradual Reduction of the Examination System as an Experiment," minimized the threat to the still potent traditional educational bureaucracy. Moreover, much of its content was devoted to reassuring those still worried over loss of their jobs or status. Provincial directors of education and Hanlin academicians would share the responsibilities of examining the school graduates with new officials such as the minister of education, the establishment of whose position was proposed by another of the five memorials. "For the aged *chü-jen, kung-sheng* and *sheng-yüan,* broad outlets will be provided; metropolitan officials will continue to be appointed as directors of education, and itinerant examiners will be even more numerous." Thus, the proposal "would be not at all an abrogation of the examination system, but in fact merely a unification of the examination system and the schools." In her edict of approval, the empress dowager accepted this misleading concept of merging the old and new systems, when in fact the new would soon supplant the old entirely.[82]

Thus was the crucial breakthrough made, the key principle established. The civil service examinations, the institution which probably most Chinese and foreign observers alike would agree was the cornerstone of the imperial government, were slated for extinction. The achievement was not easy. It had taken the unflagging perseverance of Chang Chih-tung and the cooperation of other important officials to convince the throne in the face of resistance by the old guard in Peking. Yet the accomplishment of this task is symbolic of the possibility of movement and is indicative of a growing characteristic of the imperial government, one for which it had never been noted before: the ability to generate from within itself forces sufficient to make major alterations in its basic structures. If the examination system could be abolished, any needed change could be made. From Chang's point of view, there was yet hope of successful adaptation to the needs of the times.

In 1904 and 1905, the pace of change accelerated in all areas of government concern. There were great strides in military affairs and economic development; there were still more educational reforms; and finally even the basic political foundations of the state began to be altered with the first concrete steps toward a constitutional system. Chang Chih-tung stayed abreast of events and movement for change in all of these areas.

Return to Wuchang

Chang's labors in Peking were completed, and he left the capital on February 7, 1904. After spending a few days at his ancestral home in Nan-p'i, Chihli, and at a few other places on the way, he arrived in Wuchang on March 29 to resume his regular post as Hu-kuang governor-general. He immediately plunged back into local Hupeh affairs with all his old enthusiasm, and during 1904 and 1905 reached the apex of his career as an advocate and administrator of modernizing reforms.

Chang undertook a reorganization of the Hupeh provincial educational system and established some new schools; many of his changes here were in line with his new commitment to build up primary and normal schools, as noted earlier in this chapter.[83] He reorganized and improved the training of the modern military forces in his jurisdiction.[84] During 1904, Chang also became deeply involved in the campaign to regain the construction rights to the Hankow-Canton Railroad, a campaign that would finally be successful in 1905. Chang's relationship with the provincial gentry in this "rights recovery" movement will be discussed further in a later chapter.

During 1904 and the first part of 1905, all Chinese—the court in Peking, provincial officials like Chang, representatives of the new public opinion in urban areas, and revolutionaries in China and abroad—kept one eye on the progress of the Russo-Japanese War, being fought on Chinese territory in southern Manchuria. Though the Japanese defeat of Russia was certainly less than total, and they were not able to secure an indemnity, nevertheless the impressive Japanese performance was viewed as a resounding victory all over China, and the impact of that victory was great in all strata of Chinese government and society, as it was in many other Asian countries. The net effect was to intensify Chinese nationalistic opinion, to increase the determination of the revolutionaries to overthrow the dynasty, and to spur the government itself onto a path of no return in its own reform program. In 1905 came the first use of the economic boycott as a weapon of nationalistic public opinion, in this case against the United States immigration exclusion laws.[85] In the same year, the forces of Sun Yat-sen and those of the student revolutionary movement abroad combined to form the T'ung-meng hui.[86] Meanwhile, dynastic reform accelerated as well.

Chang Chih-tung had a direct hand in securing the two most important steps of government reform taken in 1905, the final and immediate abolition of the old examination system and the commitment to build a constitutional political structure. Both of these measures reflect the sense of urgency that had overtaken many bureaucratic reformers and the court itself by 1905. To some extent, they were reactions to increasing activity and pressure for change on the part of the modern student class and the provincial gentry and merchant groups on the periphery of the political power structure. However, as Liang Ch'i-ch'ao was arguing persuasively from his position as critic in exile, and as the Japanese example now seemed conclusively to prove, expanding the new schools as fast as possible and incorporating the elite more integrally into national political life were essential to unify and strengthen the nation, despite the administrative and political headaches such steps might entail.

On August 31, 1905, Chang joined with five other major provincial officials in requesting that his earlier plan for gradual elimination of the old examinations be scrapped; rather, the exams should be abolished immediately. The memorialists were frank in admitting that this step was needed not only to hasten the time when the nation would have trained modern administrators and specialists at its service, but to increase the very stability of the state by making graduates of the new schools more certain of worthwhile positions and therefore more loyal.[87] The response of the throne was remarkably rapid; only three days later, on September 2, 1905, the civil service examinations were abolished entirely and forever.

The rapid final abolition of the examinations was consistent with the position Chang had held on this issue since 1901. But his conversion to advocacy, however lukewarm, of a constitutional political system represented a considerable departure from his past position on the issue of sharing power with provincial and local elites. Chang had become familiar with arguments in favor of constitutionalism during the spring of 1904 when the constitutionalist advocate Chang Chien saw him in Nanking, but he remained uncommitted while other officials began to advocate a constitutional system during 1904 and 1905.[88] By 1905, the issue of constitutionalism was rapidly becoming one of the foremost topics of public opinion and debate within government circles. Finally, probably in response to a specific imperial request for his opinion, Chang joined with Yüan Shih-k'ai and Chou Fu (acting governor-general at Nanking) in a memorial of July 2, 1905, which recommended that a constitutional system be implemented over the next twelve years.[89]

Unfortunately, the Chinese text of this memorial is not available in the collected papers of Chang, Yüan, or Chou, nor is it in any of the standard documentary collections for the period. However, on July 7, 1905, there appeared what seems to be an extract from this memorial in the *North China Herald*.[90] In this extract, the memorialists differed with those advocating rapid organization of a national parliament, saying that the country and the people were unprepared. But it was important to educate the people in preparation for future responsibilities, and they recommended the establishment of provincial assemblies, where gentry and other "men of ability and means," selected by cities and townships, would represent their constituencies at the provincial capital, advising the governor and other high officials, as a prelude to a national body. There is still evidence here of a reluctance really to share power with the nonofficial elite (their representatives would only "advise" officials), and a twelve-year timetable was cautious in the extreme. Nevertheless, for Chang to overcome his longstanding prejudice against *min-ch'üan* and representative parliamentarianism enough to accept it, even in diluted form, and to countenance an eventual full constitutional system, is extremely significant. It indicates the extent to which many bureaucrats had become persuaded, especially by the spectacle of constitutionalist Japan defeating autocratic Czarist Russia, that this indeed was the proper path to national strength.

The Chang-Yüan-Chou joint memorial of July 2 was followed by an edict of July 16, 1905, appointing a four-man government mission to investigate the political systems of Japan and the Western nations.[91] There was a delay when a revolutionary terrorist threw a bomb injuring two of the commissioners as the group was about to leave from Peking in September, but the mission got underway by the end of the year, and the dynasty was launched on its halting way toward a constitutional system of government.

The Significance of Government Reform

The problem of evaluating the various reforms taken at the central and provincial government levels is not an easy one. As is shown by the events described in this chapter, it was a difficult but by no means impossible task to move the government in Peking to accept and sponsor the kind of changes which officials like Chang Chih-tung believed were necessary. In the maneuvering to secure a commitment to meaningful change, Chang always had to worry about his own political security, and he resorted to various strategems in order to get his views before the throne. Even then, they might not be accepted, of course. Yet despite much hesitation, frequent backsliding, and unevenness of progress, the achievements made in generating a national reform program under central direction between 1900 and 1905 were impressive. After 1905, the pace of change increased even more, especially in the development of constitutionalism.

Many accounts of early twentieth-century Chinese history dismiss the post-1900 government reform movement as merely a final effort by the ruling Manchu dynasty to save itself.[92] Recently, however, many scholars have viewed the post-Boxer reforms more charitably, in particular drawing attention to the serious efforts made by the central government to limit the inroads of imperialism in China, and the successes scored in this area.[93]

It does seem, as pointed out by those wishing to downgrade

the importance of the government reforms, that self-preservation was one important incentive for the dynasty's willingness at last to countenance a reform movement. Increasing awareness of student dissatisfaction helped prompt final abolition of the old examination system, and realization of the importance of new public opinion groups led to consideration of constitutionalism to provide an outlet for their views and yet to control them to some extent. Yet the positive aspects of the reforms, in particular the hope that effective mobilization of national resources and the enhancement of state power would result from them, were more important to at least some leading officials, including Chang Chih-tung.

Besides the issues of motivation and specific achievements of the reforms, there was another factor after 1900 which has not been much noted by scholars, but which may have favored the long-run success of the government reform program. This was the rise of a "new generation" of officials to key positions of power and influence. Before 1900, a few men like Li Hung-chang and Chang Chih-tung had to plan and administer various reform programs in their provincial areas with little or no help from central authorities or officials in neighboring areas. Now Chang no longer had to work alone, for ever larger numbers of top officials were as convinced as he of the need for reforms. Important reform memorials were more often signed by several individuals, as were the two major ones of 1905 which Chang co-signed. A closer look at the careers of some of the major provincial and metropolitan officials in the last years of the dynasty may reveal a surprising degree of competence, effectiveness, and commitment to renovating Chinese government and society.[94]

The question of the potential for long-run achievement of the reform programs set in motion before 1911 must remain problematical, because of the discontinuity in the political system occasioned by the advent of the Republic in 1912. Yet some of the main developments in military, educational, fiscal, and even legal systems, as they were worked out during the Republic, were firmly set in motion during the decade of imperial reforms after 1900.

If the imperial reform program was to have any success in its aims, the preservation of the dynasty and strengthening of the nation through the adoption of new structures, there was a major challenge which still lay in its path. It had to come to grips with the opportunities of integration, as well as with the dangers of alienation, of those parts of society which were demanding recognition and participation in the political power structure of the nation. These were on the one hand the modern student class, and on the other the groups of gentry elite who were becoming increasingly active on the provincial level. If, as I believe, Chang Chih-tung was not unique in his appreciation of the importance of dealing effectively with these two groups, consideration of his relationship with them after 1900 may shed light on the general problem of the achievements and failures of the late Ch'ing reform program as a whole.

Chapter 7

The Student Revolutionary Movement

After 1900, and especially after 1903, revolutionary sentiments among Chinese students at home and abroad became an increasingly large problem for the government. Many members of China's modern student class, in particular those exposed to the intellectual currents of Tokyo, became alienated from their own government and dedicated to its overthrow. In 1905, they coalesced into an alliance with the older revolutionary Sun Yat-sen to form the T'ung-meng hui, or Revolutionary Alliance. Until recently, it has been an article of faith among most Chinese and Western historians that these student revolutionaries made a significant contribution to the weakening and the eventual downfall of the Ch'ing government.

Many Hupeh students were among the leaders of revolutionary activities and organizations in Japan, and they also attempted to develop a revolutionary movement in their home province. Naturally this aroused the interest of Chang Chih-tung, as much because of his concern with national educational policy as because of his desire to thwart any moves to overthrow his local administration. This chapter will describe Chang Chih-tung's relationship with the student movement after 1900. As I will try to show, Chang Chih-tung's experience with the student class shows that it probably should not be assigned such an important historical role as it has been given.

Study in Japan

One of the most important phenomena of early twentieth-century China was the surge of Chinese students who traveled to Japan to study. Before 1911, it is likely that a total of at least 18,000 students had received some sort of educational training in Japan.[1]

This tremendous movement was tied directly to Ch'ing government policy. Even though very few students were supported financially by the central government, a great many were supported by various provincial authorities. These authorities, like Chang Chih-tung in Hupeh, generally followed the guidelines laid down by the central government in sending students abroad. When edicts of 1898 and 1899 promised official employment to graduates of schools in Japan, the number of students who went there first reached significant proportions, 143 in 1899. When the edict of September, 1901, promised a number of official degrees to be set aside for those returning from study in Japan, the immediate result was a large increase in the number of students, to 727, over 250 of them not on government stipend. The edict of January, 1904, to abolish the old examination system entirely, by stages, caused a great rush to Japan; by 1905, there were probably 8,000 Chinese students there, most of them now privately supported. This was the apex of the movement.[2]

The government encouraged study in Japan and promised good positions to those who were successful. Moreover, for most of the period before 1911, the Chinese embassy in Tokyo served as the liaison between the students and Japanese educational authorities. The Chinese minister to Japan generally had the responsibility for representing the students' interests vis-à-vis the Japanese, and for supervising the students on behalf of the Peking government. The students themselves were quite aware of the official nature of their training, and most of them looked forward to good jobs in the central or provincial governments upon their return to China. In 1906, when the government tightened the rules for study abroad and raised the standards to qualify for official status and rewards, the number of students in Japan dropped considerably, to only 4,000 or so by 1909.[3]

The great majority of Chinese students in Japan were enrolled either in general studies or in special intensive courses (*su-ch'eng k'o*). Moreover, almost all were at schools set up and administered especially for Chinese students. By 1905 there were at least five major civil schools of this nature, offering mostly intensive courses, Japanese language training, and general studies preparatory courses which might qualify one for study at a bona fide Japanese institution of higher learning.[4] The level of study at these schools was not very high, perhaps equivalent to that of a Japanese junior high school, and the number of those Chinese students who eventually qualified for study above the high school level was very small. This can be seen by the extremely low numbers of Chinese who actually received degrees from authentic Japanese university-level institutions before 1908: 6 in 1903, 16 in 1904, 15 in 1905, 42 in 1906, 56 in 1907, finally over 300 in 1908, and upward from then on.[5]

The quality of the military training schools for Chinese seems to have been significantly better. In 1898, Chang Chih-tung sent four military students who were permitted to enroll at the Seijō Gakkō, a prep school for the regular Army Officers' School (Rikugun Shikan Gakkō). The following year, when Chang and Liu K'un-i sent more students, a special branch of the Seijō Gakkō was set up for the Chinese students; after 1902, this branch assumed a more separate identity and the name Shinpu Gakkō. Through 1907, this military prep school produced over 520 graduates, and more than half of them were accepted for further study at the Japanese Army Officers' School, a highly respected institution.[6]

The segregation of the great majority of Chinese students into academic enclaves largely separate from Japanese schools and society undoubtedly reinforced their instinctive tendency to stick together in a strange environment. They were undoubtedly greatly stimulated by their surroundings, especially by their relative freedom from effective supervision, and by the availability of exciting new ideas and books. But the activities and the flurry of publications which they produced even before their numbers passed the one thousand mark in 1903 were largely directed at each other and events back in China, not at their Japanese hosts.

The intellectual ferment among Chinese students in Japan in the early 1900's is well known, as is the great variety (and the ephemeral nature) of the organizations and publications of these years.[7] Well before 1903 intense feelings of anti-imperialism directed at the Western powers had brought some students to conclude that the "alien" Manchu dynasty had to be overthrown in order for China to be able to achieve the needed strength to resist foreign aggression.[8] During 1902, public meetings began to express antigovernment feelings, and in late July and August, 1902, student dissatisfaction with the Chinese authorities at the Tokyo legation erupted in a sit-in there; the Japanese police were called by the Chinese minister, and two students were deported.[9] Finally, in late 1902 or early 1903, the first avowedly anti-Manchu organization, the Ch'ing-nien hui (Youth Association), was formed; most of the approximately twenty members were students at Waseda University.[10]

Yet the militant radicals were still few, and they were far from building the sort of organization which had any chance of really overthrowing the government. The most consistently active individuals were some veterans of the Tzu-li hui revolt of 1900 and the brilliant but eccentric Chang Ping-lin.[11] The pace of literary production was furious, but that of organizing was slow. In fact, the most important characteristic of the Chinese student body in Japan before 1903 was its disunity and factionalism. Wu Chih-hui, who was one of those deported after the disruption at Minister Ts'ai Chün's legation office in the summer of 1902, later described the situation among the students at that time as one of very little cooperation or even contact between different provincial and school groups.[12] Even the Ch'ing-nien hui, the first group devoted fully to the propagation of Chinese nationalism, was not very successful. Shelly Cheng has concluded that the Ch'ing-nien hui was simply a failure in attracting any significant number of students to its views, though its members became important as writers and propagandists in 1903 and after.[13] Finally, it seems significant that there were extremely few contacts between Chinese students in Japan and Sun Yat-sen, the most experienced revolutionary there before 1903.[14]

The Chinese government was not unaware of the growing problem of student alienation, and it was willing to take some steps to make more palatable the system of supervision and regulation under which the students lived. In 1902, immediately after Minister

Ts'ai Chün called the Japanese police to clear out the students who were harassing him about admission to the military prep school, other Chinese students wired the Peking foreign ministry, complaining about Ts'ai Chün's high-handed behavior.[15] Ts'ai's actions were criticized around the court, and finally Prince Tsai-chen, who had arrived in Japan in early August on his way home from a trip to America, was directed to investigate the entire incident and see who was really at fault. In his September report, Tsai-chen blamed neither the Chinese minister nor the students, but rather the unwieldy system of assignment of students to schools and regulation of their conduct, which had been made obsolete by the rapid increase in the number of students.[16]

Tsai-chen recommended that a special Tokyo office be created to handle all the responsibilities concerning Chinese students in Japan. After some discussion in Peking, the office of general supervisor of Chinese students in Japan was created on October 31, 1902, and Wang Ta-hsieh, an official of the foreign ministry, was named to the post. The rules for admission of Chinese to Japanese institutions were also changed in the fall, and their administration was transferred from the Chinese embassy to the new office of general supervisor of students. The new rules made the assignment of students to schools less arbitrary, by requiring that all students first complete at least a half year of satisfactory work at one of three approved special schools for Chinese before being admitted to a regular Japanese school.[17] These rules remained in effect until those written by Chang Chih-tung were adopted in October, 1903. When Wang Ta-hsieh was recalled to Peking in September, 1903, the responsibility for the students was in effect moved back to the embassy: Yang Shu, who had replaced Ts'ai Chün as minister to Japan in June, 1903, was named concurrent supervisor of students, a post he held until 1906.[18]

Chang Chih-tung and the Students in Japan

Chang Chih-tung, of course, was one of the earliest and most enthusiastic advocates of sending Chinese students to Japan to receive the kind of training which Chinese schools were not yet equipped to give them. In the *Ch'üan-hsüeh p'ien* of early 1898, Chang argued that not only was study in Japan cheaper and more convenient than in Europe, and the language problem less, but it would also be easier to supervise and control students sent there. Moreover, Confucian ethics were still stressed in the Japanese school system, and that would be a good moral influence upon the Chinese students.[19] Beginning in 1898, Chang sent frequent inspection missions to Japan to learn how to build a modern school system in the Hupeh area, and he sent ever-increasing numbers of civil and military students on provincial government stipend to pursue training courses at Japanese institutions.[20]

Chang believed deeply in the value of study in Japan, and he stood firmly behind those students whom he sent there. By the testimony of one of his former students, Chang sent more young men to Japan from his jurisdiction of Hupeh and Hunan than were sent from any other area; indeed, many students from other provinces came to his schools in Hupeh for special training in order better to prepare themselves for study in Japan. Chang made a practice of talking personally to all students before they left; he always urged them to study hard, avoid bad company, and return home to be of service to the country. Perhaps most important, he was extremely conscientious in placing each returning student in a good job, or in recommending him to the central government, other provincial officials, and schools around the country.[21] Near the end of his life, Chang himself noted with pride his success in sponsoring the training of many talented students. He claimed that of those sent to Japan on Hupeh government stipends, thirty or forty had already become truly outstanding people who had made an important contribution to the country. Most of these were taken away from Hupeh by various military commands, the ministries of Finance and Education in Peking, top schools, and by Yüan Shih-k'ai for his own staff.[22]

Chang's high hopes for his students, both those in his Hupeh schools and those whom he sent to Japan, were based partially upon the assumption that the students would remain suitably grateful for their opportunities and respectful of his own and governmental authority. Unfortunately, some students showed a disconcerting degree of susceptibility to, first, the heterodox ideas of

K'ang Yu-wei, then even more radical and revolutionary doctrines. An even larger number of students resented the kind of paternalistic supervision that Chang and other older officials assumed was proper, and demanded more freedom of activity in their private lives. In Chang's eyes, the problem of insulating the impressionable students from dangerous ideas and maintaining a high level of personal morality and discipline among them was serious enough in his schools in Hupeh. To combat their occasionally alarming lawlessness and lack of respect for school authorities, he tried such expedients as reducing the size of classes, raising entrance requirements, barring older applicants, and increasing faculty power over the students.[23]

Chang's concern for the moral health and political rectitude of his students in Hupeh was multiplied severalfold for those in Japan, where they were beyond his direct supervision and exposed much more openly to political doctrines of revolution, republicanism, and anarchism. Chang sent two older men along with the first group of Hupeh students to go to Japan in the fall of 1898, and in the spring of 1899 he replaced them with one of the highest ranking members of his *mu-fu,* Ch'ien Hsün, with whom he had long been associated.[24] Ch'ien was the first Hupeh superintendent of students, an office which Chang always kept filled with his personal representative, even after the establishment in 1902 of a general supervisor of all Chinese students in Japan made it theoretically unnecessary.

I have already described how, upset with the involvement of several students in T'ang Ts'ai-ch'ang's revolt of August, 1900, Chang tried to combat the influence of K'ang and Liang among the students in Japan. His restraint and forbearance in that case remained characteristic of his reaction to the problem of discipline among students in Japan until 1903. He preferred to rely on moral admonition, at the same time reminding the students that good jobs and high prestige awaited them at home if they persevered in their studies. In June, 1902, he sent to all Hupeh students in Japan, both publicly and privately supported, a personal exhortation which was notable for its pomposity. He admonished the students to remember their basic moral code, to be upright in heart and firm of character, to turn a deaf ear to the ravings of rebels and heretics, to obey respectfully the Chinese authorities, and to please their Japanese instructors by diligence and improvement in their work, at the same time encouraging and assisting one another. If they behaved thus, they would be of service to the nation and would please Chang himself immeasurably; indeed, "the future possibilities for you all will be unlimited."[25]

By 1903, however, Chang had concluded that more strict measures would have to be used to keep the students in line. On December 30, 1902, Chang telegraphed to the Chinese minister and to both the general supervisor and Hupeh superintendent of students, directing them to put an immediate stop to a publishing venture among the Hupeh students, of which Chang had just heard. Putting out a newspaper, he fumed, was a nonsensical waste of time that could better be spent on studies or other practical activities, and potentially subversive as well. He demanded that the three officials cut off the stipend of any student persisting in this publication and request the Japanese school he was attending to expel him.[26] In February, 1903, Chang, then in Nanking, wired to Tuan-fang and Liang Ting-fen in Wuchang, who were managing educational matters there in his absence, complaining of the poor study habits of the students sent to Japan recently; he heard that the last twenty sent on government stipend did not even know what course of study they wished to pursue. He suggested making all the students from now on commit themselves in advance to courses in practical areas like agriculture, industry, and commerce.[27] Chang did not attempt to follow up on so drastic a thought at this time, however.

During 1903, while Chang was in Peking, the empress dowager gave him the responsibility of devising a whole new system for sending students abroad and yet keeping their activities within reasonable bounds while they were there. This was one of Chang's major projects in the capital, besides the renovation of the domestic educational system, and there is every evidence that he devoted considerable thought to it. After extensive consultation with Japanese officials, Chang compiled a comprehensive set of rules which he presented to the throne on October 6, 1903, and which was immediately accepted.[28] These rules struck a nice balance between the carrot and the stick.

In a short introduction to the main body of the regulations, Chang reiterated his long-standing concern with the moral qualities of the students abroad and noted that though they were young and impressionable, and some did indeed dabble in foolish political theories, nevertheless the great majority followed the rules and studied hard. What was most needed at this point, he said, was a system that would accurately punish and reward, to inhibit bad behavior and encourage the good. Thus rules for disciplining troublemakers had to be balanced by rules rewarding returning graduates, so that the government would appear fair and the students would know precisely what to expect.[29]

The new regulations were comprised of a total of twenty-seven articles. The first ten and the last seven provided for control of students in Japan and for their registration with various authorities. These were fairly stringent, putting all students, public and private, under the control of the Chinese supervisor of students. The Japanese school administrations were required to expel any student when asked to do so by the Chinese minister or supervisor, or even by provincial officials back in China when the request was forwarded through the Chinese authorities in Tokyo. Those expelled were to be deported back to China. Grounds for expulsion were any sort of disruption of public order, political activism, or even "irresponsible" political discussions. Bad risks were to be weeded out in advance by extensive background investigations of students before they were allowed to go to Japan, and quotas were put on the number of students who would be allowed to enroll in government, law, and military science programs, the latter being reserved exclusively for those on government stipends.[30]

The second group of ten articles in the regulations provided inducements and rewards for those students who put up with the supervision of the authorities and kept clear of involvement in any suspicious political activities. All graduates of Japanese institutions would be investigated and certified by the Chinese supervisor of students as to their behavior, deportment, and record of offenses, if any. Those with clean records would then be rewarded according to their diplomas and skills. Successful completion of a three-year course of study at a Japanese high school or a specialized trade school earned one the *chü-jen* degree, and those who persevered through a university program or its equivalent were rewarded with the coveted status of a *chin-shih*. Both public and private students were eligible for these and other rewards, as were those who had already graduated and returned to China before the new rules went into effect.[31]

No specific offices were attached to the rewards given returned graduates until 1904, when the January domestic educational reforms of Chang Chih-tung and Chang Po-hsi were accepted. Graduates at the middle school level were now to be appointed as assistants to prefects or magistrates; those at the level of normal colleges or high schools of technology, government, or law would be made secretaries in the Grand Secretariat (*chung-shu*), magistrates, or deputy prefects; university graduates, in addition to the *chin-shih,* would receive jobs in the Hanlin Academy or as high officials in a board (*chu-shih*).[32]

In addition to simple punishments and rewards, Chang still hoped that the force of moral example could be brought to bear upon the students in Japan. One of the five memorials on educational affairs submitted by Chang Chih-tung and Chang Po-hsi in January, 1904, suggested that older officials be given leave from their posts to go on extended tours of inspection and study abroad. Not only would this broaden their own horizons, but it would be a stabilizing influence on the Chinese students with whom they would mingle. The officials, well grounded in Confucian ethics, could help ward off heretical tendencies among the students by their steadfast example. This memorial was accepted, and several officials were sent to Japan, but to no avail. The generation gap between them and the young students was simply too great; the students found it difficult to respect them, let alone emulate them, when the older men had little knowledge of the modern subjects being pursued by the students.[33]

Moral example and Chang's continued distribution of the *Ch'üan-hsüeh p'ien* to the students he sent abroad were unlikely to be of decisive influence in keeping them loyal to the dynasty. Moreover, the rules for supervision and control of students in Japan which Chang had devised proved difficult to administer, with so many students and so few supervising officials.[34] The decisive factors in retaining or losing the students' loyalty, rather, were whether or not the dynasty found within itself sufficient vigor to defend China's sovereignty and enact reforms, and whether or not it provided adequate opportunities for the students to use their talents within the existing framework of government and society. The latter consideration was important in convincing some Peking conservatives to accept the abolition of the examination system by the end of 1903. This same concern for providing outlets for student talent was a factor in Chang's continued full support of study abroad and his confidence that, properly rewarded, the students would not go astray. Some specific cases will show that his confidence, both in the students abroad and in those at home, was not entirely ill placed.

The Student Movement: Problems of Revolutionary Commitment and Effectiveness

The Tokyo Anti-Russian Movement of 1903

While Chang Chih-tung was enroute from Wuchang to Peking in late April and early May, 1903, the Chinese students in Japan were engaging in one of their first acts of large-scale political agitation, thereby drawing to themselves the attention of major officials and the court. By the time Chang reached Peking on May 16, suspicion of the students was on the rise in conservative circles, and demands could already be heard for curtailment of modern study, especially study abroad. One of Chang's purposes in coming to court, the promotion of a greatly expanded national education system, thus seemed already to be compromised. But by mid-summer Chang received welcome news that the students in Japan were under control; as I have described, misgivings about their conduct did not prevent Chang's gaining acceptance of his educational program at the end of 1903.

By the spring of 1903, the activism of the Chinese students in Tokyo was definitely on the rise. Between November, 1902, and April, 1903, for example, four major monthly journals were founded by provincial groups: *Yu-hsüeh i-pien* (Hunan Students' Journal), *Hu-pei hsüeh-sheng chieh* (The Hupeh Student Circle), *Che-chiang ch'ao* (The Tide of Chekiang), and *Chiang-su* (Kiangsu). These journals were by no means unequivocably radical and contained a wide variety of views on subjects of academic or practical interest as well as politics. But many individual articles were anti-Manchu or otherwise politically subversive, and several members of the Ch'ing-nien hui, while unable to draw many adherents to their protorevolutionary organization, made their views known through these publications.[35] The establishment of the Hupeh students' publication in late January, 1903, might be seen as especially significant in view of Chang Chih-tung's violent reaction against such activities less than a month before. Yet its general manager and chief editor, at least at first, was Wang Ching-fang, who would prove to be a mortal enemy of the student radicals in the coming months.[36]

The students in Japan were becoming increasingly sensitive to real or imagined slights to Chinese pride and dignity by foreigners, especially by Japanese. In March, 1903, several Chinese students protested against alleged insults to China implied in the manner in which Chinese exhibits were treated at the Osaka Exhibition.[37] In late March and early April, a rumor that Governor Wang Chih-ch'un of Kwangsi wanted to use French troops from Tongking to quell popular unrest in that province prompted a protest from the Tokyo students to Peking and demonstrations in Shanghai as well.[38] These minor incidents served as preludes to the more extensive movement which began in late April.

During April, 1903, it became known that the Russians refused to honor their commitment to pull their troops out of Manchuria, large parts of which they had occupied since the Boxer Rebellion. This inflamed the already sensitive nationalistic nerve ends of the Chinese students in Japan, as well as those of students and many others back in China, especially in Shanghai, where a mass protest meeting was held on April 29. Niu Yung-chien, a firebrand from Kiangsu, in cooperation with the Ch'ing-nien hui, had no difficulty in gathering several hundred irate Chinese students for a mass meeting in Tokyo on April 29.[39] Several resolutions were drafted, and a Volunteer Corps (I-yung tui) to fight the Russians was formed. On April 30, meetings of provincial groups were held, and many telegrams were sent back to China. On May 2, at another mass meeting, the name of the students' military organization was changed from I-yung tui to Hsüeh-sheng chün (Students' Army), with an openly anti-Russian charter. On May 3, the force was divided into three sections, or battalions; a Hupeh military student was elected to lead each of them, and the overall commander was Lan T'ien-wei, also a Hupeh student.[40]

By May 7, the Japanese government was concerned over the blatantly anti-Russian and formal military character of the Students' Army and, not wishing to get involved in any diplomatic problems with Russia because of it, brought pressure to bear upon the student organization to change its public stance.[41] On May 11, the name of the organization was changed to Educational Association for a Militant Citizenry (Chün kuo-min chiao-yü hui), and its regulations were altered so as to eliminate specific reference to Russia, advocating only general military preparedness. Already on May 10, during the organization of the new society, two emissaries had been delegated to offer the services of the student soldiers to Yüan Shih-k'ai; on May 14, Niu Yung-chien and T'ang Erh-ho left on this quixotic mission. On May 17, the association sent a memorial to Tsai-chen, who had personally investigated the disturbance at the embassy in the late summer of 1902 and who was now in Japan to attend the Osaka Exhibition. Tsai-chen replied on May 18, assuring the students that the government was indeed determined to resist the Russian demands, and that the students should not neglect their studies for the sake of all these protests and petitions.

Students back in China also expressed their apprehension over the Manchurian situation in mid-May. In addition to the vociferous Shanghai students, two classes of the normal school of Peking University requested the chief educational officer, Chang Po-hsi, to memorialize on their behalf, urging the government to stand firm against Russia. Students at several schools in Wuchang received an emotional plea from "the students of Peking University" asking them to organize and make their concern known to the government; in response, students at the Wuchang Civil High School appealed to Tuan-fang, acting governor-general, lifting several points verbatim from the telegram of the Peking University group.[42]

The essence of all of these appeals was simply to ask the government to refuse the Russian demands and to fight if necessary; in that case, it could count on the students to die for their country. Several of the appeals advised turning to Britain and Japan to counterbalance Russia. Actually, this was precisely what the Peking government was trying to do. No important sector in the government, and no major official, seriously advocated accepting the harsh Russian terms at this time. Some success had been had in mustering foreign pressure against Russia in a comparable imbroglio in 1902, and the government was determined to get sufficient backing from other powers to thwart the Russian design for a permanent hold on Manchuria this time, even if it had to open some more treaty ports there as inducement for the other powers.[43]

Automatically suspicious of any sort of student activism, especially when it involved arms and military training, government officials were even more wary of the Educational Association for a Militant Citizenry because it persisted in agitation even when the government was already trying to do more or less what it advocated. The government's suspicions were well founded, for in the reorganization of the Students' Army into the Educational Association on May 11, a hard-core radical leadership around Niu Yung-chien informally pledged itself to work for the overthrow of the Manchus under the cover of the association's emphasis upon patriotic military preparedness. One of those let in on the secret deliberations, however, was Wang Ching-fang, an editor of the Hupeh student journal. Wang reported the revolutionary purpose of the leadership group to the Chinese minister, Ts'ai Chün, who relayed the information to the Peking government and other officials back in China. Meanwhile, Wang remained a member of the organization to report on its activities.[44]

Its suspicions confirmed, the government now panicked and overreacted, undoubtedly exaggerating the real danger of subversion. By late May, the worried Tuan-fang warned other Yangtze officials that the Tokyo group was going to send agents to promote rebellion in the Yangtze Valley, as T'ang Ts'ai-ch'ang's band had done in 1900. An edict from the last days of May ordered coastal officials to investigate closely students returning from Japan, for some of them were planning revolution; again, the direct parallel with the Tzu-li hui of 1900 was made. Permission was even granted for the summary execution, on the spot, of any obvious agitators, though officials were warned not to make arbitrary arrests.[45]

When the tide of revolutionary agents did not materialize on the coast, little more was said of these drastic measures. But the publicity given to this evidence of the Chinese government's mistrust of the Tokyo students (the documents were published in the Shanghai *Su-pao*) gave the government a black eye. Some students became radical because of their disappointment with the government's reaction.[46] Some even believed for a time the false rumor that the two emissaries who had gone to see Yüan Shih-k'ai had been executed.

Now it was the radicals' turn to overplay their hand. The Educational Association for a Militant Citizenry maintained a large membership through June, though it seems to have been fairly inactive. Events picked up with the return of the two frustrated emissaries, Niu Yung-chien and T'ang Erh-ho, about the first of July. They called for a meeting for July 4 or 5, at which the radical group of ten or more produced a written "statement of opinion," openly antidynastic, which tried to enlist the commitment of the whole group to revolution.[47] At this, Wang Ching-fang, the government agent, protested vehemently; he quit the society, taking several other members with him.[48] He also turned over to the authorities a copy of the radicals' position paper and the association's membership list. Wang was generously rewarded for his services; an edict of August 25, 1903, praised his loyalty and awarded him the status of *chü-jen*.[49]

It was at this point that the hard-core revolutionary element of the Educational Association went underground. Feng Tzu-yu says that the group existed until it merged with the T'ung-meng hui in 1905, all the while its revolutionary aims unknown to the government.[50] Yet Feng admits that there were no more meetings, and each member was to act on his own. The most famous supposed member of this "secret" revolutionary group, Huang Hsing, had in fact left Japan to return to China on June 4, a full month before the last open meeting in July.[51] With its statement of purpose and its membership list safe in the files of the Chinese and Japanese governments, it seems rather that the radicals of the Educational Association for a Militant Citizenry ceased altogether to function as any kind of a cohesive group.

Thus the nationalistic movement among the Chinese students in Japan in the spring of 1903, like that among their counterparts in Shanghai, resulted in many of them becoming unhappy with their government; some individuals were alienated to the point of committing themselves to revolutionary activities. But there was not a revolutionary organization worthy of the name which emerged from all the emotional turmoil in Japan, and even the degree of alienation of the students should not be overly emphasized. In the latter part of July, after the open split in the Educational Association, the supervisor of students, Wang Ta-hsieh, sent a rather optimistic assessment of student activity to Tuan-fang back in Wuchang, who in turn forwarded the report to Chang Chih-tung in Peking. Wang noted that the Hupeh military student Lan T'ien-wei, who had once been commander of the Students' Army in early May, had by now severed all ties with the radicals. Indeed, Chang was assured that "news of the Hupeh students in Japan is quite good; it should allay all your worries."[52]

Chang, who had just suffered a defeat for his educational program by being demoted to assistant examiner in the Peking special examination and by having his designated winners thrown out as a result of growing court concern over subversion, must have been relieved to hear this. Other good news was contained in Wang Ta-hsieh's report, as relayed to him by Tuan-fang. Some members of the Shanghai *Su-pao* group, whose seditious journalism had so aroused the ire of the court earlier in July, had tried to communicate with Lan T'ien-wei, but Lan had rebuffed them.[53] Indeed, I think it is significant that there were no great repercussions of the *Su-pao* case at this time among the students in Japan; no wave of protests occurred over the arrest of the revolutionary pamphleteers Tsou Jung and Chang Ping-lin. For the time being events in Shanghai far overshadowed those in Tokyo, where matters were considered by Chang Chih-tung and other managers of the educational system to be well in hand by the late summer of 1903.

"Revolution" in Hupeh, 1902–7

After the failure of T'ang Ts'ai-ch'ang's Tzu-li hui uprising in 1900, there was no significant revolutionary activity in Hupeh until Wu Lu-chen and several other graduates of Japanese schools returned to the province in late 1902 and early 1903. From then until the end of 1904, there was much radical talk among student groups in Hupeh, and even some clumsy attempts at organization, but it ended with the students scattered all over the world and some of the leaders working for the government. Moreover, since the movement did not effectively ally itself with the secret societies, Chang Chih-tung and other officials did not even pay it the compliment of taking it seriously.

Wu Lu-chen's relationship with Chang Chih-tung is intriguing. Wu had been involved in the first stages of planning for T'ang's 1900 revolt, and he had made the acquaintance of Sun Yat-sen in 1901; late in that year he also made some often quoted radical remarks at the founding of the Chinese Students' Union in Tokyo.[54] Wu was among the first group of graduates from the Japanese Army Officers' School in 1902, and he returned to Hupeh in the fall of 1902. According to the account of Chu Ho-chung, who was then a student in Wuchang, Chang Chih-tung knew about Wu's involvement in the events of 1900 and had not expected him to return to China. Therefore Chang was quite surprised when Wu presented himself with the other graduates at an audience, and he detained him for three days in a school building while deciding what to do with him. Finally, Chang, with Liang Ting-fen present, gave Wu a long interview. Wu impressed them so much with his eloquence and forcefulness that Chang placed Wu in charge of educational affairs in one of his military schools and gave him other important responsibilities as well.[55]

In a more recent article, Chu Yen-chia has suggested that Chang actually feared Wu's potential effectiveness in revolutionary activities and gave him these positions and duties to provide an outlet for his talents and thus to restrain his political activities. Chu goes on to speculate that this gave Wu a position of some advantage over Chang, for had he now turned public rebel, Chang would have been greatly embarrassed.[56] The relationship between Chang and Wu does indeed seem "subtle," as Chu puts it, but the advantage hardly seems all on Wu's side. With Chang's initial sponsorship, Wu could look forward to a successful military career, and he might be increasingly reluctant to jeopardize it by deep involvement in revolutionary politics.[57] Wu actually seems to have acquired and retained a great deal of respect, even affection, for Chang Chih-tung. In December, 1910, at about the time he was promoted to full commander in the Peiyang Army, Wu joined in a memorial requesting that a special subscription be made to construct a shrine to the late Chang Chih-tung in Wuchang, in order to honor his memory and to express gratitude for his services to the province. Other former Hupeh students, some with republican convictions, joined Wu in this request for a shrine to Chang, even if they eventually turned against the dynasty he served.[58]

By the spring of 1903, several military and civil graduates had returned from Japan, and they often met for political discussion sessions at the home of Li Pu-ch'ing (Li Lien-fang), who rented a house in the Hua-yüan shan area of Wuchang. At the time of the furor over Russia's Manchurian policy in April and May, there was much excitement and activity in the Wuhan area, with at least one public rally and several petitions to the government. Now many younger local students joined the "Hua-yüan shan discussion group," which became increasingly radical. Wu Lu-chen was one of the leading figures in this group, which met occasionally at his house. These young intellectuals avidly read the latest publications in Chinese from Japan, including Liang Ch'i-ch'ao's *Hsin-min t'sung-pao* and various revolutionary pamphlets, and tried to distribute them to a wider audience. Some of them (Chu Ho-chung claims forty or fifty) may have joined the local New Army units as common soldiers, in order to spread their radical message from within its ranks. Here they were protected by the position and influence of Wu Lu-chen in the Hupeh military education system. Wu himself reportedly used radical literature for texts in the military schools when he could.[59]

The chief characteristic of all this activity was its superficial and ephemeral nature. No specific achievements are claimed by the two major writers on the period, both of whom were participants (Chu Ho-chung and Chang Nan-hsien). Moreover, I find no evidence that the phenomenon of "intellectuals enlisting as common soldiers" (*hsiu-ts'ai tang ping*), as Chu put it, lasted very long.[60] Late in 1903, Wu Lu-chen was transferred to a position in military administration in Peking, and Li Pu-ch'ing, who had provided the main meeting place for the radical discussion group, also left town.[61]

The events described above all occurred while Chang Chih-tung was in Peking, but during these months he corresponded frequently with Tuan-fang, the acting governor-general. Moreover, Liang Ting-fen, one of Chang's closest advisers, seems to have had full charge of provincial educational matters during this period. Thus Chang certainly knew and approved of the measures to which Tuan-fang and Liang Ting-fen resorted in the fall of 1903 to handle the problem of student restlessness. Among the students being sent abroad for study by the provincial government were many who had been active in the radical political discussion group; the government was well aware of their identities. Those among them deemed most radical were sent the farthest away, to Europe; the "moderates" were sent only to Japan. Moreover, the students seemed happy to go, despite the realization on the part of some that the government's purpose was to disperse them and get them out of the way; travel and adventure beckoned, and the revolution could wait.[62]

The remnants of the radical discussion group left behind in Wuchang continued to meet on and off during the winter of 1903–4, and by spring they had agreed on the need for a more structured organization, centered in the army. Some of them enlisted in the army, giving the group representation now among both soldiers and officers, and in both military and civil schools in Wuchang.[63] In May or June they chose the name Science Study Center (K'o-hsüeh pu-hsi so) for their group and soon thereafter chose officers.[64] In the late summer of 1904, Huang Hsing came up from Changsha to visit the Science Study Center. Huang had impressed many Wuchang people when he passed through there in June, 1903; at that time he purportedly made a radical speech at his alma mater, the Liang-hu Academy (now the Civil High School), and distributed some revolutionary literature.[65] Now he informed members of the Science Study Center of the plot of his

Hunan revolutionary organization, the Hua-hsing hui, to revolt against dynastic authority on the empress dowager's birthday in November, 1904, and he enlisted their cooperation. They would lead an uprising in Hupeh in coordination with his in Hunan.

The Science Study Center busied itself in preparations for the fall uprising. A house was rented to serve as a headquarters and arms depot. Each member tried to establish a liaison with a different school or army unit, to win support for the revolt and new participants. This campaign does not seem to have been overly successful, for only the engineering battalion of the Eighth Army Division and the Civil High School have been claimed as fruitful recruiting grounds (and I suspect that the engineering battalion was the army unit joined by most of those enlisting earlier in the year). At any rate, all was for nought. The Hunan plot leaked in October, and when the connection with the Science Study Center was discovered by the authorities, the Hupeh plotters also had to disband. Luckily, they received sufficient warning from their Hunan allies to clear out all the weapons and incriminating documents from the headquarters; the premises were bare when the police arrived.[66]

By this time Chang Chih-tung had long since returned to his post at Wuchang and had taken up the reins of power there as vigorously as ever. His response to this revolutionary conspiracy was absolutely minimal, and in striking contrast to the witch hunt prompted by T'ang Ts'ai-ch'ang's plot of 1900. The names of many participants were known, but only two were put on a public wanted list: Ou-yang Jui-hua, who signed the rental agreement for the headquarters house, and Sung Chiao-jen, the chief liaison man with the Hunan group, whose name was known there.[67] Even these were not arrested, and no other action was taken. Chang Nan-hsien claims that this was because Liang Ting-fen was rather embarrassed at the number of students and faculty in the provincial educational system who were participants, and therefore he persuaded Chang Chih-tung not to press the investigation. This is simply not credible, especially when Chang's sensitivity to subversive activities and the comparison with 1900 are kept in mind. The only reason that Chang would have foregone a more drastic reaction was his estimation that the Science Study Center was really not much of a threat to the established order of the province. With his natural predilection to be lenient to students and intellectuals, he must have felt that he could afford to overlook revolutionary agitation as long as it remained impotent.

Why would Chang and the authorities judge the 1904 plot to be fairly harmless? Comparison with the Tzu-li hui of 1900 is most instructive. In Chang's eyes, and in those of the entire higher provincial elite, the great crime of T'ang Ts'ai-ch'ang and his friends in 1900 had been their alliance with the secret societies. The Science Study Center had no such alliance; in fact, it had no contacts at all with the societies. Thus it appeared frivolous. In Hunan, Huang Hsing had tried to achieve effective coordination with the Hunan Ko-lao hui leader Ma Fu-i, but had failed to do so. Huang and his group of student revolutionaries were no more vigorously hunted down than were those in Hupeh. Indeed, they were protected and assisted to escape by several prominent Changsha gentry of a liberal bent.[68] The main threat to the old order was still the secret societies; the radical intellectuals carried little weight unless they successfully stirred up the societies.

The association of student revolutionaries with the alarming P'ing-Liu-Li uprising of December, 1906, would once again put their activities beyond the pale and would bring about a rigorous suppression by Chang Chih-tung and other officials in central China, indeed one comparable to that of 1900. Interestingly, radical intellectuals were not the prime movers in this brief but powerful mass rebellion which erupted in the adjoining counties of P'ing-hsiang in western Kiangsi and Liu-yang and Li-ling in eastern Hunan.[69] Rather, the popular forces involved developed spontaneously out of the depressed and unstable socioeconomic conditions in the border area. Several Hunanese student revolutionaries, reacting against the tightening of control over their activities by the provincial gentry and educational authorities during 1906, attempted to link up with the secret societies in rebellion, and did so to some extent, providing one of the manifestos issued during the revolt. However, the students were at best catalysts, releasing forces already present, and were even less able to control the secret societies than T'ang Ts'ai-ch'ang had been in 1900.

Nevertheless, after the rapid and brutal crushing of the P'ing-Liu-Li revolt by government troops sent from several provinces, the student activists of central China, even those not in any way connected with the uprising, paid dearly for the association of some of their number with the secret society rebellion. Unlike 1904, but as in 1900, a wave of arrests and executions swept Changsha in the first weeks of 1907, and the student movement was practically destroyed. In Hupeh, Chang Chih-tung was also moved to drastic action in early 1907. Not only had Chang sent some of his best troops, including three artillery batteries, to crush the rebels in Hunan, but afterwards he demolished what remained of activist student organization in Wuchang, the Jih-chih hui (Society for Daily Improvement), and condoned an overall suppression of all suspected of radical sympathies.[70]

The Jih-chih hui, a direct descendent of the disbanded Science Study Center of 1904, had been under official surveillance for some time during 1906, without any action being taken against its members.[71] But as soon as the spectre of student-secret society collaboration again appeared at the end of 1906, Chang Chih-tung wasted no time in smashing it. Nine of the Jih-chih hui leaders were arrested and given long jail terms, and many secret society suspects perished in an atmosphere of arrests and executions described by Consul General Fraser as "a regular reign of terror."[72] Once again, Chang's sense of discrimination toward student activism, depending on the seeming presence or absence of secret society links, was clearly manifested. His reaction was consistent with that of 1900, although perhaps somewhat more edgy, since in this case there was no evidence of direct student-secret society contacts in Wuchang as there was in Hunan.

Chang and the Tokyo Student Strike of December, 1905

As the main features of the educational reform program he had long advocated were achieved in 1905, Chang also began to reach the limits of his tolerance of student dissent. In April, 1905, Chang directed the Hupeh Office of Education to be more thorough in its background investigation of students before sending them abroad; better to weed out troublemakers in advance and avoid later regret over their behavior.[73] In May, Chang had an unfortunate confrontation with a group of Governor Tuan-fang's Hunan students enroute to Japan on government stipends. As they passed through Wuchang, Chang, as was his practice, planned to receive them in audience, give them copies of his *Ch'üan-hsüeh p'ien,* and exhort them to study hard. But the students refused to kneel before him, as was customary. After eleven days of an embarrassing standoff, during which Tuan-fang lost much face, threats were issued on all sides, and the students grew increasingly resentful of Chang's stuffiness; a compromise bowing ceremony was agreed upon, and the students went on their way.[74]

By late 1905, the major steps of immediately ending the old examinations and beginning deliberation of a constitutional political system had been taken by the court. The government, moreover, had enjoyed some success in resisting further inroads on China's sovereignty by the imperialist powers; for example, it had just recovered construction rights to the Canton-Hankow railway.[75] Keenly aware of these achievements, Chang was inclined to have little patience with further outbreaks of student complaints and disruptions, at home or abroad.

Meanwhile, in Japan, the Chinese student community was becoming even more radical, and more students than ever before were in favor of doing away with the Manchu government. The T'ung-meng hui was formed around Sun Yat-sen in August, 1905; for the first time, large numbers of students were linked in a common organization, and in a common program of sorts. Three hundred of the students joined the T'ung-meng hui soon after its establishment, and many more by the end of the year; through 1906, almost nine hundred students in Japan would enroll in the T'ung-meng hui. This was a significant percentage of the total number of students there, which probably reached eight thousand in 1905 and was somewhat less in 1906.[76] The revolutionary atmosphere in Tokyo was further enlivened by Japan's exciting victory over Russia in 1904–5 and by the Russian Revolution of 1905.

Japan's victory over Russia, however, also set off a new trend of suspicion and fear of Japan among the Chinese students, including those who joined the T'ung-meng hui. The students had long viewed Japan, to some extent at least, as just another imperialist power, and had few illusions that Japan entered into war with Russia in 1904 in order to defend Chinese national interests. Nevertheless, the Chinese students in Tokyo were almost unanimous in their support of Japan against Russia, largely on the basis of race and their sensitivity to the racist elements of the attitudes toward China held by the Western nations, represented by Russia.[77] After the war, however, as it became apparent that Japan had replaced Russia as the chief threat to Chinese sovereignty in southern Manchuria, and especially after Japan openly tightened her control over Korea, the factor of common racial identity was overpowered by a resurgent fear of Japanese aggressive designs on Chinese territory and rights.

The sensitivity to Japanese intentions toward China shared by many of the Chinese students in Japan surfaced in their reaction to an attempt by the Japanese government in late 1905 to impose a new set of regulations on the schools they attended in Japan. The rules previously devised by Chang Chih-tung, in effect since late 1903, already attempted to regulate the content of the programs of study, and especially the extracurricular activities of these students, to an ambitious degree. The Japanese government was less concerned with censoring the politics of the students. Rather, it was interested in putting the schools at which the Chinese students enrolled under the close supervision of the Japanese Ministry of Education and in requiring these institutions to meet certain minimum standards of facilities and curriculum. It was also eager to weed out students who performed poorly academically or otherwise proved troublesome (this latter goal matched the objectives of the Chinese legation in Tokyo, of course).

There was actually good reason for the Japanese Ministry of Education to be concerned about these matters. To serve the demand from the tide of Chinese students who arrived between 1903 and 1905, a number of schools had been established to offer intensive courses in the Japanese language and other subjects; many student rooming houses catering especially to Chinese had sprung up, as well. Some of these schools had deplorably low academic standards, and some of the rooming houses apparently charged exorbitant rent for unsafe and vice-ridden lodgings. Moreover, among the thousands of Chinese students present there were not a few who did little studying and moved constantly from school to school, where they would invariably be accepted by tuition-conscious administrators.

On November 2, 1905, the Japanese government, after consultation with the Chinese Minister Yang Shu, issued a set of fifteen regulations to correct some of these abuses.[78] These regulations provided that, in order to qualify for Ministry of Education certification, the schools had to submit to inspection of their facilities and equipment, qualifications of teachers, and content of examinations. Moreover, they had to report admissions, withdrawals, and graduations to the Ministry of Education and to the Chinese government sponsoring office, as well. If any student changed programs of study or withdrew from one school, he would have to present an affidavit from the Chinese legation registering its acknowledgment before another school could accept him; a student expelled for bad behavior could not reenroll in any certified school. Finally, the schools were charged with responsibility for supervision of the living conditions of their students outside the classroom.

The timing and manner of promulgation of the rules, as well as their content, caused a hostile reaction among many Chinese students. The rules were first put forth in association with regulations for Korean students, and since Korea had recently become a protectorate of Japan, such an association seemed threatening to the Chinese students. Moreover, there was resistance to two particular articles, those regulating lodging places and providing for no reenrollment of students expelled for bad behavior. Already during November, some students wrote a petition to make some changes; Minister Yang Shu, not unsympathetic, received it and passed it along to the Japanese Foreign Ministry, which promised to discuss it with the Ministry of Education. But meanwhile, a group of activist students began to agitate among their fellows, calling the regulations an intolerable infringement of their rights and an insult to their patriotism; they organized a United Association of Students in Japan (Liu-Jih hsüeh-sheng lien-ho hui). By early December, 1905, the response was sufficient for them to confront the Ministry of Education with a demand to rescind all the new regulations, on threat of a total student strike and an exodus back to China.[79] For these students, many of whom were T'ung-meng hui members, the threat from Japan overrode their anti-Manchuism for the moment.

This seeming overreaction on the part of the students prompted scathing criticism in the unsympathetic Japanese press, which only served to inflame the sense of outrage they felt and spread it to others.[80] On December 8, the Hunanese revolutionary Ch'en T'ien-hua drowned himself in the sea as a protest against the press's description of the students as dissolute and worthless.[81] By mid-December, emotional enthusiasm, coupled with physical force employed to block school entrances and to coerce those reluctant to join the movement, had resulted in almost total effectiveness for the strike. Hundreds of students were even leaving Japan, crowding onto boats for Shanghai. At its peak, this mass movement was quite impressive. Announcements of compromise by the Chinese minister and the Japanese government were ignored, as was an appeal by the faculty of Waseda University which pointed out the students' misunderstanding of the intent and content of the regulations. All clarifications and explanations were of no avail.

Chang Chih-tung disapproved of the students' activities when he first heard of the dispute in early December. On December 8, he sent a message through the Hupeh superintendent of students, Li Pao-sun, warning the students against actions that could harm Sino-Japanese relations or endanger the program of study abroad, while offering to help settle their grievances if they would tell him what they were. Soon after this, Chang received a request from Superintendent Li for permission to provide all of the Hupeh students (about 1,200, by the figures involved) with money for passage back to China, indicating that Li himself was affected by their mood of patriotic indignation. While Chang was still reeling from his shock at this request, there came news from Li that he had already permitted the students to return to China and had advanced some of them two or three months' stipends to make the trip; now he asked Chang to wire him more money so he could finance the rest. Chang was absolutely flabbergasted. On December 21, he wired his rage to Superintendent Li, berating him for permitting himself to be intimidated by the students. He gave Li an ultimatum: those students who had already left Japan could never return, and the others had to give back immediately the money Li had advanced and behave themselves, on pain of forever losing their future career chances. Spluttering, Chang ordered Li to report at once.[82]

The adamant opposition and threats of Chang and other

officials may have indirectly affected the outcome of the student strike, but it was ultimately broken by a countermovement from among the students themselves. On December 24, a Society of Comrades in Support of Study Abroad (Wei-ch'ih liu-hsüeh chieh t'ung-chih hui) was established to work for a return to classes. For the next two weeks, during which classes were normally recessed for the winter vacation anyway, the two organizations fought verbally, and occasionally physically. Those advocating calling off the strike won, and virtually all those students remaining in Japan registered again for classes when they resumed on January 13.[83] Several hundred, perhaps as many as a thousand students, had actually returned to China at the height of the strike. Of these, some now went back to Japan, while others remained in Shanghai.[84] Minister Yang Shu sent a list of nineteen strike leaders back to Peking, requesting that their names be put on a blacklist for employment by the central government or local governments, and that they not even be permitted residence in China.[85] Chang Chih-tung himself does not seem to have followed through on his most dire threats against those who left Japan, despite all his blustering. He sent one Shuang Shou to Tokyo as his personal representative in late December to assist Superintendent Li, and he sent other officials to Shanghai to reason with those students who had returned in order to persuade them to go back to their studies in Japan.[86]

Chang Chih-tung and other officials were not very perceptive in their interpretation of the Tokyo student strike, at least not publicly. Chang was plainly relieved that most of the students returned to class, and he claimed that this represented a victory over the revolutionaries. Minister Yang Shu did likewise.[87] However, the split among the students over the strike issue was not on revolutionary-conservative lines; Yang Shu, at least, must have been aware of this. Indeed, members of the T'ung-meng hui were on both sides of the issue. Sung Chiao-jen and Hu Ying, representing those students most sensitive to Japanese intentions toward China, were leaders of the pro-strike forces; Wang Ching-wei and Hu Han-min, both very close to Sun Yat-sen and representing an overriding anti-Manchu emphasis, were active participants in the organization to counter the strike.[88]

Thus the initial success and eventual failure of the strike is not a commentary on the vitality of the student revolutionaries, but on the ambiguity of their short range target—Japan and the other imperialist powers, or the Manchu government. Ironically, Chang Chih-tung himself, in taking the lead to engineer an important victory for Chinese nationalism in the recovery of the rights to the Canton-Hankow railroad line in 1905, had lined up on the same side of the anti-imperialist issue as the Tokyo student strike leaders. As I will argue below, more such effective government action in defense of Chinese sovereignty might begin to dilute those revolutionary commitments which were ultimately based mainly on anti-imperialism.

Though the Chinese government misread the student strike, it was not unaffected by it. As the largest of the disruptions among the students in Japan, which embarrassed the Ch'ing government greatly, this was probably the last straw in prompting a considerable tightening of the rules for study abroad in 1906 and after. There would be no mass movement among the Chinese students in Japan to rival this one before 1911.[89]

Revolution or Cooptation?

What conclusions can be drawn from this survey of the points at which diverse currents among the post-1900 generation of students impinged upon the perceptions and policies of Chang Chih-tung? As Chang himself seemed to perceive with varying degrees of acuity, Chinese students and intellectuals were torn in several different directions in the decade after 1900. They tended to be emotionally nationalistic, and many of them became increasingly alienated from the Manchu government in their desperate search for a means to resist effectively imperialist encroachment. On the other hand, their position as members of the traditional political and social elite class, as well as fears of heightening the danger of national political dismemberment by undermining the existing government, made their alienation equivocal and their political stance inconstant.[90]

In his educational policies for a domestic school system and for study abroad as well, Chang Chih-tung showed full appreciation for the tendency of youthful radicals to gravitate back into the established political order, if that order made a place for them and if it seemed to be responding to the need for vigorous action to ensure China's survival. Many of the students returning from Japan or graduating from the new schools at home, with the dual advantages of upper-class background and prestigious credentials, found it easy to slip into interesting and well-paid positions after the old examinations were abolished in 1905. Moreover, this seemed to be the main ambition of the majority. Even those of the minority who considered themselves revolutionaries, and talked of subverting the old order by working from within, may have actually contributed more to its staying power by serving it. It was much easier to be a flaming radical among fellow students in the liberated atmosphere of Tokyo or Shanghai (or even the provincial capital) than it was back home, with the pressures of family and career dampening the old revolutionary ardor.

Among the students abroad, many examples can be listed of young men who returned from Japan to government positions of considerable responsibility from 1903 on; and Chang Chih-tung had started using his own sponsored graduates even before this, of course.[91] The total number of students abroad remained a function of government policy and requirements, with a position in the bureaucracy as inducement. In 1906, partly as a reaction to student restlessness, most recently the strike of December, 1905, higher academic qualifications were required for admission to approved Japanese schools, and the Chinese Ministry of Education withdrew its approval of degrees granted by intensive study institutions. In 1908, the performance levels to qualify for government positions after graduation in Japan were raised once more, this time as a result of an actual surplus of those returning to compete for available jobs. In 1909, there were only about four thousand students in Japan, half of the peak reached in 1905, and they had a higher academic level than the 1905 group.[92] Students continued to return from Japan for jobs at home through 1911, and with ever better qualifications. Indeed, they outnumbered the good job opportunities by that time, and the role of some of them in the 1911 Revolution might be that of frustrated job hunters rather than that of dedicated revolutionaries.

As in radical student movements in other times and other places, flirtation with revolutionary ideas sometimes resulted partially from personal problems of alienation from family or culture, or of general disorientation in a rapidly changing world. In his educational policies and in his specific treatment of Hupeh students at home and abroad, Chang Chih-tung showed some understanding of these factors. So too did Yang Shu, who as minister to Japan and concurrently supervisor of Chinese students from 1903 was a key figure between the often mutually suspicious Chinese government in Peking and the Chinese student community in Tokyo. Unlike his predecessor Ts'ai Chün, who showed hostility and mistrust toward the students in the legation sit-in of 1902 and the anti-Russian movement of 1903, Yang Shu was very sensitive to the concerns and the problems of the students.

A 1904 report on the students by Yang showed great perception and sympathetic understanding, put to the service of control and management; it was a model of manipulative educational administration. Yang tried to convince the court that the students were under great personal and academic stress and acutely aware of their freedom from immediate government sanctions, so that in their disruptive activities over public issues they were actually playing out private grievances. Yang described his methods of dealing with the students, which emphasized communication. He told the students that the door to his office was always open, and meant it; he kept close contact with the Student Union and often visited the students at the schools they were attending to receive in person any complaints they had. By taking the students' part and working vigorously on their behalf when they had a valid grievance against their schools or the Japanese authorities, he was able to keep the majority of them satisfied.[93]

Yang's report obviously ignores the fact that the students had well-founded fears concerning the seeming aggressiveness of foreign imperialism and the ineptness of the Manchu government, and that some of them would remain revolutionaries even if all their personal problems were solved. Indeed, it would be grossly incorrect to describe the revolutionary students in Japan and in China solely as opportunistic careerists whose occasional forays into emotional mob actions or adventurous conspiracy stemmed from private psychological problems of cultural and self-identity in a disturbing world. One cannot ignore what they said troubled them, mainly the imminent demise of China—as culture, race, or nation. The nationalism which they felt was a very real and tangible phenomenon, chiefly taking the form of an intense anti-imperialism that very easily shifted to anti-Manchu sentiment. At this point nationalism fed the fires of revolution and impelled many students to join the T'ung-meng hui in 1905 and after. Yet, Liang Ch'i-ch'ao was eloquently warning after 1905 that anti-imperialism in the form of overthrowing the dynasty was misguided, and would only cause further imperialist aggression to quell the resulting chaos. The haunting fear that this might after all be true nagged at even the most dedicated revolutionaries, and it made their commitment to overthrow the political order potentially less than total.

In particular, if the Ch'ing government could somehow reverse its consistent record of humiliation at the hands of foreign powers and begin to defend and enhance China's eroded sovereignty, many "revolutionaries" were open to cooperation with it. They might even defect back into its ranks. The prospects for effective government action to defend China's sovereignty looked poor in 1900, but the government's record between 1900 and 1911 was actually quite respectable. And every success in defense or recovery of China's rights ate away at the foundations of the revolutionary movement. Chang Chih-tung had an important role in one of the most important victories of the "rights recovery" movement, the regaining of the rights to the Canton-Hankow railway line in 1904–5. I will examine this movement in the next chapter in relation to the participation of provincial gentry interest groups, but it was also important in fulfilling some of the students' demands for concrete results in resisting imperialism.

As Chang Chih-tung seemed to sense, a revolutionary movement built around student enthusiasm and based in Japan was not a mortal threat to the government, unless it could effectively tap into the ever-present reservoir of mass energy through the secret societies. When it seemed to be in danger of doing so, as in 1900 in Wuhan and in late 1906 on the Hunan-Kiangsi border, Chang was willing to use extreme measures to suppress it. But this was seldom necessary.

Moreover, individual members of the student-intellectual group dedicated to revolution showed a remarkable propensity to drift back into the service of the government. Wu Lu-chen was a full commander in the Peiyang Army by 1911; Ts'ai Yüan-p'ei, an original Shanghai radical leader in the early 1900's, was working in a government translation bureau and seeking a stipend to go abroad by 1906; Ts'ai O, Hunanese veteran of the Tzu-li hui uprising of 1900, returned to China after graduation in 1904 and spent most of the time until 1911 as an energetic reforming military administrator in Kwangsi province; Liu Shih-p'ei, an ardent revolutionary nationalist who dabbled in socialism and anarchism and worked for a time on the T'ung-meng hui's *Min-pao,* joined the secretariat of Tuan-fang in 1909 and served him faithfully until 1911; Ch'ien Hsüan-t'ung, younger brother of longtime Hupeh superintendent of students Ch'ien Hsün, joined the T'ung-meng hui when he went to Japan in 1906, but ended as a provincial educational official in Chekiang before 1911.[94]

The above examples are only crudely indicative, but they tend to corroborate Chang Chih-tung's own belief that, given important things to do and some status, and (all-important) a decent amount of government success in reform and resisting imperialism, China's modern student class and young intellectuals, even the revolutionary vanguard in Japan, were not irrevocably alienated from the dynasty.[95]

Chapter 8

The Provincial Elite and the Recovery of the Canton-Hankow Railway Rights, 1904–5

In many ways, Chang Chih-tung seemed to find it easier to manage the students than to handle the increasingly assertive gentry class after 1900. Despite his longstanding reluctance to share the power of the central government with the gentry elite as a class, Chang came to realize that this was necessary. He himself had predicated the success of the new national educational system upon the cooperation and participation of the gentry, and after the abolition of the exams in 1905 they responded, taking a leading role in the new provincial school systems. Moreover, as already described, in 1905 Chang finally reconciled himself to allocating a portion of formal political power to this class in some form of constitutional system.

In the campaign to recover China's rights to the Canton-Hankow railway line in 1904–5, Chang encouraged, and put to effective political use, expressions of nationalistic protest and the organizing abilities of the provincial gentry class, especially that of Hunan. However, he discovered that in so doing he had acquired a fractious ally. The gentry class was itself in a transitional, increasingly differentiated state, and it proved impossible for Chang to keep it fully under control after the initial success of the rights recovery campaign. Moreover, in casting about for allies on the railway issue in 1904–5, Chang found himself cooperating not only with the provincial gentry, but with the forces of that new "public opinion" which we saw emerging in 1900, including the new students, journalists, and some merchants, especially in Shanghai. These proved even less amenable to Chang's leadership over the course of the rights recovery campaign. Indeed, Chang found that the various elements whose participation in the railroad campaign he had originally encouraged and welcomed eventually operated to limit and obstruct his own plans for China's national railroad development under central direction.

The Strategic Interest: Chang Chih-tung's Initiative

Chang Chih-tung, mindful of China's need for secure internal communications and transport lines in the face of foreign pressures, had long been in favor of constructing a great interior trunk railway line. As early as 1889 he recommended building the Peking-Hankow line, which eventually would extend all the way to Canton.

In the flurry of grabbing for economic concessions in 1898, the Peking-Hankow line was allocated to Belgian financial interests.[1] At the same time, the Chinese government wanted to avoid giving the Belgians a position of advantage along the entire line, and likewise to deny the British a further consolidation of power in their own "sphere of influence," the Yangtze Valley and south China. Therefore, the loan and concession rights to the Canton-Hankow line, amounting to four million pounds sterling, were granted to the American China Development Company, an agent of United States financial interests. During the spring and summer of 1900, the contract between the Chinese government and the American company was renegotiated on the basis of raising an additional forty million United States dollars in loan capitalization, more than twice the original amount.[2]

The desire of the Chinese to keep this concession in American hands, as a counterweight to the position of other nations in China, was shown clearly by article seventeen of the supplementary agreement of 1900. This stipulated that the rights attaching to the loan could not be alienated to any other nations or their citizens. In fact, however, quite soon after the conclusion of the supplementary agreement of 1900, and before it had been ratified by the Chinese government, rumors began circulating in international financial circles that certain Belgian interests, in particular King Leopold II himself, had bought up large amounts of shares in the American China Development Company. Already in 1901 the Chinese minister in Washington, Wu T'ing-fang, inquired as to the truth of these rumors, and by 1902 it had become apparent to Wu, to Director of Imperial Railways Sheng Hsüan-huai, and to all other interested observers, that the Belgians had indeed gained an important position within the company.[3]

Wu and Sheng, the chief representatives of the Chinese government in the matter, were assured by the United States government that control of the company was still firmly in the hands of United States citizens, and on this basis the two officials recommended that the supplementary agreement of 1900 be ratified by the court. Chang Chih-tung, stationed at Hankow, one terminus of the line, was also an interested party, and he was undoubtedly aware of the problem concerning the Belgian interest in the company. However, at this time he accepted in good faith the United States assurance as to continued American control. The last thing he wanted to do was to reopen the question of the assignment of the concession and loan, and thereby risk other nations wedging themselves in on the arrangement, with endless complications. Thus he also favored ratification of the 1900 contract, which was formally approved in July, 1902. At the same time, Chang urged Sheng Hsüan-huai to speed up the actual construction process, which had been lagging. Chang wanted a railroad as soon as possible, and preferably one involving only American interests in the concession and the loan.[4]

By early 1904, the situation had changed drastically. In the first place, no construction to speak of had taken place anywhere on the line. This failure alone would have been sufficient to justify reappraisal of the dependability of the American company. Even more disturbing, it was obvious that despite claims of the company's management to the contrary, Belgian interests now controlled the company. Extremely unhappy with this development, Sheng Hsüan-huai began to talk about cancellation of the 1900 contract due to violation of article seventeen's prohibition against alienation of the company's rights. Sheng worked through Minister Liang Ch'eng in Washington (Wu T'ing-fang had by now returned to become a high official in the Ministry of Foreign Affairs in Peking). Sheng also sent his own representative, John C. Ferguson, director of his Nan-yang school in Shanghai, to the United States to argue the Chinese case, and he even hired former U.S. Secretary of State John W. Foster as legal adviser on the matter. In the spring of 1904, Sheng was exerting considerable pressure upon both the company and the United States government to recover those shares owned by the Belgians, and thus to restore full American control. High U.S. State Department officials had to admit privately the strength of the Chinese case. Sheng, it is clear, did not really want to cancel the American contract; he merely wanted to force the reestablishment of full and permanent United States control, and he used the threat of cancellation as a bargaining device.[5]

Chang Chih-tung did not enter the arena of the Canton-Hankow railway dispute until late April and early May, 1904, well after Sheng's campaign had begun. But when he did take an interest in it, he dominated the scene until the successful redemption was consummated in September, 1905. After his 1903 tour of duty in Peking, Chang had returned to Wuchang in late March, 1904. Less than three weeks after his arrival, his old friend, the British consul general E. H. Fraser, had a long interview with Chang. Fraser warned Chang that the Belgians had their sights set on controlling the entire Canton-Hankow line through domination of the American company.[6]

Fraser hardly had to remind Chang that Belgian financial interests, already controlling the Peking-Hankow railway, were tied very closely to the French and Russian financial and political position in China. In the context of the Russo-Japanese War, which had just broken out in February, 1904, Chang suddenly perceived the threat of a grand coup by Belgian-French-Russian interests which would gravely impair China's sovereignty. If Russia defeated Japan and dominated Manchuria, and if Belgian interests gained control of the Canton-Hankow line, the result would be a unified line of communication and transport from Siberia to Canton, directly through the Chinese heartland and all under the control of the same interest group. Mortified at this apparition, Chang threw himself wholeheartedly into preventing its realization.

In late April, Chang began to urge Sheng Hsüan-huai to pursue more ambitious aims vis-à-vis the American China Development Company; he should try to renegotiate the whole contract on more favorable terms, or even terminate the agreement entirely. Unhappy with the evasive replies he received from Sheng, who shrank from such a drastic step, Chang then looked for allies to help him exert pressure on Sheng. On May 7, Chang telegraphed Governor Chao Erh-sun of Hunan, requesting him to help in this effort and to enlist the energies of all the officials and gentry of the province as well.[7]

Here, I think, Chang was making an appeal for influence to be exerted in a fairly traditional manner. His hope was that prestigious gentry, members of the "national elite," whose background of higher degrees, national office, and interprovincial personal connections gave them many channels of influence into the Peking bureaucracy, would exert pressures to prod Sheng Hsüan-huai in the direction Chang wished him to move. These men, rather like Chang himself in age and status, were natural allies for Chang to seek in this situation. However, other elements within the gentry class, representing a provincial corporate identity as well as personal influence, and components of national public opinion from outside the two provinces as well, also threw themselves into the fray. This was considerably more than Chang had bargained for.[8]

The Nationalistic Interest: Successful Redemption of the Railway Rights

The strategic interests which prompted Chang to take part in the Canton-Hankow railway issue dovetailed nicely with a growing and widespread sense of grievance against the whole range of Western economic privileges in China. Local friction with Western surveying and engineering crews on railway and mining projects, the continued irritation of missionary cases, increased sensitivity to the foreign drain on China's wealth, the activities of students and the energetic press, and rising resentment over the stringent United States anti-Chinese immigration laws, which would come to a head in the boycott of 1905, were all part of this picture.

Chang Chih-tung himself shared some of this heightened national resolve to ward off further imperialist exactions. After his return from Peking in the first part of 1904, there was a noticeably more distant, though quite correct, relationship between Chang and his old acquaintance Consul General Fraser, whom he knew better than any other foreign diplomat in his career and with whom he had been through so much during the dangerous summer of 1900 and the vicissitudes in his political position from then until 1903. In particular, no more appeals for British support, such as he had made during those earlier years, reoccurred.[9] In the summer of 1905, Fraser remarked that Chang was growing "more and more jealous of the rights and privileges of China," and was suspicious of all proposed foreign concessions. By 1906, Fraser noted that Chang was strictly enforcing restrictions on foreign economic activities and foreign investments in Chinese enterprises, matters on which he had been quite lax in previous years.[10] Before Chang left Wuchang for good in the late summer of 1907, Fraser had several times noted the gradual cooling of relations between them.[11] Chang saw him infrequently and, though always cordial, did not confide in him as before.

In the spring of 1904, Chang saw a chance to recover some ground which had been swept away in the race for concessions in the late 1890's. Thus his pressure on Sheng Hsüan-huai for cancellation of the American contract and his appeal for help to the gentry of Hunan. His appeal struck a responsive chord in Hunanese provincial opinion, which was in fact already mobilizing against the railway. In late April, 1904, Hunan Governor Chao Erh-sun, on behalf of the officials and leading gentry, had telegraphed both Sheng Hsüan-huai and Chang Chih-tung to protest the continuation of the American contract and a proposed Belgian branch line in their province.[12] After receiving Chang's May 7 telegram of encouragement, the Hunanese went into high gear; within days they exerted their influence at several key points in the Chinese government.

First, spokesmen for the Hunanese gentry assured both Governor Chao and Chang that they were prepared to build the railway themselves. Then they contacted their fellow Hunanese holding high posts in Peking and in the provinces. These included Ch'ü Hung-chi, head of the Ministry of Foreign Affairs; Chang Po-hsi, head of the Board of Revenue; and in the provinces, two governors-general and at least one governor. The Hunanese provincial leaders themselves were men of national stature, good examples of the "national elite." Wang Hsien-ch'ien, Lung Chan-lin, Chang Tsu-t'ung, T'an Chung-lin, and others could all command attention by their demands, and combined with their fellow provincials in office in Peking and elsewhere, their influence was formidable. During May and June, these men exerted increasing pressure on Sheng Hsüan-huai in Shanghai, both by telegram and by sending representatives to remonstrate with him in person; one of the latter was Wang Chih-ch'un, former governor of Kwangsi. Hunan Governor Chao also sent a personal representative to Shanghai to urge Sheng to stand firm against the American company.[13]

An interesting feature of this first mobilization of gentry power, in light of later developments, was that there was originally no onus attached to borrowing foreign money, if necessary, to build a railroad, as long as full control was in Chinese hands. The memorial which Hunan Governor Chao sent to the throne on May 10, 1904, requesting permission on behalf of the Hunan gentry to construct two small branch lines off the main trunk, specified that if the necessary capital could not be raised by subscription, the remainder could be obtained through foreign loans. It was the Ministry of Foreign Affairs in Peking which expressed reservations on such a loan in its reaction to the proposal, which it rejected as premature.[14] The goal of the Hunan gentry establishment, it is clear, was not so much practical—actually building a railroad—as it was political—preempting a rumored foreign interest in building such branch lines. And in principle, taking a foreign loan to do so seemed acceptable at the time.

At the same time that Hunanese officialdom and gentry were protesting the American company, Chang Chih-tung was following up on his initiative by peppering Sheng in Shanghai and the Ministry of Foreign Affairs in Peking with telegrams, several of them sent jointly with Hupeh Governor Tuan-fang and Hunan Governor Chao. Moreover, some representatives of the Hupeh gentry, led by the financial commissioner Li Shao-fen, now joined in the campaign with the Hunanese, although they did not cause as much stir as the latter. The Kwangtung gentry were also aroused, and like the Hunanese, they sent two representatives to Shanghai, the better to argue the case for cancellation of the contract.[15]

These expressions of gentry opinion were precisely what Chang had hoped for. However, by the early summer of 1904, the campaign against the Canton-Hankow railway concession had begun to spread beyond official and higher gentry circles to the entire urbanized, semi-modern sector of Chinese society. The campaign was picked up by other important sectors of public opinion, including key newspapers, journals, and students abroad in Japan and the United States.

One of the first to join the fight was Chang Chih-tung's old associate Wang K'ang-nien and his Shanghai newspaper, the *Chung-wai jih-pao*. Already on April 19, Wang's newspaper editorialized on China's right to cancel the United States contract, under terms of the supplementary agreement of 1900. In the following weeks and months, the *Chung-wai jih-pao* consistently advocated cancellation, and did so in emotional and nationalistic terms. *Tung-fang tsa-chih,* the Shanghai journal of news and opinion which rapidly attained the high stature it would maintain in Chinese journalism for a half century, was founded on March 11, 1904. It, too, took up the issue of recovery of rights to the Canton-Hankow railway and devoted much space to it in the summer of 1904. In the early fall, the Shanghai *Shih-pao,* a daily paper reflecting the views of the K'ang-Liang monarchist reform party, joined the campaign for full rights recovery on the railway, as did a major paper in Chang Chih-tung's own metropolitan area, the *Han-k'ou jih-pao*.[16]

It seems especially significant that the famous reform leader Liang Ch'i-ch'ao fully supported his old nemesis, Chang Chih-tung, in the latter's campaign to override Sheng Hsüan-huai and cancel the American contract. Throughout 1904, Liang frequently dealt with the Canton-Hankow railway issue in his *Hsin-min ts'ung-pao,* published in Japan but widely read in China as well. Liang enthusiastically favored cancellation, and went so far as to say that Chang Chih-tung, "by his achievements today, can atone for his sins of seven years ago" (referring to Chang's supposed betrayal of the radical reformers around K'ang Yu-wei, including Liang, in the failure of the "100 days" of reform in 1898).[17]

The railway issue naturally attracted the interest of many Chinese students abroad. During the summer and fall of 1904, Chinese law students in the United States drew up a series of legal briefs, based on United States contract law, supporting the right of China to cancel the contract in view of its violation, and sent these to Sheng Hsüan-huai and Chang Chih-tung. The students from the three provinces who were in Japan were unanimous in their urging that the contract be abrogated and the railway built with China's own resources. Yang Tu, a Hunanese student who contributed several articles on the railway issue to Liang's *Hsin-min ts'ung-pao* during 1904, was sent to Shanghai by the students of the three concerned provinces as their official representative at the end of the year, in order to badger Sheng Hsüan-huai in person.[18]

For his part, Sheng Hsüan-huai in Shanghai felt himself being squeezed from both ends in the early summer of 1904. In order to bring some pressure on the company, Sheng passed on to the United States consul general many of the protests pouring into his office during May and early June.[19] But on June 10, the United States government officially informed Sheng that it was unwavering in its support of the company's rights (despite its private doubts). Sheng calculated that the best he could do would be to renegotiate parts of the contract, or perhaps transfer it to another, more responsibly managed, American group. Thus for a time he tried to introduce to the protestors visiting his office a new scheme by which Chinese investors and provincial governments would send agents to America to buy up a majority of shares in the American China Development Company; the Chinese shareholders could then force a policy of renegotiating the contract on terms favorable to China. At the same time Sheng also sounded out A. W. Bash, the American financial adventurer who had brought together the original investors in the American company in the 1890's, about forming a new company to take over the railway concession.[20]

These maneuvers bought Sheng only a few weeks' respite. Some of the gentry representatives, and Chang Chih-tung himself, were intrigued with the idea of share recovery, but they were soon disillusioned with this approach by the lack of funds to repurchase the shares. Moreover, Sheng's contacts with the disreputable Bash became known, and both Chang and the provincial gentry interests became suspicious that Sheng was trying to deceive them by renegotiating the contract with the same company under a different name.[21]

Therefore, Chang reignited the campaign against the contract and against Sheng's approach to it in the fall of 1904. He appealed to the gentry of the three provinces to renew their pressures. The gentry responded magnificently, showering the Ministry of Foreign Affairs and Peking officialdom with telegrams. The Hunanese censor Huang Ch'ang-nien picked up the campaign and carried it directly to the throne, marshaling all the evidence and arguments in favor of cancellation of the contract. By now, the Shanghai press and students abroad were also strongly reinforcing the demand for cancellation. In response, the throne dropped the whole issue in the lap of Chang Chih-tung. On November 27, an edict gave Chang Chih-tung full authority over the negotiations to recover China's rights to the railway, although Sheng was still partially responsible as well.[22] Despite some misgivings in the central government about the danger of alienating the United States government, the agitation of public opinion and the determination of some officials, led by Chang, had convinced the court that more was to be gained by trying to engineer a foreign policy coup and reap the prestige of successfully recovering the rights to the railway.[23]

The edict of November 27, 1904, had tied Chang's own prestige to the outcome of this railway rights recovery campaign. Chang pushed ahead with his strategy of cancellation of the contract, dragging Sheng in his wake; Sheng himself was probably happy enough to be associated with Chang, if only to ward off the vituperation to which he had been subjected recently. On December 19 and 21, Chang and Sheng issued joint instructions to Minister Liang Ch'eng in Washington, and on December 22 Liang officially informed the United States government of the Chinese intention to cancel the contract.[24]

Ever since the summer of 1904, when it was requested to do so by some American shareholders in the company, the U.S. State Department had tried to facilitate recovery of control by American interests, so as to avoid violation of the supplementary contract. The Belgians dug in their heels until late in the year, when the apparent determination of the Chinese made them take seriously the possibility of the company losing the entire concession. In early January, 1905, J. P. Morgan was finally able to purchase twelve hundred of the shares held by Leopold II, and control of the company reverted to American hands. Immediately, on January 6, Minister Liang Ch'eng was informed that control was now definitely in American hands, and that the United States government intended to stand behind the company.[25]

The last-minute American rally to regain control of the company revived Sheng's hopes of avoiding complete cancellation. Sheng was still in a position of at least technically equal authority with Chang Chih-tung on the matter, though Chang was supposed to devise the recovery strategy. At any rate, Sheng took the initiative and responded to the American announcement of support for the company by pointing out that other matters remained to be cleared up. Sheng was trying to improve the Chinese position, but he was obviously leaving open the possibility of continuation of the contract if the Americans would meet further conditions.[26]

Sheng seems to have miscalculated the strength of the diverse alliance that had been formed by Chang Chih-tung, the provincial gentry groups, and other spokesmen of public opinion during the preceding months. Chang was dismayed at Sheng's reaction to the American stiffening of early January, when he considered himself to have charge of the negotiations, and the provincial gentry groups were absolutely enraged. The latter were by now fully determined to eradicate all traces of foreign influence over the railway line and were supported by public opinion in general. The Hunanese gentry, led by Wang Hsien-ch'ien and Lung Chan-lin, telegraphed Chang, attacking Sheng in the most scurrilous terms and threatening physical obstruction of any attempts by the American company to lay a foot of track in their province. They warned,

> If the U.S. government still insists on completely supporting the few thousand people involved in the company, how can the Chinese government use force alone to restrain the several tens of millions of people of the three provinces? . . . If we don't fight the contract with all our strength, the people of Hunan will become no better than Negro slaves, and the land of the province another Manchuria.[27]

The gentry of the other two provinces soon joined the new campaign of denunciation against Sheng, as did the Chinese students in the United States and Japan, the *Tung-fang tsa-chih,* and daily newspapers. Chang very effectively channeled this burgeoning tide of public opinion against Sheng. On January 17, 1905, he telegraphed Sheng that he believed the gentry groups were sincere in their claim of lack of trust in the company, and that he simply could not suppress this popular sentiment. He even expressed some concern that, if the contract were allowed to remain in force and company crews would actually try to build the line, popular violence by the people and troops in Hunan would be likely.[28]

After this rejection at the hands of both Chang Chih-tung and public opinion, Sheng retired from active participation in the issue. Even though Sheng was still mentioned in an edict of February 22, 1905, as co-responsible with Chang, Chang now had an open field in which to exercise the initiative as chief negotiator. For the next few months, Chang still feared from time to time that Sheng, in collaboration with Wu T'ing-fang in Peking, was trying to undercut him, but there seems to be no evidence that this was the case.

Early in 1905, Chang realized that if the railway rights were going to be recovered fully, some approach other than simple cancellation of the American contract was necessary. With the United States government standing more firmly behind the company now, outright cancellation was politically not feasible. Chang soon hit upon the device of redemption, rather than cancellation, of the contract with the company. If the American China Development Company itself could be induced to sell the rights back to China, of its own free will, then the United States government could hardly protest. China's unilateral repudiation of the contract would have ruptured relations with the United States; it was hoped that redemption would avoid this.

By late February, 1905, Chang was urging this approach as hard as he could. At the end of that month and in early March, he fired off volleys of telegrams to Liang Ch'eng in Washington, laying out in considerable detail the strategy Liang was to follow. First, he was to approach the company directly, avoiding the interposition of any United States government representatives. He was to arrange a series of conferences to discuss China's purchase of the American company's rights on the railway line; no time was to be wasted over the question of right and wrong as far as violation of the agreement of 1900 went, although this had set off the whole issue. Liang should not haggle too much over the price, but put all his energy into recovering the full rights, with no residual American strings. Time was of the essence, for Chang was convinced that a long, drawn-out negotiating process would only give tricksters on both the American and Chinese sides a chance to undermine the deal. He specifically ordered Liang to pay even an exorbitant price, if necessary, if he could thereby achieve rapid and total redemption of the entire concession.[29]

Liang Ch'eng carried out his mission well and found the Americans receptive to Chang's approach. Discussions between Liang's representatives (former Secretary of State Foster and another American railroad lawyer) and those of J. P. Morgan (Elihu Root and George L. Ingraham) commenced in March, and the first formal negotiating session took place on April 5, 1905. Progress was rapid, and a draft agreement was initialed by Liang and the company's representatives on June 7, pending ratification by the Chinese government and the shareholders of the company. The sum of the redemption, U.S. $6,750,000, was indeed exorbitant, considering that practically no work had been done beyond surveying, but following his instructions, Liang had emphasized the recovery of full sovereignty, and this was achieved.[30]

As the redemption negotiations gained momentum and showed prospects of success, they were jeopardized briefly by developments on both the American and Chinese sides. W. W. Rockhill, the new American minister to China who took up his duties in Peking on June 1, 1905, adamantly opposed the company's giving up its concession rights and protested to Secretary of State John Hay. President Theodore Roosevelt also took a brief interest in the issue after a personal appeal by King Leopold, who claimed that J. P. Morgan had deceived him. However, the company's shareholders approved the deal of June 7 at a meeting in late August, 1905.[31]

On the Chinese side, Chang Chih-tung soon perceived that major difficulties would be encountered in raising the sum demanded by the Americans for the redemption of the contract. In December, 1904, before making his final commitment to recover fully the railway rights under his own responsibility, Chang had canvassed the provincial gentry groups who had been so enthusiastic in their support of cancellation. The officials and gentry of the three provinces had assured him that they were dedicated to raising the necessary sums to build the railway themselves through various bond issues and other revenue raising devices. But by the late spring of 1905, just when redemption looked likely, it was obvious that the provinces were not raising money rapidly enough. There were as yet insufficient funds even to redeem the rights to the railway, let alone actually to build it.[32]

In these circumstances, Chang turned to his old friend Fraser, the British consul general. Over the course of the summer, they managed to reach an acceptable agreement by which the government of Hong Kong would lend Chang enough money to meet the American schedule of redemption payments. This loan would be secured on provincial sources of revenue, not on the railway line itself, a prime consideration from Chang's point of view. But the British hopes for future involvement in the line were satisfied by Chang's firm private commitment that if the British offered the best or equal terms on any future loans for the railway or its branches, they would get the contract.[33]

Chang, suspicious to the end that some last-minute hitch would wreck his plans, memorialized on August 12, 1905, that the draft agreement which Liang Ch'eng had signed with the company in the United States on June 7 be approved; the edict came down on August 15. After a flurry of activity in the first few days of September, due to the short notice given by the shareholders' meeting of the company at the end of August, the final redemption agreement was signed on September 6. On September 9 the loan contract with the government of Hong Kong was consummated. Chang could at last breathe a sigh of relief. His work was beyond sabotage. He had personally carried through to success a movement which constituted the first "rollback" of the position of imperialist privilege in China.

The significance of this achievement was lost on neither the court nor public opinion. The central government, and Chang personally, reaped much prestige from it.[34] Moreover, the diverse coalition of provincial gentry, Shanghai journalists, and students abroad who had contributed to the success of the campaign all rejoiced in this victory for Chinese sovereignty. Many foreign observers caustically noted the unfavorable financial terms to which the Chinese had agreed, but this was not the point. Chang had engineered an important, if largely symbolic, reassertion of Chinese sovereignty and dignity, not a simple business deal, and Chinese opinion acclaimed it as such.[35]

The Power of Provincial Interests

The leadership of Chang Chih-tung was probably crucial to the success of the campaign to redeem the rights to the Canton-Hankow railway line. Chang not only committed his own personal prestige to the movement, but orchestrated the pressure of public opinion both inside and outside the government; this brought the central government into line and overcame the reluctance of Sheng Hsüan-huai. Chang was also responsible for changing the emphasis of the campaign from cancellation of the contract to redemption, and for negotiating directly with the company, thus avoiding the potential obstruction of the United States government.

Yet Chang was not in control of the forces with which he had allied in the redemption movement. For example, he did not bring into being the provincial protests against the American contract; these already existed before he himself became alarmed, as Hunan Governor Chao's telegrams of late April, 1904, showed. Much less was Chang in control of the other elements of the anticontract alliance. These forces, even stronger after the successful redemption campaign, now worked to thwart the policy Chang wanted to follow in the fall of 1905 in regard to railway development.

It will be recalled that Chang's first motivation for plunging into the movement to recover the railway rights was to prevent the strategic and geopolitical disadvantage to China which would result from the same group of foreign interests having control of the transport system from Manchuria to Canton. He also hoped to negotiate new terms of the concession and loan agreement, recovering China's full rights of sovereignty in the supervision and control of the railway line. During the course of the cancellation and redemption campaign, however, the provincial gentry groups and the organs of public opinion in urban centers became infatuated with the concept of China building this important railway herself, with her own resources. No foreign loan would be needed; only a few foreign engineers would be hired. *Tzu-pan* (self-management) became the major slogan in the campaign.

This constituted a distinct shift of emphasis from the period of the beginning of the campaign in April and May, 1904, when, as noted, the first members of the Hunan gentry to respond to Chang's appeal for pressure on Sheng Hsüan-huai left open the possibility of taking a foreign loan to finance actual construction of a railroad. This approach was now no longer tenable, in light of the natural acceleration of hopes for success and especially the expectations of the other members of the redemption coalition. It is likely, in fact, that this escalation of goals to include complete Chinese capitalization signified the entry of a somewhat younger, more urbanized and economically sophisticated group within the gentry class, one that might be termed a "modern provincial elite," as opposed to the "national elite" of older gentry. This group, lacking the interprovincial political connections of the national elite, found it more natural to operate entirely within the province, based in the provincial capital, and to cooperate with the students and the press as well. It was anxious not only to deny foreign control of Chinese resources, as was the national elite, but also actively to develop those resources, in mining, railroads, and manufactures, under its own control. Thus its members may have been more sensitive to the manner of capitalization than their elders had been the year previous.[36]

After the successful redemption of the rights to the line in early September, 1905, Chang was primarily interested in commencing its construction as rapidly as possible. As long as Chinese sovereignty was not compromised, he was not adverse to taking another foreign loan to do the job. Moreover, he had been disappointed in the poor showing made by the three provinces in raising funds for the redemption of the railway contract in early 1905. Thus it was only reasonable that he turned to Fraser and the British for the necessary capitalization, as he had agreed to do if a loan was needed. Within only a few days after the redemption agreement with the company and the redemption loan agreement with the government of Hong Kong had been signed, Chang informed

Fraser of the terms on which he invited bids for a large British loan, approximately two or two and a half million pounds, with which to build the Hupeh section of the railway.[37]

As Chang began to negotiate with the British over a new loan, on mutually acceptable terms, he unexpectedly found that the gentry groups and public opinion in general were turning against him, and moreover that they could muster enough influence to block his plans. During late September and October, 1905, a furor arose from the gentry, the students of the three provinces in Japan, and Chang's other allies in the redemption campaign.[38] By the end of October, Fraser reported from Hankow that this opposition had effectively stymied Chang's plans for a British loan. The Ministry of Foreign Affairs and the throne had forbidden any and all foreign loans, even for the Hupeh section of the line alone. Chang fought this, "trying by telegram to overcome the clamour in Peking in favor of using Chinese capital for railway building," but to no avail.[39] As British Minister Satow reported at this time to Foreign Secretary Lansdowne back in London, the opposition was "so vehement that it is not at present possible to hope for the loan to receive sanction . . . in spite of the fact that the Viceroy points out that Hupeh is not rich enough to raise money for its section of the railway."[40]

Chang Chih-tung himself tended to blame the machinations of Sheng Hsüan-huai and Wu T'ing-fang for fomenting the opposition to his plans, and the British for a time suspected that threats by the Germans and the French may somehow have contributed to Peking's caution.[41] Yet the decisive factor was authentic and irate public opinion. In late October, Chang appealed to Ch'ü Hung-chi, head of the Ministry of Foreign Affairs, for help in overcoming the unfavorable attitude of the court. Fraser reported that Ch'ü replied to Chang, fully approving of Chang's proposed loan, but claiming that he did not dare, "in the face of the clamour for keeping China for the Chinese, 'open his mouth.' "[42] In early November, Satow himself interviewed some high officials of the Ministry of Foreign Affairs in Peking, and was told that "they must humour the agitation in the provinces lest they should be swept off their legs."[43]

Chang quickly found himself on the defensive in this matter and felt compelled to justify his position. In late October, 1905, he tried to placate the ire and reduce the clamor of the students in Japan by sending them an explanation of his policy through Minister Yang Shu and the Hupeh superintendent of students.[44] He explained that no sovereign rights whatsoever would be compromised in a loan such as he evisaged. Soon Chang had to explain himself to the throne. The censor Huang Ch'ang-nien, who in the fall of 1904 had helped to obtain the throne's support for Chang in the contract cancellation movement, indicted him in November, 1905, for promising the British a loan on the southern trunk line and now acting as their agent in trying to obtain it for them. An edict demanded an explanation of Chang, and reaffirmed the ban on any foreign loans to build the railway.[45]

On January 21, 1906, Chang submitted a lengthy memorial summarizing the entire cancellation and redemption campaign, and also submitted two more memorials defending himself against the charges of Huang Ch'ang-nien and others.[46] He quoted the entire text of his letter of understanding to Fraser concerning the conditions under which the British might be eligible to lend funds or provide engineers for the project. Chang pointed out how he had made it clear that this agreement would be operative only if such assistance were needed by China and if no one else's terms were better. He demolished Huang's insinuations point by point, accusing him of simplemindedness, if not outright idiocy. Chang asked if it were preferable to have no railroad at all than to make a financially and politically sound deal that could provide the funds at less than half the rate of interest prevailing in China at the moment.

This was an eloquent defense, and no more was heard of Censor Huang's partisan accusations, but it was unavailing on the point at issue. Already in late November, 1905, Chang told Fraser that his hopes were gone—Hunan and Kwangtung were so set against a loan that he had no choice but to let them first try to raise sufficient Chinese capital. He admitted that there was not the slightest chance that Hupeh, relatively poorer than the other two provinces, could raise the money.[47] Chang also began repairing his bridges in regard to the gentry of the three provinces. To Fraser's disgust, in December, 1905, Chang held a banquet for "the gentry who prate of China's sovereign rights being impaired by the use of foreign capital to build railways," and photos of the guests with their host were put on public sale afterwards.[48] No more was heard of taking a foreign loan to build the Canton-Hankow railway until 1908, when it was again Chang Chih-tung, this time in a powerful position in Peking, who raised the issue.

Aftermath

The successful redemption of the Canton-Hankow railway rights had a direct effect on other campaigns to reclaim rights alienated to Western nations and financial groups. During 1905, the gentry and students of Kiangsu province began a campaign to redeem the Shanghai-Nanking railway line from the British. The movement went on until 1908, with much emotion and enthusiasm if little concrete success. Between 1905 and 1907, Kiangsu interests combined with gentry groups from Chekiang to fight for Chinese control of the railway line running from Shanghai through Hangchow to Ningpo. In this case, the provincial interest groups actually raised a fair amount of capital, but the nervous British saw the case as a test of their whole position in China and insisted on retaining the loan rights in the original 1898 concession. The vigor of the protests in the two provinces when redemption was finally denied in late 1907 was quite alarming, both to foreigners and to the Chinese government. In both of these cases, the success of the movement led by Chang Chih-tung and the Hunanese gentry provided initial high hopes for the redemption forces.[49]

Chinese began to reclaim their rights of sovereignty not only in the area of railways, but also in that of mining concessions. In several provinces, mining rights which had been granted to foreign interest groups were contested by Chinese officials, provincial gentry, merchants, and public opinion in general during the last years of the dynasty. In some cases, the alienated rights were recovered through an indemnity or significantly altered in China's favor. In the successful mining rights recovery movements, regional and local officials, who were themselves sometimes returned students from abroad, took the lead in mobilizing and applying the pressure of public opinion against both the central government and the foreign interests, as Chang Chih-tung had done.[50]

These various rights recovery campaigns, as well as the vigorous central government reforms which had gotten well underway by the end of 1905, showed that the driving force of modern nationalist sentiment motivated not only Chinese revolutionaries, but also government officials and the provincial elite groups as well. This phenomenon gave China a very different atmosphere, which was starkly apparent to many foreign observers who were familiar with the "old" China. Experienced Western diplomats noted the appearance of a new, more confident and assertive generation of Chinese officials, and were especially impressed (though often angered) by the strident nationalistic tone of the press in major cities. Western journalists agreed. British Minister Satow even perceived "the consciousness of national solidarity, which is entirely a new phenomenon in China."[51]

In addition to a more impressive performance by the central government, it is clear that a major part of what all these observers perceived as new forces at work in China was the mobilization of the provincial gentry class. This class, both old "national elite" and especially the emerging "modern provincial elite," provided the political and economic muscle behind an increasingly activist and nationalistic interest group operating at the provincial level. These provincial nationalists not only impressed foreigners, but, as shown, they were able to frustrate one of the foremost men of the country, Chang Chih-tung, in his plans for railway development strategy in late 1905.

It seems to me that here in 1905, we can see the firm start of a trend which became the most important factor in Chinese politics by 1911. The provincial gentry groups, and within them the modern provincial elite more so than the traditional national elite, were demanding that China conduct her own modernization, for the national goals of survival, strength, and pride. It was assumed that they, as members of the dominant social and economic class, would naturally play the leading role in programs of modernization at the provincial level. However, they had neither the resources nor, more important, the national cohesiveness and unity as a group to carry out this leading role on a systematic, nationwide basis. At the same time, some national bureaucrats, for example Chang Chih-tung, were becoming increasingly committed to implementing effective and coordinated domestic reform and anti-imperialist programs on a national basis. These programs began to run head on into the suspicion and resistance of the would-be provincial elite managers of the same kind of projects.

This can be seen in the provincial agitation against taking a British loan, even on acceptable financial terms and with no political strings attached, to build the Canton-Hankow railway after the redemption of the United States concession. The provincial opponents of Chang's loan plan prevailed despite their failure to come up with any significant financial commitment to the capitalization of the railway in 1904 and 1905. This failure of capitalization and lack of results prevailed until the central government, led by Chang, finally renewed its interest in the problem in 1908.

Actually, the inability to attract Chinese capital into the various companies set up to build the Canton-Hankow railway may not have been entirely due to the simple lack of resources. Joseph Esherick has pointed out that there was in fact a fairly impressive amount of Chinese private investment in several enterprises in Hunan and Hupeh during the years 1904–9. He speculates that there was some distrust of the semipublic nature of the Chinese railroad companies, and especially of the managerial skills of the old line gentry who tended to have charge of them. This resulted in a proliferation of railroad companies in Hunan, for example, and may have confused and discouraged potential investors.[52] On the other hand, Chang Chih-tung was clearly convinced that the resources to capitalize Hupeh's portion of the railway, and Hupeh's section of the Hankow-Szechuan line as well, were simply not present in the province.

Besides the problem of resources, interprovincial jealousies and rivalries detracted from the ability to get anything accomplished in actually constructing the line. In November, 1905, general offices for both the Canton-Hankow and the Hankow-Szechuan railway lines were set up under Chang's supervision in Wuchang.[53] But this ostensibly unified administration was already a dead letter. As early as September 20, 1905, Fraser sent Satow a long analysis of the railway situation, in which he noted the problems of provincial rivalry: Hupeh and Hunan were trying to get Kwangtung to use the profits of the small but lucrative Canton-Fatshan section of the line to help finance the entire line, but Kwangtung "blandly suggests that the length of line in each province should alone govern the apportionment of pecuniary responsibility"; also, "Hunan would like to put some extra share on the other two as having the termini."[54]

These problems of capitalization and coordination did not improve during the years after 1905. The sensitivity of provincial interests to rights of control over their section of the railway made difficult even the most rudimentary joint planning for the entire trunk line. Moreover, contention between competing groups within each province for government approval to build the road, and for subsidies and special provincial taxes to supplement their lagging sale of shares, also was an obstacle to construction.[55] Finally, it is apparent that many of the individuals in charge of railway development after 1905, representing both the traditional and modern elements within the gentry class, used an anti-imperialistic, patriotic public stance to shield the pursuit of prestige and profit for themselves, family, and friends.[56] For all these reasons, the real national interest in having an operating railway line between Canton and Hankow was submerged, much to the regret of those with a national point of view, such as Chang Chih-tung.

Chapter 9

Return to the Center

It is a significant clue to the political currents of the times that in his last years Chang Chih-tung found himself being drawn inexorably toward the political center, Peking, and that he spent his last two years as a practicing official in the capital. Other than for the purpose of his temporary educational duties in 1903, he had not had a substantive appointment in Peking since the early 1880's. Yet, by 1907 both the demands of the dynasty he served and his own calculation as to where he could be most effective led him back to Peking, where he died in office in October, 1909.

Between 1905 and 1907, while he finished his remarkably long tenure as governor-general of Hu-kuang, Chang seemed to carry the various projects in which he had long shown such interest as far as he could hope to carry them, given his limited provincial power and resource base. But unlike the years before 1900, when no central initiative existed to pick up the slack inherent in uncoordinated provincial programs, the years after 1905 witnessed an accelerating central activism in some of the areas in which Chang had long labored. This quickening central government interest in various reforms was in no small measure due to the work of Chang himself. At any rate, the issues of national educational reform and economic development, to name two that Chang had long promoted, and those of administrative reorganization and implementation of a constitutional system, of which Chang was rather more chary, were being tackled in Peking after 1905, even if in less than a wholly effective manner. In the turmoil of these issues and of others as well, Chang played out the last two years of his life in

Peking. This chapter will attempt to recount both the realities of Chang's political position in the last four years of his life and his role in some of the major issues confronting the dynasty in its last years.

Chang as Politician and Official, 1905–9

Final Years in Hupeh

Nothing in Chang's last years of service in Hupeh matched the success and prestige he had enjoyed in the redemption of the construction rights to the Canton-Hankow railway in 1905. Indeed, during 1905 probably no inducement could have lured him away from his Wuchang post. During the summer of that year, when the redemption campaign was in its last stages, Chang heard rumors from Peking that he was scheduled for transfer to the governor-generalship at Nanking, to replace the politically ailing Chou Fu. He at once telegraphed Grand Councillor Ch'ü Hung-chi that he would not have it, threatening to plead sick and retire first.[1] Two years later, the situation was very different. Chang was still unwilling to be transferred to another governor-generalship, but he proved to be quite amenable to recall to Peking, once he was certain that the conditions were satisfactory.

Between 1905 and 1907, Chang and his various reform projects ran into a series of dead ends in his Hu-kuang post. The last chapter describes how the protests of elite and public opinion groups in Hupeh and Hunan had stymied his hopes of soon commencing railroad construction in the two provinces under his authority by means of a foreign loan. At the time of his transfer to Peking in the late summer of 1907 the situation had not improved; not a mile of track had been laid in either Hupeh or Hunan, and the project was deeply mired in mistrust and tension between officials and private investors, as well as in interprovincial conflict.[2] If trunk line railways were going to be built, obviously it would require the imposition from the national level of development schemes that would override local and provincial squabbles. Chang became involved in the development of one such railway plan when he was made, with Yüan Shih-k'ai, co-manager of the financing of the line between Tientsin and Pukou (Chinkiang) in March, 1907. Already by May of that year Chang and Yüan had basically agreed upon the strategy that would culminate in a German loan, on very favorable terms, in early 1908: that is, in effect to use the protests of provincial gentry groups (in this case those of Chihli and Shantung) as leverage against the foreign banks in bargaining for the loan, but not to let their protests prevent taking the loan altogether, for this would mean no financing at all, as the situation on the Canton-Hankow line had already proved.[3] A position of authority at the national level, if used to generate pressure from the center, might be expected to facilitate the accomplishment of a similar plan for moving the Canton-Hankow railway project off dead center.

In addition to his inability to push ahead with development schemes for the future from his present provincial post, Chang found it increasingly difficult after 1905 even to maintain the progress he had made in years past, due to shortage of funds. In particular, Chang's various schools suffered cutbacks in teachers' salaries and equipment and began to charge tuition, which reduced the student body of some schools. This was evident already in the spring of 1907, and the problems continued after Chang's departure later in the year, so that some of the schools were on the verge of shutting down completely by early 1908.[4] At the same time, Chang was forced to reduce the work force at some of his industrial projects, and in spite of his economies had to impose an extra land tax in 1907 to meet his obligations.[5] Finally, there were the related dangers of popular unrest and undependability of the provincial troops, even those with modern training. The P'ing-Liu-Li uprising of December, 1906, is indicative of how close to the surface was the former, and the latter was attested to by several observers during 1906 and 1907.[6]

During these years, when the problems of his jurisdiction seemed more intractable than ever, Chang was nearly seventy years of age (he turned seventy in 1906, by Chinese calculation). His health was not always good, a problem undoubtedly compounded by his irregular, generally nocturnal, working hours. Thus he was probably more in need of capable assistants in his personal secretariat than ever. However, he had no first-class personnel in this area. After the departure of Liang Tun-yen in 1904, Chang went through several chief assistants; he was apparently unhappy with all of them.[7] It should be noted that by this time attractive positions in the changing bureaucracy in Peking were opening up for men who only a few years before could have hoped to do no better than the secretariat of a major provincial official. Men like Liang Tun-yen were finding employment in the ministries of foreign affairs, posts and communications, commerce, education, army, and other bodies in Peking. As a result, Chang and other provincial officials were finding it difficult to surround themselves with the array of talent and wisdom that they could attract in earlier years.

While Chang struggled along in his provincial post, major initiatives were being taken in Peking, threatening to bypass him. Between 1901 and 1905, most of the major reform measures had been secured by pressure and persuasion mobilized from among provincial officials like Chang, Yüan Shih-k'ai, Liu K'un-i, and others. But after the watershed year of 1905, when the examination system was totally discarded and a commitment was made to the eventual adoption of constitutional government, the initiative passed to Peking. As some of the nation's ambitious young men, many of them foreign educated, began to be employed in subordinate positions in the Peking bureaucracy, their ability to draft reform proposals and propel them through the power structure there restored to the central government some of its role in marking out the course of future national development, even if it could not always realize its plans. For example, during 1906 and 1907 important measures of administrative reorganization and plans for the first steps toward constitutional government were generated in Peking itself, with major provincial officials consulted only on a post facto basis.

Thus the possible attractions for Chang of a post in Peking were, I think, apparent. But the only post in which he could be interested was a seat on the Grand Council, the highest advisory body to the throne, and this was not offered until September, 1907. Another means of enhancing his influence in the face of the flow of power toward Peking was to enter into a close degree of cooperation with Yüan Shih-k'ai, the Chihli governor-general, with whom Chang had already collaborated in several joint memorials and projects in previous years. Interestingly, Liang Tun-yen, who had been a protégé of both Chang and Yüan before starting his immensely successful career in the Ministry of Foreign Affairs, in 1906 expressed his hope of facilitating a closer Chang-Yüan alliance.[8] The possibilities for closer cooperation between the two were enhanced by their simultaneous transfer to Peking in September, 1907.

Transfer to Peking, 1907

Almost a year of political instability and vacillating leadership in Peking preceded the transfer of Chang and Yüan in 1907. The instability resulted mainly from a factional feud between groups striving for dominance at court. On the one side was Prince Ch'ing, with whose power position Yüan Shih-k'ai was closely associated; on the other was a group consisting of Grand Councillor Ch'ü Hung-chi, Ts'en Ch'un-hsüan, and others who enlisted several censors in their struggle to unseat Prince Ch'ing and reduce the power of Yüan. The battle raged from September, 1906, on the issue of administrative reorganization of the empire, to June, 1907, by which time it had degenerated to a bitter personal vendetta, with Prince Ch'ing finally digging up accusations dating back to the 1898 reforms to finish off Ch'ü and Ts'en.[9] Relative, though still precarious, stability was restored with Ch'ü's removal from the Grand Council on June 17, 1907.

Corresponding to the factional political struggle, and undoubtedly contributing to it, seems to have been a prolonged period of hesitant and indecisive leadership on the part of the empress dowager, lasting for the first eight months of 1907. During this period some of the administrative changes decreed in late 1906, to be dealt with below, were being carried out. Meanwhile, pressure was growing from newspapers and provincial associations for a speedy implementation of constitutional forms. Many officials, Chinese and Manchu alike, also were advocating the abolition of remaining legal distinctions between the two races, and especially an end to favoritism toward Manchus in government. At the same time, revolutionary groups were launching attacks on the persons of major officials; on July 6, 1907, they succeeded in assassinating En-ming, the governor of Anhui province. The mood of apprehension and outright fear as to personal safety, and the aimless drift of domestic and foreign policy, were repeatedly emphasized in the communications of, for example, British Minister Jordan through the summer of 1907.[10]

Beginning in June, 1907, Chang Chih-tung step by step became an integral part of this uncertain Peking scene.[11] On June 19, two days after Ch'ü Hung-chi's fall, Chang's relative Lu Ch'uan-lin was restored to the seat on the Grand Council which he had lost the previous November, at a moment of Ch'ü's ascendancy. On June 21, Chang himself was appointed a junior grand secretary (*hsieh-pan ta-hsüeh shih*), a nonsubstantive but important honor which he had never before enjoyed, perhaps indicating that he might be under consideration for a change in job. July was a month of growing rumors as to the future roles of both Chang Chih-tung and Yüan Shih-k'ai, and attacks on both. On July 2, Chang was criticized by a capital censor for his recent opposition to some of the administrative changes of late 1906. On July 10 Yüan Shih-k'ai, pleading illness, requested a month's vacation, and within the next few days was severely denounced by two court censors for having too much power. On July 23, Chang was given the honorific title of senior grand secretary (*ta-hsüeh shih*), and Lu Ch'uan-lin was made a junior grand secretary.

By early August, 1907, Chang heard that the throne had decided to move Yüan Shih-k'ai to the Grand Council, to replace Yüan in Chihli with Tuan-fang, who was presently governor-general at Nanking, and to move Chang to Nanking. He reacted strongly against this. On August 6 he telegraphed Lu Ch'uan-lin in Peking, warning that he would retire rather than be transferred to Nanking, and on August 7 he wrote a memorial requesting twenty days' leave due to illness.[12] The next day, August 8, as if to test the intentions of the court on a major issue which had been in the air for months and which seems to have especially troubled Chang, he sent in a major memorial requesting that the legal and political distinctions between Manchus and Han Chinese be abolished.[13] On August 10 came an edict abolishing racial distinctions, and an edict of the same day called Chang speedily (*hsün-su*) to come to Peking for an audience.

He was either really ill or still unwilling to go immediately, for on August 12 Chang reiterated his request for leave, estimating that he could manage to depart for the capital by about August 28.[14] This request was now approved. After a hiatus in activity lasting about two weeks, on August 24, 1907, Yüan Shih-k'ai was ordered to Peking for an audience; Yüan arrived there on August 30. On September 4, the appointments of Yüan as foreign minister and grand councillor and of Chang as grand councillor were announced. Only now, with his elevation to the Grand Council already made public, did Chang come to Peking; he left Wuchang on September 10 and arrived in the capital on September 12.

Two important problems of interpretation involved with Chang's transfer to Peking concern the question of the throne's intention and that of Chang's own attitude toward this important change. It has been claimed that the aim of the empress dowager and the Manchu officials around her was simply to reduce the real power of Yüan and Chang, the two most powerful governors-general, thus to advance the cause of centralized Manchu dominance by "promoting" the two to positions where they could be more easily controlled.[15] This assumes the existence of a rather systematic plan of procedure on the part of the throne, or some group in a position to dominate it. In actuality, as described, the throne and the court seem to have been afflicted with a great degree of uncertainty in the summer of 1907, beset as they were with a myriad of intractable issues. Rather than hoping to reduce the influence of either Chang or Yüan through their transfer, it is more likely that the throne was hoping to shore up the authority of the central government as a whole by incorporating the two most respected Chinese officials of the empire into its highest policy body. Jordan reported to London in late August that there was a growing call to transfer Yüan to the center in order to "save the situation," and after the appointment of the two to the Grand Council he opined that the regime was "attaching to themselves the Chinese who carry most weight in the country."[16] If this was the case, then both Yüan and Chang were coming into a situation where they might hope to have a good deal of influence, rather than into a trap designed to reduce them to impotence.

Chang Chih-tung's own perceptions, to the extent that they

can be pieced together, support this view. Considering his age and the fact that he seemed ready to retire in early August rather than accept a post he did not want, his willingness to take up new duties in Peking indicates his presumption that he would not be a supernumerary there. Chang was aware of the confusion in which the court was operating; in late July or early August, 1907, he had received a personal letter from one Lu Pao-chung, senior vice-president of the Censorate in Peking (*tso-fu tu yü-shih*), which stressed the indecisiveness and lack of leadership which had been prevailing there for months.[17] The rapid, if token response to his August 8 memorial on Manchu-Han relations may have been a signal that his opinions would make an impact. Moreover, he apparently could still count on his long-standing good relationship with the empress dowager; at the time of his seventieth birthday in 1906, she had been very generous in bestowing rewards and symbolic honors upon him.[18] Nevertheless, Chang's customary caution in political matters characterized his reentry into court politics. As noted, he did not leave Wuchang until the empress dowager had publicly committed herself to making Chang a grand councillor. Even after his arrival in Peking there were rumors that he would make an attempt to regain his Wuchang post, and one account claimed that when he appeared in the Forbidden City for his first audience he had a servant supporting him on either side, so as to have an excuse to decline office if he wished to.[19]

Whatever apprehensions Chang may have harbored concerning his new situation seem to have been allayed within the first few days in Peking, during which he had several audiences with the empress dowager. According to an account of one of these audiences, the empress dowager appealed to Chang to help her make sense of the bewildering and conflicting array of advice being offered her, and solicited his opinions on several issues, including management of the students abroad, constitutionalism, and the fitness of various high officials.[20] On September 21, Chang was given charge of all the affairs of the Ministry of Education, a position of great responsibility.[21] From this time until increasingly debilitated by sickness in the summer of 1909, Chang fulfilled his Grand Council obligations faithfully, in addition to his educational duties and other special tasks assigned him by the throne.

Chang as Metropolitan Official, 1907–9

During the last two years of his life, Chang was involved in a variety of major issues in Peking. These will be described in later sections of this chapter. My purpose now is rather to analyze the political presence, as it were, of Chang during these years, including his relationships with other important centers of power. My conclusion is that the political stature of Chang during this period was indeed important enough for his opinions and actions on several issues and problems to be taken seriously into account in any attempt to understand the last years of the dynasty.

From September, 1907, until early 1909, the most influential single official in Peking, below the throne, was undoubtedly Yüan Shih-k'ai. In his analysis of the nature and extent of Yüan's power base during these years, Stephen MacKinnon has concluded that Yüan controlled the Grand Council and the Peking bureaucracy down to the ministerial level as well.[22] Without detracting from Yüan's preeminence at this time, I should like to modify the picture somewhat from the point of view of Chang Chih-tung. First, it is possible that Yüan's dominance of the Grand Council was by no means complete. The council during this period was composed of six members—Yüan, Chang, Prince Ch'ing, Prince Ch'un (to be regent after the two majesties' deaths in November, 1908), Shih-hsü, and Lu Ch'uan-lin. Yüan and Prince Ch'ing often acted in consort, it is true, and may have been able to influence Shih-hsü. But Chang was hardly Yüan's puppet. Moreover, Chang and Lu were relatives and had a long relationship; Lu is usually characterized as anything but pliant, in fact as quite opinionated and stubborn, although he was advanced in age. Prince Ch'un's behavior on the council is more difficult to guess at, though of course as regent he would strip Yüan of all offices in January, 1909. Likewise, Yüan's ability to manipulate the Peking bureaucracy can be overestimated by noting only that a good number of the ministers, vice-ministers, and other high ranking personnel during these years had had links to Yüan in the past.[23] At least some of these, for example Liang Tun-yen, also had strong ties to Chang Chih-tung, and perhaps to other officials as well, if in fact such links do constitute the elements of a power base for anyone.

Thus I would argue that focusing attention upon Yüan Shih-k'ai for the 1907–8 period, while certainly justified, should not be exclusive; the lens should be widened to include Chang Chih-tung as well. And to many observers at the time it was apparent that the role of both of these men—each a grand councillor, each head of a major ministry, and each with a lifetime's worth of former protégés and old associates scattered throughout the government—was crucial. Moreover, the relationship between them was of obvious importance. As friend of both, Liang Tun-yen speculated in early 1906 that "in combination they would be irresistible"; whereas working at cross purposes they could partially neutralize each other's influence, to the detriment of both.[24]

Although Chang and Yüan had cooperated on such matters as their joint memorials to end the examination system and to chart a course toward constitutionalism in 1905, and had communicated heavily via telegraph on many other affairs in which they had a mutual interest, for example joint policy during the Boxer Rebellion, they had never been on close terms in an official or a personal capacity. Chang had often expressed suspicion and dislike for Yüan to his intimates.[25] When it became known that both were coming to the capital as grand councillors in September, 1907, the British minister John Jordan was convinced that the two were "opposing forces . . . perhaps intended to neutralize each other," and that the court conservatives would rally around Chang, while Yüan represented reform and progress.[26]

In fact, what can be discovered of their personal relationship during this period in Peking indicates that there was a fair degree of mistrust between them. After Chang Chih-tung came to Peking, he found the long journey each day between his residence and their majesties' location, which had been moved to the Hsi-yüan palace for the winter, to be burdensome. Yüan Shih-k'ai lent Chang one of his residences, quite near the palace, but then had his servants spy on Chang and give him a daily report on who came to visit his distinguished lodger.[27] Chang, as a scholar who prided himself on his elegant prose, was rather contemptuous of the low academic background of some of those in Yüan's camp, for example Yang Shih-hsiang, who succeeded Yüan as governor-general of Chihli; it seems that he made fun of Yüan's own written style on more than one occasion. For his part, Yüan considered Chang to be an "old bookworm" (*lao shu-sheng*), and claimed that Chang was only "half the man" that Hsü Shih-ch'ang and Yang Shih-hsiang were.[28] I have no doubt that factors such as this did exist, which must have made it hopeless for Chang and Yüan ever to be friends. The real question is whether the impossibility of their personal friendship prevented them from working together effectively or reflected a similar gulf between them on major issues of the day. I do not think that either was the case. Rather, the evidence indicates a fair congruence of views on matters which both men were working on during the 1907–8 period, despite continuing indications of personal incompatibilities.

Chang, for example, had been ordered to collaborate with Yüan in managing the loan negotiations for the Tientsin-Pukou Railway even before their transfer to Peking in 1907, and despite differing initial preferences for strategy, they succeeded in gaining the best financial and political terms China had yet achieved in any major railway loan when the final agreement was signed in January, 1908.[29] On another important issue, one which the Grand Council often grappled with, that of the best timetable for implementing a constitutional system, Chang and Yüan did not always agree, but apparently they were usually closer together than each was to some of the other members. Both believed that the reasonably speedy implementation of a bona fide constitution was desirable, or at least politically necessary.[30] *The North China Herald* in January, 1908, even spoke of Yüan and Chang as a reform team, jointly fighting the influence of conservatives like T'ieh-liang.[31]

At various times during 1908 there were rumors of personal friction between Chang and Yüan, and the possibility of Chang's leaving the Grand Council on his own volition was mentioned more than once.[32] But apparently the empress dowager valued the services of both men very highly, and herself took the initiative in helping to make peace between the two by forcing the betrothal of their children; before the end of 1908 Chang's daughter was indeed betrothed to Yüan's son.[33] The two men seem to have maintained a satisfactory working relationship until Yüan's sudden forced retirement in early January, 1909. It is claimed by some sources that at the time of Yüan's fall from power, the prince regent wanted to kill him, but that Chang Chih-tung's vigorous opposition prevented this.[34] Another account reports that in late September, 1909, as Chang lay near death, the regent inquired of Chang as to who should succeed him on the Grand Council if he was unable to resume his duties; Chang replied that Yüan should.[35] Thus, to summarize the fragmentary evidence, there certainly seems to have been no conservative-reformist dichotomy between the role of these two important officials; neither was there any insurmountable personal rivalry between them which prevented their cooperation.[36]

Chang's relationship with the Manchu throne was of course at least as important as his position vis-à-vis Yüan, and from 1907 to 1909 that relationship remained fairly constant. Until her death in November, 1908, Empress Dowager Tz'u-hsi relied heavily upon both Yüan and Chang, although Yüan received such extravagant gifts and favors upon the occasion of his fiftieth birthday in 1908 as to indicate special preference. But with the accession to power of Prince Ch'un, Kuang-hsü's brother and father of the child emperor Hsüan-t'ung, upon the occasion of the practically simultaneous death of Kuang-hsü and Tz'u-hsi in November, 1908, Yüan's position began to recede, and Chang emerged as the Chinese official most trusted and relied upon in the Grand Council and the inner precincts of the court. Both Yüan and Chang contributed greatly to the smooth transition of power to the regency, a transition which many observers had feared would be impossible to conduct peacefully. But Chang seems to have drafted single-handedly most of the edicts and decrees of the first few weeks of the new regime in late 1908, and he also seemed to receive a greater share of honorific appointments during these weeks.[37] Then, of course, Yüan dramatically departed the political scene altogether, stripped of power in early January, 1909, leaving Chang alone in terms of prestige and influence at the top of Chinese officialdom.

From January until July, 1909, when increasing physical debilitation forced him to take extended leave from his daily Grand Council duties, Chang played an important role as one of the few disinterested yet competent sources of opinion available to the regency. At a time when his personal inclinations were perhaps to withdraw from an active political role, he found himself as one of only two reasonably effective grand councillors, the other being Na-t'ung, who had replaced Yüan; at the same time that Chang was burdened with continuing duties in railroad loan negotiations and in the Ministry of Education, the regent refused to let Chang resign from the Grand Council, citing the fact that only he and Na-t'ung were doing their jobs. With Yüan Shih-k'ai's guiding hand in foreign policy gone, Chang was even being harassed by other officials for opinions on how to handle various problems in foreign relations as late as August, 1909, when he was confined to his home and gravely ill.[38]

While demands upon Chang did not lessen in his last few months, and his influence was considerable, his power position actually seems to have declined in practical terms. This was because the prince regent chose increasingly to consult kinsmen and other Manchus, bypassing the bureaucratic apparatus of government where Chang's influence and expertise lay. Already in March, 1909, British Minister Jordan reported the existence of an "inner Grand Council" consisting of the prince regent's two younger brothers and T'ieh-liang, while the regular Grand Council was enfeebled.[39] As a result, the government bureaucracies and offices which had received considerable attention and had gained some important functions in the last years of Tz'u-hsi, even though the overall national reform program under her direction may have left much to be desired, under the regency began a steady decline into disorganization, uncoordination, and ineffectiveness.[40] By the time of Chang's death on October 4, 1909, the dynasty he had served for practically all of his adult life was already displaying the signs of ineptitude which would contribute to its rapid demise in 1911 and 1912.

Chang and Dynastic Policy, 1905–9

In his last years, Chang continued to maintain an active hand in most of the areas of reform in which he had long been interested. Educational matters remained especially close to his heart, as they had throughout most of his career, and he had considerable responsibility for national educational policy as director of the Ministry of

Education from September, 1907, until his death. After the abolition of the old examination system in 1905, Chang at times displayed concern that classical learning not be neglected altogether; he approved of the use of a special selection procedure to recognize scholars proficient in the old curriculum, and even established a School for the Preservation of Antiquity (Ts'un-ku hsüeh-t'ang) in Wuchang just before his transfer to Peking in 1907.[41] However, he was by no means preoccupied with this concern, and the bulk of his educational activities in his last years was in the direction of expanding and improving the modern sector of the educational system, both in its facilities for specialized training and in its ability to offer to a greater number of people some modicum of general education, as the empress dowager had charged him to do in turning the Ministry of Education over to him in 1907.[42]

In 1908 he secured a special grant of two million taels to upgrade the curriculum and facilities of the Imperial University of Peking; he advocated the establishment of a second national university at Nanking; and he obtained permission to establish a national women's normal college at Peking. At the same time, he worked to achieve standardization of educational quality throughout the nation, and tried hard to win approval for the adoption, at least in principle, of the desirability of a minimum level of compulsory education for all citizens. Although this last goal was clearly a long-term one, Chang saw it as absolutely crucial if China was ever to make a success of a constitutional system.[43]

As might be expected, Chang maintained a particular interest in the Chinese students in Japan and other foreign countries, even after his move to Peking. Chang sometimes took personal charge of the "palace examination" administered to these students upon their return to determine the positions for which they were qualified. To some extent Chang may have been disillusioned by this time with the quality of the education these students had received, especially those trained in Japan. In addition to expressing concern, as he had in years past, that the Chinese diplomats abroad exercise proper vigilance over the personal welfare, moral health, and political opinions of the Chinese students abroad, he also warned against overhasty hiring of students with apparently sound credentials from Japanese educational institutions. He requested provincial officials not to hire such students until they could prove completion of their course of study, and recommended rigorous examinations for such students to see if their command of general knowledge and the Japanese language matched their pretensions.[44] Conviction that China could in the near future provide her own advanced training for most of these students, thus reducing the expense and risk of their going abroad, lay behind Chang's 1908 campaign to pour great resources into the upgrading of the Imperial University in Peking.

The educational issues described above were important, and of some intrinsic interest, but they were not foremost on the policy agenda of the dynasty during these years. The issues which increasingly preoccupied the dynasty, rather, and on which its fate eventually hinged, were those of constitutionalism and national railway development; in both of these the dynasty found itself challenged by that provincial consciousness and assertiveness discussed in previous chapters.

The Path to Constitutionalism

In July, 1905, Chang Chih-tung had joined with Yüan Shih-k'ai and Chou Fu in a memorial which may have been influential in the launching that same month of a government mission to investigate the constitutional political systems of foreign nations. However, for the next year and a half Chang consciously refrained from participating in the continuing debate on the subject and the growing clamor for a constitution. Meanwhile, steady though slow movement toward implementation of such a political system continued.

On November 18, 1905, the throne ordered the Office for the Management of Political Affairs to consider an overall plan (*ta-kang*) for the adoption of a constitution, and on November 25 established the Commission for Investigation of Government (K'ao-ch'a cheng-chih-kuan) to begin work on the details of planning. Interest in constitutionalism accelerated with the return of the investigative mission from abroad in July, 1906, when two of its leading members, Tai Hung-tz'u and Tuan-fang, revealed their opinion that China should adopt a constitution on the Japanese model.[45] Yüan Shih-k'ai again memorialized in favor of a constitution in August, as did other officials, and Tai and Tuan-fang argued for their recommendations in person before the throne. On August 25, 1906, the Grand Council and the Office for the Management of Political Affairs were directed to consider the documentation compiled by the mission of investigation.

At this time, Chang could have registered his opinion; in fact he was requested to do so by the returned commissioners in late July, 1906. But he declined and in the process gave the distinct impression that he was not as enthusiastic about a constitution as they were. On August 2, 1906, Chang sent a short telegram to Tai Hung-tz'u and Tuan-fang, who were still in Shanghai preparing for their trip to Peking to report the results of their mission; interestingly, Chang sent copies of this telegram to seven other major provincial officials, including Yüan Shih-k'ai, Chao Erh-feng, Ts'en Ch'un-hsüan, Chou Fu, and Hsi-liang. Chang noted tersely that establishment of a constitutional system was an extremely grave undertaking. If in the future he were to receive orders to discuss and memorialize on the subject, naturally he would do his best to make a sensible recommendation, but for now he did not dare recklessly (*wang*) to join in petty discussion (*mo-i*).[46] This was a fairly clear statement of his refusal to be pressured on the subject, and was probably a suggestion to the recipients that they might do likewise.

The court responded to all the enthusiasm for a constitution by taking one more step toward its realization. An edict of September 1, 1906, announced that in order to prepare for a constitutional system, some administrative reorganization in the bureaucracy would be required, and major provincial officials were directed to send representatives to Peking to join metropolitan officials in determining what form this would take. On September 6, an Administrative Reorganization Office (Kuan-chih pien-chih kuan), under Sun Pao-ch'i and Yang Shih-ch'i, was established to handle the paperwork and drafting details that would be necessary.[47] Since a large number of officials had a right to express opinions on this matter, the debate became rather thorny over the next two months. The question of reorganization also became closely tied in with the power struggle involving Prince Ch'ing, Yüan Shih-k'ai, Ch'ü Hung-chi, and others. The result was that the recommendations for central government reorganization presented to the throne by the Administrative Reorganization Office on November 2, 1906, which actually provided for a significant degree of restructuring at the upper levels, including a strong executive leader rather than the collegial Grand Council, could not be divorced from the factional political struggle. Mindful of this, and perhaps uncertain how best to proceed, the empress dowager opted for a minimum of reorganization in her decrees of November 6, leaving the Grand Council as it was while combining and streamlining several minor offices into larger ministries.[48] At the same time, extensive changes in the structure of provincial administration were promised for the future.

It is not clear what Chang Chih-tung thought of this limited reorganization of the Peking bureaucracy. But the projected changes at the provincial level quickly drew his attention. On November 5, 1906, the Administrative Reorganization Office sent to all top provincial officials a long draft version of proposed changes, soliciting their reactions.[49] The draft took as its stated purpose the fostering of more popular participation in government and the increased efficiency of government through functional specialization at the provincial and local levels. Specifically, it provided that each prefecture, department, and district (*fu, chou* and *hsien*) would convene a deliberative assembly (*i-shih hui*) chosen by the people (*jen-min*), to meet and discuss its affairs. A smaller management council (*tung-shih hui*) would also be chosen by the people, to assist the local officials in carrying out matters discussed by the deliberative assembly. After the system of assemblies and councils was operating in these units of administration, it would be extended as well to cities, towns, and townships (*ch'eng, chen* and *hsiang*). All of the above measures and new bodies were to be supervised by local officials, and would come under the direction of the taotais, who themselves were to be given province-wide functional jurisdictions, rather than their former territorial jurisdictions.

In addition to these provisions, the draft proposal specified that an independent hierarchy of judicial officers, from the provincial down to the district level, should be set up under the direction of the judicial commissioner (*an-ch'a shih*). The scope of authority of governors-general and governors was to be further narrowed by designating certain jobs as the responsibility of the lieutenant governor (*pu-cheng shih*) and by the establishment of a new provincial office for financial administration (*ts'ai-cheng ssu*).[50] Local branch offices for finance, commerce, education and other functions would come under the direction of the responsible provincial officer through the functional taotais, not that of the local prefect or magistrate where they might be located.

Chang's reaction to these proposals for the reorganization of provincial administration did not come for almost two months, but when it did it was highly critical of both the theme of popular participation and that of functional differentiation of responsibility.[51] In an extremely long telegram of protest sent on January 2, 1907, he pointed out many defects in the scheme, but he reserved his most vigorous denunciations for those aspects of it which opened the way for extensive participation in local government by the gentry, who would inevitably dominate the proposed deliberative assemblies and management councils at the local level.[52] Here, as he had on many occasions in previous years, Chang displayed his apprehension that the local elite, if given the chance, would pursue their own interests, regardless of the interests of good government or those of the dynasty. He pointed out that the proposed two kinds of local elected bodies offered great opportunities for self-serving to the gentry (*hsiang-shen*), and he insisted upon at least two precautions: first, these bodies should be called *chü,* or bureaus, rather than *hui,* to indicate their subservience to government officials; second, the regulations must specify clearly the limits of power for these groups, so that deliberative groups could not make the final decision, and so that management groups would listen to the local officials, not the gentry. Otherwise, official control would be a farce.[53]

In his January telegram Chang also opposed the establishment of specialized bureaus at the prefectural and district level and the replacement of territorial taotais by functional ones. Finally, he rejected the idea of an independent judiciary at all levels; he elaborated his case against the proposed judiciary in another telegram of February 6, 1907, arguing that this would constitute excessive and unnecessary copying of the Western concept of separation of powers, which was inappropriate to Chinese conditions and might shackle provincial and local officials in a time of crisis.[54] In sum,

Chang argued in his January 2 protest that he did not oppose constitutionalism, but all this reorganization was not necessary for the successful adoption of a constitutional system. It was fine to have some elected gentry representatives to play a minor role in local government, but if the overall welfare of the people was to be improved, it would be better to establish some new economic enterprises than to have elections. Anyone getting an education these days, he said, and especially the students overseas, arrogantly presumed that they should be able to play a role in public affairs, and to interfere in dynastic prerogatives. He reminded the court that "the original aim of establishing a constitution was to preserve the autocracy." Clearly, Chang felt that the effectiveness of central government control could be eroded rather than enhanced by the proposed reorganization.

Chang apparently was the most important figure in the opposition to the proposed changes; most other provincial officials approved them, or at least did not protest.[55] Thus Chang should be given partial credit (or blame) for the fact that the actual steps of provincial reorganization taken later in 1907 were considerably short of the 1906 draft proposal. After measures of April and May which set up a regular civilian administration for Manchuria, dividing it into three provinces, a decree of July 7, 1907, outlined the first alterations in the structure of provincial authority.[56] The old judicial commissioner was replaced with a new provincial commissioner of justice (*t'i-fa shih*), who was given charge of all judicial affairs down to the local level. Moreover, all territorial taotais were abolished and replaced by functional intendants (still called taotais) for police and industrial affairs. In these respects, the measures corresponded to the draft proposal which Chang had opposed. However, it was directed that the new structure was to be fully implemented only in the three newly established northeastern provinces; it was to be tried on an experimental basis in selected areas of Chihli and Kiangsu, and implemented gradually in other provinces over the next fifteen years. Moreover, there was no mention of the establishment of local participatory organs, which Chang had opposed most vigorously; directives to plan for these were not issued until later in the year, when Chang was sitting on the Grand Council.

In his January and February telegrams of commentary on the provincial reorganization draft, Chang had emphasized that he did not oppose constitutionalism per se; indeed he conceded that it was necessary. However, it seems that his acceptance of it was due as much to his recognition that so many other people expected and demanded it as it was to his appreciation of its intrinsic merit. He still may have seen it as a possible route to a more powerful state, as he had in 1905 when he recommended it, but he was also aware of its pitfalls for central authority, as seen in the specifics of his opposition to the provincial reorganization recounted above. During 1907, however, the pressures for more rapid movement toward a constitutional system mounted. The modern Chinese press of Shanghai and the other major treaty ports was almost unanimous in its advocacy of speedier action; Yüan Shih-k'ai and several Chinese diplomats also memorialized on the subject in late July.[57] The court responded in a minimal way on August 13 by changing the name of the old Commission for Investigation of Government more specifically to the Commission for Constitutional Preparation (Hsien-cheng pien-ch'a kuan), but the problem of how quickly to proceed was still up in the air when Chang arrived in Peking to take up his new post in September, 1907.[58]

In the fall of 1907 Chang advised the throne to take more rapid steps toward constitutionalism. Both he and Yüan Shih-k'ai did this, in separate audiences and in at least one joint appeal.[59] But Chang's motives were at least partially preemptive, according to one account of an audience with Tz'u-hsi. In response to her question as to how to stop the antigovernment agitation among students abroad, Chang replied that the rapid granting of constitutional government would do this.[60] At any rate, with Chang and Yüan now on the Grand Council, and presumably with the acquiescence of both, an edict of October 19, 1907, directed provincial officials to make preparations for the speedy convocation of provincial assemblies (*tzu-i chü*), and to make plans as well for deliberative assemblies (*i-shih hui*) at the prefectural, departmental, and district levels.[61] Yet at the same time that these steps were taken toward broadened participation in government at the provincial and local level, some measures of November and December, 1907, seemed to narrow the grounds of such participation, reflecting the same kind of apprehension that Chang had long shown over irresponsible and self-serving localism. The Ministry of Education was given responsibility for seeing that students kept to their books and did not interfere in political matters; and the Commission for Constitutional Preparation was directed, in conjunction with the Ministry of the Interior, to draw up regulations governing the formation and operation of political societies, so that gentry, merchants, and other men of influence likewise could not unduly interfere in politics other than in approved structures of participation.[62]

During the year 1908, the tempo of debate and action on constitutionalism grew, culminating in the promulgation on August 27 of the throne's nine-year plan for gradual implementation of a constitutional system. We cannot be sure what precisely was Chang's attitude toward the final product, but the topic was certainly frequently discussed in the Grand Council in the months before the August promulgation, and at times rumors were circulated as to how the grand councillors stood on the issue of the proper timetable for implementation of the constitution. Although Chang, along with Prince Ch'ing, was characterized by one of these accounts as favoring the rather slow introduction of a constitutional system, other reports paired Chang with Yüan Shih-k'ai as advocating swifter action and attainment of a full working system within five years; one even claimed that Chang wanted to proceed more quickly than did Yüan, though I doubt that this was the case.[63] At any rate, it seems likely that Chang thought it wise to move at least as rapidly as the nine-year plan which was in fact adopted, and he could well have favored a five-year plan.[64]

Thus there does not seem to be any question but that Chang fully accepted the coming constitutional system for China. However, his special concerns about the vulnerability of central power to the depredations of local and provincial assertiveness led him to view constitutional government as a venture which held great risks for effective government, as well as one which promised a more legitimized, and therefore stronger, regime. Some of those concerns may well have contributed to the cautious and rather hesitant manner in which the throne finally embarked upon this important new departure in government.

The Issue of National Railway Development

In the last year of his life Chang Chih-tung was burdened with the responsibility for dealing with what may have been, from the point of view of a government official, the most complex and frustrating issue of the day. This was the task of finding adequate and dependable financing for the backbone of China's national railway system in the southern part of the country and for its extension into Szechuan, all in the face of the competing and conflicting demands of many interested parties, foreign and domestic, each of which hoped to shape events to its own advantage. The basic story of what came to be termed the Hukuang railways loan issue is not an unfamiliar one; other scholars have recounted its main events.[65] I would like to examine it more specifically from the position of Chang Chih-tung and his special interests in the effective national direction of railroad development.

There was of course ample reason for the central government to hope for the speedy construction of trunk railway lines through the major parts of the nation. The Peking-Hankow line had been completed in 1905, and its extension south to Canton and west into Szechuan, from Hankow, would complete the outline of a transportation-communications system which would enhance both the military capabilities and the prospects for economic development of the nation and the dynasty. Unfortunately, the central government was not able itself to capitalize such a huge project. Moreover, great parts of the as yet unbuilt lines were hedged about with loan concessions and other promises of participation previously given to various foreign powers. Finally, these railway lines had become particular objects of attention and emotion on the part of China's new public opinion and the provincial elite groups who were participating enthusiastically in the rights recovery movement; to these elements, anything short of complete Chinese control of the construction of the lines, and their own leading role, was anathema.

Chang Chih-tung was quite aware of the danger of railway development falling into limbo due to the unresolvable tension between the need for massive capitalization, the inability of the provincial groups to supply it, and the capability of the same groups nevertheless to block other methods of financing, especially a foreign loan, by their political protests. As I have recounted in the last chapter, Chang successfully used the provincial agitation in 1904–5 to improve China's position of rights on the Canton-Hankow line, only to see construction postponed because of the reluctance of the throne to fly in the face of the provincial groups by taking a British loan. It was necessary first to permit the provinces to attempt financing and construction on their own. Between 1905 and 1908, it became apparent to any objective observer that not only was far too little capital being raised by the three provinces with responsibilities for building sections of the line, but that even these small sums were being squandered in inefficient, uncoordinated, and competing activities. Already in early 1907 Chang recommended that Hunan's railway affairs could best be straightened out by imposing a single *kuan-tu shang-pan* (official supervision, merchant management) structure on the present diverse array of companies and groups claiming construction rights in the province.[66]

Significantly, it was to Chang that the throne turned when it finally moved to prod these two major rail lines toward realization in 1908. In June, 1908, after almost three years of negligible progress on the part of the provincial railway companies set up immediately after the redemption of the Canton-Hankow line, the throne directed the Ministry of Posts and Communications to send a team to inspect these companies.[67] Perhaps partly due to its report, and also at the request of Kiangsu Governor Ch'en Ch'i-t'ai that a respected individual be appointed to override local squabbles holding up railway development, on July 18 Chang Chih-tung was made director-general (*tu-pan ta-ch'en*) of the entire Canton-Hankow line, with authority over provincial officials and private groups alike on matters relating to the line.[68] There seems little doubt that the intention was that Chang would confront head-on and force into line any recalcitrant provincial groups as he worked out a development plan; the British consul picked up signs of apprehension among the leaders of Kwangtung's railway company within hours after the announcement of Chang's appointment.[69] Of course, Chang's previous predilection for taking a foreign loan to capitalize the line was well known, so his appointment itself was indirect indication that such a course would be followed, in spite of the desires of the provincial interests.

On October 28, 1908, Chang's authority to shape strategy for the Canton-Hankow line was further buttressed by a strong edict which affirmed his preeminence over all other officials on any matters relating to the railway, and charged him with bringing action against private gentry, merchants, or company directors who were engaged in practices detrimental to the best interests of the line as a whole.[70] At this same time, late October and early November, 1908, it was rumored that Chang was greatly determined to bring the provinces to heel behind his strategy of unified financing through a foreign loan, and that he planned personally to visit the southern provinces to work his will.[71] If he was so intending, this plan had to be laid aside due to the uncertainties and the great demands upon Chang after the death of the emperor and the empress dowager in mid-November, 1908. Nevertheless, Chang proceeded with his railway strategy. In early December he requested that representatives from Hunan and Hupeh come to Peking to discuss the matter of a foreign loan, and negotiations with the British began later that month.[72] Chang's scope of authority was broadened still more on December 28, 1908, when the prince regent appointed him director-general of the Hupeh portion of the Hankow-Szechuan rail line as well.[73]

Now Chang was in a position to realize his vision of establishing the foundation of a rational and coordinated national rail system by arranging for the next two crucial links in it, the lines from Hankow to Canton and to Szechuan, respectively. But to do so he would have to hold the disruptive provincial interest groups at bay while he negotiated a satisfactory loan from abroad. Had he been able to do the latter within several months, he might have been able to succeed, since it would be hard for the provincial groups to mobilize effective protests once loan terms favorable to China could be publicized, thus undercutting the accusation that a foreign loan per se compromised China's sovereignty.[74]

Unfortunately, a long negotiating process and, eventually, international rivalries doomed Chang's chances. He had assumed that it would be possible to deal with Britain alone, along the lines of his 1905 promise to Consul General Fraser at Hankow, and that the British would be willing to match the terms of the January, 1908, Tientsin-Pukou loan agreement, which were quite satisfactory to most informed Chinese. Indeed, Chang seems to have hoped that the negotiations would take only a few days and might be completed before the end of 1908.[75] This was not to be. The British banking interests involved held out for terms more onerous to China than Chang was willing to accept; Chang had to turn to a German bank for leverage; and the delay enabled France to insert herself into the negotiations as well. After some tortuous adjustments among those three parties, Chang was still able to sign a draft agreement with a consortium representing all three nations on June 6, 1909, now covering the Hankow-Szechuan as well as the Canton-Hankow line. At this point the entire edifice was toppled by the demand of the United States for an equal share of the multilateral loan rights.[76]

By mid-summer, 1909, all chance of a speedy conclusion to the loan negotiations was lost. Before China could work out a final agreement with the four powers, it was first necessary for the powers to sort out their own allocation of loan prerogatives and rights among themselves, and this was not done until 1910. Chang, his work ruined, was dismayed and disgusted at the course that events had taken. Chang was very hostile to the United States interjection, and had not President Taft taken the unusual step of a personal appeal to the prince regent on the subject, Chang might have insisted on rejecting American participation.[77] Chang was already very sick, and this further delay made it likely that he would not be able personally to carry through this last major assignment to its conclusion.

Even more serious, the delay called into question the likelihood of the loan ever going through in an acceptable manner, for it provided time in which opposition forces in the provinces could mobilize themselves against it. Chang seems to have been able to keep the provinces in line through the first half of 1909.[78] Moreover, the provincial elite groups were somewhat distracted during these months by the holding of elections and other preparations for the convening of the first provincial assemblies in the fall of 1909. Had the loan agreement been concluded during this time it might have stuck. But by September it was too late. Provincial opinion was focusing on the issue, especially in Hupeh, Hunan, and Kwangtung. As the provincial assemblies geared up for their opening sessions on October 14, they found the stalled Hukuang loan project an easy target. The manner in which successive foreign nations had interfered with the consortium gave to the whole affair an aura of rapaciousness which Chang and other officials could not dispel by pointing to specific terms since there were as yet no specific terms agreed upon. The protests against the Hukuang loan which began in earnest in the fall of 1909 would eventually escalate to a firestorm after the final agreement was signed in 1911, by which time no terms, however favorable to China, could have counteracted the political damage which had already been done to the dynasty through the long and faltering negotiations.

It was the impression of many observers at the time that the untimely death of Chang Chih-tung in early October, 1909, accelerated the provincial protests against the Hukuang loan. Jordan noted that Chang was the only man who could "control the turbulent spirits in Hunan and Hupeh"; with his passing, no one had the prestige and evenhandedness to prevent provincial opposition from arising.[79] With Chang's death, responsibility for the loan negotiations was taken over by the Ministry of Posts and Communications, under Hsü Shih-ch'ang, rather than being assigned to another special director-general. Jordan commented pessimistically upon the likelihood that Hsü could withstand the rising provincial protest movement as well as Chang could have.[80]

To my mind, the idea that Chang somehow could have put down or turned aside the growing provincial opposition to the whole Hukuang loan effort is a very misleading one. Had he lived, he undoubtedly would have been vilified by the provincial assemblies convening in mid-October, and may well have had to back off from his earlier aims. Indeed, even in his last few days, as he lay dying, it was rumored that a Peking censor was about to launch an attack on Chang for having run roughshod over provincial interests in his management of the loan negotiations.[81] Indeed, the failure to conclude the negotiations in a timely manner and on acceptable terms earlier in 1909 had probably already doomed the project, even had Chang lived to continue his personal direction of it. With a solid institutional forum now in the provincial assemblies, the gentry, merchants, and other provincial elite leaders who demanded from the dynasty ever increasing political, as well as economic, prerogatives, were not easily to be turned aside. Chang perceived this, even if the prince regent's regime as a whole did not.

Chang Chih-tung and the Politics of Dynastic Survival

In the last years of the dynasty, and especially after the passing of the Empress Dowager Tz'u-hsi in late 1908, the question of the central government's performance on a variety of specific reform measures gradually evolved into a more basic issue. That was the threatened loss of the intangible, yet crucial, aura of legitimacy and acceptance which underlies the continuity of all political regimes. By mid-1909, several months of government under the prince regent had created grave doubts among both domestic and foreign observers as to the perspicacity and leadership abilities of his regime. Chang Chih-tung finally came to share these doubts and died in October, 1909, rather pessimistic about the dynasty's future.

Chang's views on the exact course of action necessary for the central government to contain all the centrifugal elements which were tearing at the fabric of national political authority by 1909 were never specifically articulated. Indeed, there was probably no single action or set of policies which could be pointed to as necessary for the survival of the dynasty. In these last years, nuances were significant, and the general impression of good or bad faith in the intentions of the central government was all important.

Some felt that it would be an expression of sincere commitment to real reform and national progress, as well as a correction of past injustices, if Liang Ch'i-ch'ao and K'ang Yu-wei were permitted to return to China and given government posts. Liang and other leaders of the reform group, still based in Japan, clearly hoped for this. They tried to lend their influence to the task of overthrowing their accused betrayer of 1898, Yüan Shih-k'ai, both before and after the death of Tz'u-hsi, and in the process flirted with the idea of enlisting Chang Chih-tung as an ally; Liang may have written to Chang both in 1908 and in 1909.[82] But Chang was unresponsive, if Liang did in fact approach him; he passively acquiesced in, and perhaps personally requested, the prohibition of Liang's chief political organization, the Cheng-wen she, in August, 1908.[83] And in 1909, when the chief obstacle to the return of Liang and his associates, the empress dowager, was dead, Chang still held out against the reported eagerness of the prince regent to pardon the 1898 reformers and bring them back with honors.[84]

Liang, of course, never did make his way back into national politics before the fall of the dynasty in 1912.

Chang did not deem it necessary for the dynasty to engage in any dramatic but superficial displays of sincerity such as the rehabilitation of K'ang and Liang. Rather, he seemed to feel that steady, unspectacular progress in all the major affairs of state, foreign and domestic, if carried through in a spirit of impartiality and primary concern for the national welfare, would be evident to those who might suspect the competence and the sincerity of the government, and would win their adherence. Thus, while Chang certainly had his reservations about granting new rights of political participation to the nation's social elite, and wanted to prevent provincially oriented economic interests from disrupting a sensible overall plan of national economic development, nevertheless he showed great sensitivity to one particular issue which involved the ultimate motivations of the Manchu regime. This was the issue of continuing Manchu-Chinese racial distinctions, which existed on a number of levels from legal to informally political. At its most extreme, this issue posed the question of whether the dynasty was working first and foremost in the interests of the Chinese nation, or whether it was selfishly promoting mainly its own continued dominance as the ruling group. In the years before 1911 the overt manifestations of discrimination against Chinese were abolished. But the reform-minded Chinese provincial interest groups whose loyalty the dynasty in the last analysis had to retain, to say nothing of the revolutionary groups, remained highly suspicious of continuing covert forms of discrimination as evidence of dynastic contempt for their aspirations.

Already in 1903, Chang urged the empress dowager in an audience to abolish distinctions between the races.[85] In 1907, as noted, Chang expressed particular concern over this issue on the eve of his transfer to the Grand Council in Peking. A great many other officials and organs of public opinion were also advocating racial equality during 1907, and the throne did respond with a series of decrees in the late summer and fall of 1907 which provided for this.[86] Moreover, as the measures for China's constitutional system were promulgated, provisions were included to guard against racially based distinctions. Nevertheless, suspicions of Manchu intentions remained, and seemed to be lent substance by the high percentage of Manchus who were appointed to important office in Peking in the various measures of reorganization taken during these years; T'ieh-liang, among others, was especially singled out by critics as a major advocate of a policy of systematic discrimination against Chinese.[87]

From Chang Chih-tung's vantage point, this continuing suspicion of Manchu intentions was a dangerous phenomenon, because it compromised the integrity of the various reform measures under way. If the programs for political constitutionalism and economic development under way after 1907, many of which had centralizing tendencies, caused those centralizing features to be associated with suspected Manchu exclusiveness, the viability of the programs and of the dynasty itself would be called into question. As I have argued, the vigorous provincial assertiveness so evident during these years was not, in the view of Chang, to be uniformly embraced; it had to be constantly restrained and guided along acceptable paths. But neither could it be blithely ignored or dealt with in an arbitrary manner. There were forces of constraint now working on the central government as well, which it could ignore only at its peril.

Unfortunately, these concerns were not sufficiently appreciated by the regime of the prince regent in 1909 or thereafter. By July, 1909, Chang Chih-tung himself began to despair of the political acumen of the regent. That summer was not a pleasant one for Chang. In early June, he had finally achieved agreement with the three-power consortium on the Hukuang railways loan, only to be pushed back to the starting line by the American intrusion. In late June or early July, he began to have serious pain in his right side, the first major sign of the illness that would kill him; his doctors told him his liver was ailing. Chang's leading biographer describes his mood at this time as despondent, not only because of his illness but because of the aimless actions of the throne and the extensive employment of relatives of the imperial house and other Manchu nobles.[88] He fought against an edict of July 15 which concentrated military power in the hands of the regent by making him commander-in-chief of the army and navy, independent of the Ministry of War.[89]

On July 17 things seemed to come to a head. A censor had been criticizing the manager of the Tientsin-Pukou railway, Li Teshun, and its director, Lü Hai-huan, as well. At a Grand Council meeting that day, it was revealed that the Manchu clique around the prince regent had picked one of their number, Ts'ai-k'an, to succeed Lü. Chang protested that public opinion would not stand for this. Prince Ch'un sneered that these were merely the words of a member of the Chihli gentry. Chang repeated his protest, warning that the adverse reaction to an unqualified Manchu being named to such an important post might even approach rebellion. The regent replied coldly, "We have troops [*yu ping tsai*]." Chang withdrew, sighed, and said, "Who would have thought I would hear words indicating the collapse of the dynasty [*wang-kuo*]?"[90] On this same day he hemorrhaged quite badly, and three days later he submitted his request for a few days' leave from duties. He never took up regular Grand Council attendance again, although he kept watch on a few items of particular responsibility, such as the Hukuang railways loan; less than three months later he was dead. The dynasty limped on for over two more years, but one might argue that its fate had been adumbrated in the exchange recounted above.[91]

Conclusion

Having submitted a farewell memorial, Chang Chih-tung died a dignified death, surrounded by friends and family, on October 4, 1909.[1] He was extensively eulogized by both Chinese and foreigners, from the prince regent to most major newspapers and British Minister Jordan as well. The major themes of the tributes to Chang's long career were his unblemished reputation for honesty (all remarked that he was unique in not having enriched himself in office), and the great personal respect in which he was held for his scholarship, forthrightness, and integrity.[2] Within the next few months, several provincial officials from areas where Chang had served in the past submitted memorials of praise, and Wu Lu-chen, the former revolutionary student whom Chang had knowingly employed in 1902, now an army commander in north China, led a group who requested that a memorial shrine to Chang be erected in Wuchang.[3]

For my purposes in this study, Chang's significance has been in his functioning position within the overall late Ch'ing political structure and in the changing political life of the nation. Of those who had achieved high enough position to take an important part in the initial post-1895 reform movement, Chang was the sole major official who survived still to be playing a significant role as late as 1909. His career is thus in many ways an ideal one through which to gain a broad sense of the changes of the 1895–1911 period, as experienced and perceived from within the imperial bureaucracy. This study has provided some insights into the relations between a major central government official and several other sectors of the political scene, as well as into the manner in which more abstract forces like nationalism and reformism were beginning to work changes in China as a whole.

As I have stressed throughout, Chang Chih-tung's self-identity as a part of the central dynastic apparatus of government was basic. During the years covered, and especially after 1900, the central bureaucracy was extending its capabilities for initiative in reform, definition of goals, resource control, and program management. As a national bureaucrat, Chang Chih-tung welcomed and promoted these trends. However, he was aware of the need for the central government to proceed circumspectly with regard to other, nonbureaucratic participants on the political scene after 1900, and near the end of his life he showed apprehension at the disregard for the constraints of the time being shown by the regime of the prince regent, in particular its resurgent Manchu chauvinism. Chang was not blind to the defects of the dynasty, and at times doubtless wished that he had the power to purge the court of its sycophants and incompetents, but his loyalty to and identification with the center never wavered.[4]

Chang was also quite consistent in his relations with the nation's gentry class and its various emerging subsections after 1900. As part of the central government bureaucracy which was extending its reach into many new areas in pursuit of a national reform program, Chang, as he had even before 1895, viewed the local and provincial elite's particularistic interests with a jaundiced eye. He was always alert to the need for the central government to exert maximum control over these elite groups as reform programs involving them, especially the constitutional system, developed. As Chang seemed to sense, the same reform programs that enhanced central control also often provided openings for expanded elite activities as well, especially at the provincial level, and these activities might not be in the ultimate best interests of the center.[5] In view of what happened after 1911, Chang's long-standing reservations about elite self-interest being potentially destructive of dynastic, and indeed of all central authority, seem well founded.

In contrast to his great concern for the dangers of gentry or provincial elite power, Chang had relatively fewer worries about the modern student class and the revolutionary movement founded upon it. As Chang seemed to realize, to the extent that nationalism was a major motive of most of the student revolutionaries, they were open to cooptation by reformist or government forces which satisfied their desire to see a vigorous assertion of national energies. And to the extent that the great majority of them were of upper-class or gentry family background, upon their return to China they were susceptible to reabsorption by this dominant social, economic, and political class. This factor of upper-class background may have also been partly responsible for the generally poor showing made in their occasional attempts to join forces with the other end of the social spectrum, the secret societies. This combination of factors ultimately left the students as an ineffective revolutionary force.

Chang's concern for the dangers of revolution rose only when secret societies were involved. Chang always reacted very quickly to evidence of large-scale secret society activities and did not hesitate to use force, even terror, to quell unrest. Nevertheless, he did not view the societies in and of themselves as having the ability to topple the dynasty, only to cause chaos. He feared their power only in alliance with the leadership and organization that could be provided by the upper classes. Thus he reacted strongly when students and intellectuals seemed to be making progress in effectively linking their efforts to those of the secret societies. Then, as with the Tzu-li hui plot of 1900 and the P'ing-Liu-Li uprising of late 1906, he suppressed violently both student and lower-class rebels.

In the introduction, I postulated two large themes, reformism and nationalism, as dominant for the 1895–1911 period. I think that their omnipresence has been evident in the body of the study. However, on the basis of this examination of the career of Chang Chih-tung, there were two basic varieties of each of these themes. One was "bureaucratic," deriving from a viewpoint centered within the national government, and the other, less well defined but more extrabureaucratic in nature, was what might be called "provincial."

It is apparent that in the first decade after 1900, there was developing a significant degree of cohesion and integration of action at the provincial level. This was led mainly by the modern-minded members of the gentry class, the "modern provincial elite"

I have discussed in chapter 8. Such effective organization and action at this level was unheard of only a few years before; it was far beyond anything feasible in 1900, for example. Concentrated especially in the provincial capitals (where newspapers and the best modern schools, as well as the provincial assemblies after 1908, were also present), a real provincial consciousness emerged, taking the province as its natural scope of action.

Both these provincial forces and national bureaucrats like Chang Chih-tung were alike motivated by nationalism (chiefly in the form of anti-imperialism) and reformism. But the provincial varieties proved a nettlesome problem for Chang and the central government in their last years. To the extent that a potent nationalistic public opinion expressed itself after 1900, the central government could effectively utilize it to make headway against the foreign position in China, as Chang did in leading the recovery of the Canton-Hankow railway rights. And participation in national reform programs in education and other areas by important sectors of the gentry elite was essential to the success of these centrally sponsored programs. Yet, to the extent that nationalism and reformism coalesced and grew in provincial capitals, and paralleled the lines of emerging provincial social and economic interest groups, they tended actually to reinforce the gap between the newly activist central government and the provinces, which it naturally wished to control.

Chang Chih-tung's "bureaucratic" variety of these two elemental currents, although an understandable and indeed highly defensible outgrowth of his position and experience, was in the end insufficient. His bureaucratic reformism included a basic desire to implement new reform programs and to construct new institutions systematically, on a national basis. It therefore assumed an important component of central direction, and the primacy of the old imperial central structure over all the new power elements—reforming gentry, students, newspapers, provincial assemblies. The result was that many of these elements were alienated from the center, especially from 1909 onward, as Chang himself was aware at the end of his life.

Chang's bureaucratic nationalism was the natural result of his being a power holder, not a power seeker. It included a fairly realistic appraisal of China's resources and needs for some foreign capital and an appreciation of the limits to China's action within the bounds of the treaty system. I think that the story of Chang's relationships with foreigners as presented in this study shows that he was by no means a pushover for Western diplomats, much less a spokesman for foreign interests. Like some other officials after 1900, Chang was actually rather effective in dealing with foreigners and promoting China's interests. But Chang had to be concerned, for example, with building a national railway system, not with decrying imperialism in the abstract, and as a result he was willing to take foreign loans if the terms were right. And in the post-1900 period, all such associations with imperialism, no matter how realistic and necessary, were immediately suspect. The taint compromised Chang and the entire dynasty, and eventually made easier the final defection of various interest groups which ended the dynasty. The impossible demands of an aroused Chinese nationalism made a marvelous stick with which to beat the central authorities from 1909 to 1911.

One might argue that Chang Chih-tung's bureaucratic nationalism, in an era of China's abysmal weakness in the face of the power of imperialism, was in the end no more effective in halting imperialistic inroads than was the ranting of an emotional public opinion. The achievements of both were quite limited. It would be necessary to await the formation of a national political regime with a strong mass base before imperialism could begin to be rolled back. In this sense, both Chang, the bureaucratic nationalist, and the more vociferous provincial nationalists were limited by their basically elitist stance. They were cut off from the mass base upon which the Chinese Communist party eventually would build a real national strength.

However, Chang's bureaucratic reformism did not have the same practical implications as the reformist activities of his provincial counterparts. Again, both were equally elitist in the sense of not including a large percentage of citizens among those qualified to debate upon and administer reform programs. But Chang's was a centralizing elitism, always concerned with systematization, uniform national administration, and ultimately with the national welfare over that of any particular class. That of the provincial reformers was a decentralizing elitism, destructive not only of central power but eventually of national welfare, and increasingly after 1911 tied to the privileged interests of the nation's elite groups, urban and rural. In this sense, Chang's bureaucratic reformism is closer to the post-1949 stress on the elimination of elite class domination of local and provincial administration than was the rapacious interlude of 1911–49, during which there was no consistent countervailing central force preventing the aggrandizement of power by various elite groups all across the land. Chang Chih-tung was perhaps nowhere more prescient than in sensing the dangers of unrestrained pursuit of elite self-interest.

A final word seems in order on Chang Chih-tung as an individual figure in the broad sweep of Chinese history. As I said at the outset, I have no desire to make him bigger than life, better than he was, or more significant than good history warrants. I have not studied Chang for his own sake alone, but as a way of getting at some of the crucial issues of an important period of modern Chinese history. And yet, a basic concept of Confucianism has always been that the upright official is not a mere "utensil"; as he should be more than this to his ruler, so should he be to the historian as well. Chang Chih-tung, who was at the height of his career after 1895, and who remained one of the pillars of the central government until his death in 1909, has enabled me to make a somewhat different cross section of late Ch'ing political life than could have otherwise been achieved. But he has also provided us with an example of one of the most important products of the traditional Chinese political system, the civilized scholar-statesman. In his energy, in his unflagging loyalty to the dynasty, and in his broad interests and abilities, Chang embodied the best qualities of the Confucian public servant. Yet in his willingness to move with the times, to become an insistent if always a moderate reform spokesman, and to show the sensitivities of modern Chinese national pride as well as traditional cultural pride, Chang also manifested the depth to which the forces of history were beginning to touch China early in the twentieth century.

Abbreviations

CC	*Chang Wen-hsiang-kung ch'üan-chi* [Complete works of Chang Chih-tung], ed. Wang Shu-t'ung. 6 vols., 229 *chüan*. Taipei, 1963.
FO	Public Record Office, London. Files under Foreign Office.
HHKM	*Hsin-hai ko-ming* [The 1911 Revolution], ed. Ch'ai Te-keng, et al. 8 vols. Shanghai, 1957.
Hsü *nien-p'u*	Hsü T'ung-hsin, *Chang Wen-hsiang-kung nien-p'u* [Chronological biography of Chang Chih-tung]. Taipei, 1969.
KKWH	*Chung-hua min-kuo k'ai-kuo wu-shih-nien wen-hsien* [Documents on the fiftieth anniversary of the founding of the Republic of China], ed. Chung-hua min-kuo k'ai-kuo wu-shih-nien wen-hsien pien-tsuan wei-yüan-hui [Committee on the compilation of documents on the fiftieth anniversary of the founding of the Republic of China]. Vols. 1–. Taipei, 1963–.
Kuo T'ing-i	*Chin-tai Chung-kuo shih-shih jih-chih* [Daily record of events in modern Chinese history]. 2 vols. Taipei, 1963.
NCH	*North China Herald* (weekly, Shanghai).
PRO	Public Record Office, London. Files under Public Record Office.
WHPF	*Wu-hsü pien-fa* [The reform movement of 1898], ed. Chien Po-tsan, et al. 4 vols. Shanghai, 1953.

Notes

Introduction

1. For a representative statement of the theory, see the long introduction by Franz Michael to Stanley Spector, *Li Hung-chang and the Huai Army: A Study in Nineteenth-Century Chinese Regionalism* (Seattle, 1964). Also Michael's earlier study, "Military Organization and Power Structure of China During the Taiping Rebellion," *Pacific Historical Review* 18 (1949): 469–83.
2. See my article, "The Nature of Provincial Political Authority in Late Ch'ing Times: Chang Chih-tung in Canton, 1884–1889," *Modern Asian Studies* 4.4 (1970): 325–47; David Pong, "The Income and Military Expenditure of Kiangsi Province in the Last Years (1860–1864) of the Taiping Rebellion," *Journal of Asian Studies* 26.1 (November 1966): 49–65; Kwang-Ching Liu, "Li Hung-chang in Chihli: The Emergence of a Policy, 1870–1875," in Albert Feuerwerker et al., eds., *Approaches to Modern Chinese History* (Berkeley and Los Angeles, 1967), pp. 68–104, and "The Limits of Regional Power in the Late Ch'ing Period: A Reappraisal," *The Tsing Hua Journal of Chinese Studies*, n.s. 10.2 (1974): 207–23; Stephen R. MacKinnon, "The Peiyang Army, Yüan Shih-k'ai and the Origins of Modern Chinese Warlordism," *Journal of Asian Studies* 32.3 (May 1973): 405–23.
3. Kenneth E. Folsom, *Friends, Guests and Colleagues: The Mu-fu System in the Late Ch'ing Period* (Berkeley and Los Angeles, 1968), who is concerned mainly with Li Hung-chang; Spector also analyzes Li's case, of course. Jonathan Porter, *Tseng Kuo-fan's Private Bureaucracy* (Berkeley, 1972). I deal with Chang Chih-tung's *mu-fu* in "Chang Chih-tung in Canton, 1884–1889," pp. 339–40.
4. All of the sources in note 2 demonstrate this for some particular official and area of activity.
5. Perhaps something much like rationalization and centralization of political power within the *han* during the Tokugawa period indirectly contributed to effective national action in the Meiji state. See John W.

Hall, "The Nature of Traditional Society," in R. Ward and D. Rostow, eds., *Political Modernization in Japan and Turkey* (Princeton, 1964), pp. 14–41; also his "Feudalism in Japan—a Reassessment," *Comparative Studies in Society and History* 5 (1962): 1–51, especially 45–51.

6. Philip A. Kuhn, *Rebellion and Its Enemies in Late Imperial China: Militarization and Social Structure, 1796–1864* (Cambridge, 1970), pp. 183–88.
7. See the development by Joseph R. Levenson, *Confucian China and Its Modern Fate,* vol. II, *The Problem of Monarchical Decay* (Berkeley and Los Angeles, 1964), pp. 25–73; also Albert Feuerwerker's analysis in Ping-ti Ho and Tang Tsou, eds., *China in Crisis,* vol. I, book 1 (Chicago, 1968), pp. 179–93, where he looks at this dichotomy in terms of "Polity I" and "Polity II."
8. Kuhn, passim. This is an extremely significant work, perhaps the most important one among the recent literature for understanding the problem of the political "center of gravity," as I have put it.

Chapter 1

1. For accounts of his career, see Hsü *nien-p'u,* the basic biography; Hu Chün, *Chang Wen-hsiang-kung (Chih-tung) nien-p'u* [Chronological biography of Chang Chih-tung], *Chin-tai Chung-kuo shih-liao ts'ung-k'an* [A compendium of historical materials on modern China], ed. Shen Yün-lung, vol. 47 (Taipei, n.d.), which is based on Hsü *nien-p'u;* William Ayers, *Chang Chih-tung and Educational Reform in China* (Cambridge, 1971); Meribeth E. Cameron, "The Public Career of Chang Chih-tung, 1837–1909," *Pacific Historical Review* 7.3 (September 1938): 187–210; Cameron's contribution to Arthur W. Hummel, ed., *Eminent Chinese of the Ch'ing Period* (Washington, D.C., 1943), pp. 27–32; Li Kuo-chi, *Chang Chih-tung te wai-chiao cheng-ts'e* [Chang Chih-tung's foreign policy] (Taipei, 1970); Chang Ping-to, *Chang Chih-tung p'ing-chuan* [The life of Chang Chih-tung] (Taipei, 1972).
2. Hao Yen-p'ing, "A Study of the Ch'ing-liu Tang: The 'Disinterested' Scholar-Official Group (1875–1884)," *Papers on China* 16 (1962): 40–65; also Lloyd Eastman, "Ch'ing-i and Chinese Policy Formation During the Nineteenth Century," *Journal of Asian Studies* 24.4 (August 1965): 595–612.
3. Bays, "Chang Chih-tung in Canton, 1884–1889," pp. 335–37; Thomas L. Kennedy, "Chang Chih-tung and the Struggle for Strategic Industrialization: The Establishment of the Hanyang Arsenal, 1884–1895," *Harvard Journal of Asiatic Studies* 33 (1973): 156–63.
4. For two sound accounts of this incident, see Li Kuo-chi, *Chung-kuo tsao-ch'i te t'ieh-lu ching-ying* [Early railroad enterprise in China] (Nankang, Taiwan, 1961), pp. 74–85, and Wu To, "Chin-t'ung t'ieh-lu te cheng-i" [The dispute over the Tientsin-Tungchow railroad],

Chung-kuo chin-tai ching-chi shih yen-chiu chi-k'an [Researches in modern Chinese economic history] 4.1 (May 1936): 67–132.

The Peking-Hankow Railroad was not seriously begun until 1896, however. After the initial two million-tael appropriation of 1889, which actually went into the Hanyang Ironworks to make rails for the railroad, later monies were given to Li Hung-chang to build a line north from Tientsin into Manchuria, as the court became more worried about Russian moves there. Li Kuo-chi, p. 85.

5. Li Han-chang, elder brother of Li Hung-chang but not very vigorous, was governor-general at Canton from 1889 to 1895, and also acting governor of Kwangtung, 1889–92. Kang-i was governor, 1892–94. Li's refusal to continue Chang's fledgling industrial projects in 1889–90 is some indication of his level of interest. Later, Li's administration in general was lethargic, and it seems that Kang-i actually closed down the Canton military academy and tied up the new flotilla of gunboats at the docks. See Harold Z. Schiffrin, *Sun Yat-sen and the Origins of the Chinese Revolution* (Berkeley and Los Angeles, 1968), p. 92. A newspaper which Kuang Ch'i-chao, a member of Chang's *mu-fu,* began in 1886 also expired after it ran afoul of Li Han-chang in 1891; Roswell S. Britton, *The Chinese Periodical Press 1800–1912* (Shanghai, 1933), p. 103.
6. For the mill, James Morrell, "Two Early Chinese Cotton Mills," *Papers on China* 21 (1968): 43–98 (be careful of footnotes, they are not properly aligned with citation numbers in the text). For the arsenal, Wang Erh-min, *Ch'ing-chi ping-kung-yeh ti hsing-ch'i* [The rise of the munitions industry in late Ch'ing times] (Nankang, Taiwan, 1963), pp. 93–103, and Thomas L. Kennedy, "Chang Chih-tung and the Struggle for Strategic Industrialization." For the ironworks, Albert Feuerwerker, "China's Nineteenth-Century Industrialization: The Case of the Hanyehping Coal and Iron Company, Limited," in C. D. Cowan, ed., *The Economic Development of China and Japan* (London, 1964), p. 79; a rich source of materials on the early years of the ironworks is Sun Yü-t'ang et al., eds., *Chung-kuo chin-tai kung-yeh-shih tzu-liao, ti-i-chi, 1840–1895 nien* [Materials on the history of modern industry in China, first collection, 1840–1895] (Peking, 1957), II, 743–892.
7. Bays, "Chang Chih-tung in Canton, 1884–1889," pp. 331–32, 343–44.
8. Ayers, pp. 28–29, 70–74, describes these two incidents.
9. Lloyd Eastman, *Throne and Mandarins: China's Search for a Policy During the Sino-French Controversy 1880–1885* (Cambridge, 1967), pp. 103–4.
10. Hsiao Kung-ch'üan, "Weng T'ung-ho and the Reform Movement of 1898," *Tsing Hua Journal of Chinese Studies,* n.s. 1.2 (April 1957): 120–22.
11. Hsü *nien-p'u,* pp. 84–85. On August 19, Governor Wu Ta-ch'eng of Hunan received permission to lead a body of troops to the north, and other units were sent from Hu-kuang in September and October.

12. The edict was in response to a memorial by Hsü Shih-ch'ang, then a compiler in the Hanlin Academy. Chang's biographer quotes Weng T'ung-ho's diary to the effect that Hsü's request was indeed a result of Chang's overbearing generosity with his advice on war strategy; the implication is that Chang was to be neutralized by making him an adviser on war policy. Hsü *nien-p'u,* p. 85. See Shao Hsün-cheng et al., eds., *Chung-Jih chan-cheng* [The Sino-Japanese War of 1894–1895] (Shanghai, 1956), V, 1–150, for Chang's voluminous telegrams. Also *CC,* 76:1–8b; most of the latter were addressed jointly to the Tsungli yamen and Li Hung-chang in Tientsin.
13. Hsü *nien-p'u,* p. 85. See *CC,* 34: 21–28b, 35:1–26.
14. Hsü *nien-p'u,* p. 85. It is difficult to determine whether Chang was really sick; whether he delayed his departure in October for political reasons, hoping to avoid going to Peking; or whether his presence in Hupeh really was necessary for the completion of various duties—e.g., he may not have trusted Governor T'an to carry on as he would have liked.
15. Kuo T'ing-i, pp. 889–90. Tz'u-hsi may well have been upset by the humiliating defeats suffered by the Chinese forces in Manchuria, which cast a pall over her approaching birthday festivities.
16. Hsü *nien-p'u,* pp. 86, 89. This and later edicts also approved Chang's plans for expansion of the arsenal and textile mill in Hupeh; Kuo T'ing-i, p. 894.
17. Hsü *nien-p'u,* p. 89; Kuo T'ing-i, p. 894. This preeminent role in defense matters in central and south China permitted Chang to play an important part in events on Taiwan in the spring of 1895. See Harry J. Lamley, "The 1895 Taiwan Republic," *Journal of Asian Studies* 27.4 (August 1968): 739–62.
18. Li lost his most important posts, those of Chihli governor-general and Northern Trade Commissioner, on February 12, 1895.
19. Edward Le Fevour, *Western Enterprise in Late Ch'ing China* (Cambridge, 1968), pp. 126–28. Keswick hired Rev. Timothy Richard to see Chang at Nanking and learn what he could of his plans, or at least Richard sent him intelligence reports gratis.
20. Feuerwerker, "The Case of the Hanyehping Coal and Iron Company, Limited," p. 87. Thomas L. Kennedy, "The Kiangnan Arsenal 1895–1911: The Decentralized Bureaucracy Responds to Imperialism," *Ch'ing-shih wen-t'i* 2.1 (October 1969): 21–25. Proponents of the regionalism theory could of course point to both of these as examples of Chang strengthening his own Hupeh power base.
21. Kuo T'ing-i, p. 903; Hsü *nien-p'u,* p. 92. See Ayers, pp. 105–6, for a concise list of these schools.
22. Before the end of 1895, he had even sent foreign engineers to survey the lower Yangtze lines, and before he left Nanking had arranged for tentative official financing of these lines. Hsü *nien-p'u,* pp. 93, 96, 99.

23. It is quite likely that Liu was largely responsible for blocking the investigation of the Kiangnan Arsenal. Kennedy, "The Kiangnan Arsenal," pp. 25–26.
24. Ralph L. Powell, *The Rise of Chinese Military Power, 1895–1912* (Princeton, 1955), pp. 60–68; Hsü *nien-p'u,* p. 99. Chang did take back a few of the German officers to begin a troop training program in Wuchang; Powell, p. 69.
25. Hsü *nien-p'u,* pp. 90–91. *CC, chüan* 36–37, 77–78, passim.
26. Hsü *nien-p'u,* p. 94. It seems that this did silence him for awhile. There was a hiatus in his transmission of telegraphed memorials for over a month, from September 22 to October 29, and a later gap in his regular memorials, from October 26 to December 27. Hsü *nien-p'u,* p. 94, also quotes Weng T'ung-ho, who at one point in his diary during the autumn noted with surprise that no telegraphed word from Chang had been received for over thirty days.
27. Kennedy, "The Kiangnan Arsenal," pp. 25–26.
28. Hsü *nien-p'u,* pp. 94–95, 100–101; Feuerwerker, "The Case of the Hanyehping Coal and Iron Company, Limited," pp. 87–88.
29. The *wei-hsing* lottery involved betting on the surnames of examination candidates. It seems to have been an especially popular pastime among Cantonese. The lotteries were originally licensed in 1885 to help pay the debts of the Sino-French War.
30. Bays, "Chang Chih-tung in Canton, 1884–1889," p. 341.
31. Ayers, pp. 61, 125.
32. Ibid., p. 61.
33. Public Record Office, London, Foreign Office (F.O.) 228/889, Consul Gardner to Minister Walsham, September 2, 1890. Also Wesleyan Methodist Missionary Society Archives, London, letter from Samuel Barber, July 19, 1890.
34. Hsü *nien-p'u,* pp. 78–83, has extensive coverage of this entire incident, including full quotes of all the memorials and reports involved. It is worth noting that Hsü Chih-hsiang had attacked Chang at least once before. This was in 1884, when it was rumored that Chang planned to build a railroad for the Shansi coal mines. Hsü, then a sub-chancellor of the Grand Secretariat, vilified both the plan and Chang. Li Kuo-chi, *Chung-kuo tsao-ch'i te t'ieh-lu ching-ying,* p. 76.
35. Chao had also been a member of Chang's staff in Canton, and accompanied him to Hupeh in 1889.

Chapter 2

1. Lloyd E. Eastman shows that some such ideas were current before 1894, though he probably overstates his case. "Political Reformism in China Before the Sino-Japanese War," *Journal of Asian Studies* 27.4 (August 1968): 695–710.

2. For K'ang Yu-wei's version of these events, see his autobiography translated in Lo Jung-pang, ed., *K'ang Yu-wei: A Biography and a Symposium* (Tucson, 1967), pp. 63–66. Further references to "K'ang's autobiography" are taken from this translation. Chang sent many telegrams to Peking in April and early May of 1895, counseling rejection of Japan's demands; Kuo T'ing-i, pp. 913–17.
3. K'ang's autobiography, p. 69. It seems clear that the newssheet was separate from the Ch'iang-hsüeh hui in origin, though Liang Ch'i-ch'ao later seems to have fused the two in his memory (Lo Jung-pang, ed., *K'ang Yu-wei,* p. 153, n. 33). The two were for practical purposes merged by autumn.
4. Basic sources on the Ch'iang-hsüeh hui are K'ang's autobiography, p. 72; Ts'ai Erh-k'ang's comments in his annotated translation of Young J. Allen's work entitled *Chung-tung chan-chi pen-mo* [A full account of the war between China and Japan], excerpts from *WHPF,* IV, 386–87; and a fairly complete membership list in T'ang Chih-chün, ed., *Wu-hsü pien-fa jen-wu chuan-kao* [Draft biographies of persons in the 1898 reforms], 2 vols. (Peking, 1961), pp. 339–41.
5. Liang Ch'i-ch'ao, in his *Wu-hsü cheng-pien-chi* [Account of the 1898 coup d'etat]; *WHPF,* IV, 395–96. An apparently more complete list of societies alone appears in T'ang Chih-chün, pp. 335–38. Also see the classified list of societies in Wang Erh-min, *Wan-Ch'ing cheng-chih ssu-hsiang shih-lun* [Essays on late Ch'ing political thought] (Nankang, Taiwan, 1969), p. 135 ff.
6. *WHPF,* IV, 395–96. K'ang's autobiography, p. 73; Hummel, p. 855.
7. Ts'ai Erh-k'ang, pp. 386–87, and K'ang's autobiography, p. 74. Members are also listed in T'ang Chih-chün, pp. 342–43.
8. This organization, complete with two periodical publications, was founded in March, 1896; Sun Chia-nai was the director. It never achieved the stature of its predecessor, however. Kuo T'ing-i, pp. 944–47; Britton, *The Chinese Periodical Press,* p. 103.
9. The best description of the original "statecraft" collection in English is Frederic Wakeman, "The Huang-ch'ao ching-shih wen-pien," *Ch'ing-shih wen-t'i* 1.10 (February 1969): 8–22. For a description of editions put out after 1895, see the bibliography in *WHPF,* IV, 574–75. For missionary writings, see Wang Shu-huai, *Wai-jen yü wu-hsü pien-fa* [Foreigners and the 1898 reforms] (Nankang, Taiwan, 1965), pp. 112–15.
10. Though Chang's preface is dated late summer, the collection itself did not appear until near the end of the year.
11. John Schrecker has characterized the dominant pre-1894 attitude toward foreign policy as the "mainstream" approach. "The Reform Movement, Nationalism, and China's Foreign Policy," *Journal of Asian Studies* 29.1 (November 1969): 43–53.
12. Benjamin Schwartz has referred to this often neglected aspect of tradi-

tional ideology as "muscular Confucianism." *In Search of Wealth and Power: Yen Fu and the West* (Cambridge, 1964), p. 15.

13. Schrecker, "The Reform Movement," pp. 50–52.
14. Richard C. Howard, "Introduction" to "The Chinese Reform Movement of the 1890's: A Symposium," *Journal of Asian Studies* 29.1 (November 1969): 12–13; John Schrecker, "The Reform Movement of 1898 and the *Ch'ing-i:* Reform as Opposition," in *Reform in Nineteenth-Century China,* ed. Paul A. Cohen and John E. Schrecker (Cambridge, 1976), pp. 289–305.
15. Hao Chang, *Liang Ch'i-ch'ao and Intellectual Transition in China, 1890–1907* (Cambridge, 1971), p. 122, has some very perceptive comments here.
16. See Frederic Wakeman, Jr., "The Price of Autonomy: Intellectuals in Ming and Ch'ing Politics," *Daedalus* 101.2 (Spring 1972): 56–60. He argues that the study societies from 1895 to 1898 were for the most part nonissue oriented, stressing arousal of the elite's energies, and focusing on Peking and "national" connections. After 1900, however, they developed real local foci, both in issues and organization, which put them outside the old Peking-centered political structure and its assumptions.
17. Kuo T'ing-i, vol. II, appendix, p. 60. K'ang's autobiography, p. 72, claims that at the organizing dinner for the Ch'iang-hsüeh hui, Shen Tseng-chih nominated Chang Hsiao-ch'ien just because of his intimacy with Li Hung-tsao. Also see Hsü *nien-p'u,* p. 116.
18. For a short biography of Liang Ting-fen through 1898 see T'ang Chih-chün, pp. 256–60. For Chang's recommendations, *CC,* 38:11b–15b.
19. K'ang's autobiography, p. 43. K'ang says he declined the offer because "some people" spoke against him.
20. Noted in Schrecker, "The Reform Movement," p. 51.
21. It is interesting that in 1900 Li Ping-heng would become one of the most zealous Boxer supporters, fighting to his death against the allied forces advancing on Peking, while Chang Chih-tung did his utmost to limit the Boxer calamity to the north. Thus, although Li and Chang represent two of the strands of "militant" foreign policy after 1895 (and it is significant that K'ang grouped them together in 1895), the events of 1900 show what different practical results ensued.
22. Onogawa Hidemi, *Shimmatsu seiji shisō kenkyū* [Studies in late Ch'ing political thought] (Kyoto, 1969), p. 122.
23. K'ang's autobiography, pp. 72–73, 153 n. 35; Ts'ai Erh-k'ang, in *WHPF,* IV, 386.
24. This list is in T'ang Chih-chün, pp. 342–43. The eleven included: Liang Ting-fen and Ch'en Pao-ch'en of his *mu-fu;* Huang Tsun-hsien, recently of Chang's *mu-fu* and soon to play an important role in the Hunan reform movement; Huang T'i-fang (an original *ch'ing-liu* parti-

san, recommended by Chang in 1895) and his two sons, Huang Shao-chi and Huang Shao-ti; Wang K'ang-nien, former tutor to Chang's grandsons and teacher in schools sponsored by Chang; and Tsou Tai-chün, Chih-chün (the only Manchu member in either Peking or Shanghai), Li Shu-ch'ang, and K'uai Kuang-tien, all four of whom Chang recommended in memorials between 1895 and 1898. *CC,* 38:11b–15b, 42:13–16b; *WHPF,* I, 391–92.

The "probables" were Liang Ch'i-ch'ao (who is not included in this Shanghai membership list—he was then still in Peking), T'u Jen-shou, a Hupeh censor associated with the *ch'ing-liu* group in Peking in the 1880's, and Ch'en San-li, son of Governor Ch'en Pao-chen of Hunan, who was highly regarded by Chang.

A total of ten of the individuals specifically recommended by Chang in memorials from 1895 to 1898 were members of one of the Ch'iang-hsüeh hui units. For the contribution of 1,500 taels, see Hsü *nien-p'u,* p. 96.

25. K'ang's autobiography, p. 74.
26. Ibid.
27. *P'u-t'ien chung-fen chi,* 9:3–7; the preface is on 9:3 alone. Note that this is separate from the preface to the collection as a whole which Chang wrote several months before publication, in the late summer of 1895.
28. The editors of the *WHPF* collection state that the preface here ascribed to Chang was actually written by K'ang, although they offer no specific evidence to support this claim. *WHPF,* IV, 385–86.
29. K'ang's autobiography, p. 74. For K'ang's ideology, the various writings of Hsiao Kung-ch'üan are basic. "K'ang Yu-wei and Confucianism," *Monumenta Serica* 18 (1959): 96–212; "The Philosophical Thought of K'ang Yu-wei: An Attempt at a New Synthesis," ibid., 24 (1965): 1–83; "K'ang Yu-wei's Excursion into Science," in Lo Jung-pang, ed., *K'ang Yu-wei,* pp. 375–407.
30. The best general account of the paper is in Chang P'eng-yüan, *Liang Ch'i-ch'ao yü Ch'ing-chi ko-ming* [Liang Ch'i-ch'ao and the late Ch'ing revolution] (Nankang, Taiwan, 1964), pp. 257–73. Also see Britton, pp. 91–92, and Lo Jung-pang's note in K'ang's autobiography, pp. 162–63.
31. T'ang Chih-chün, pp. 90, 249.
32. Both translations from Britton, pp. 88–89, 99–101. Also see Hao Chang, p. 107.
33. *WHPF,* IV, 547–48. At four silver dollars (*yüan*) per annual subscription, this amounted to a yearly sum of 1,152 *yüan,* of which Chang forwarded half in advance as payment for the remainder of 1896. The newspaper had fund raisers in several cities of central and north China. Those in Hupeh were Wang Ping-en and Yeh Han, both either members of Chang's *mu-fu* or very well acquainted with him. The

names of ten other fund raisers in various places are in T'ang Chih-chün, p. 354.

34. Chang P'eng-yüan, *Liang Ch'i-ch'ao,* pp. 268–71, has laudatory quotes from these and several other officials who subscribed to the *Shih-wu pao;* also see *WHPF,* IV, 549–51.

 The *Chih-hsin pao,* published in Macao beginning in 1897 by a group of K'ang Yu-wei's followers, including his brother Kuang-jen, also attracted this kind of support from several officials; *WHPF,* IV, 552–53, 555–56.

35. See Joseph Pittau, S.J., *Political Thought in Early Meiji Japan* (Cambridge, 1967).

36. As early as 1895, Chang protested T'ang Ching-sung's use of the related term *min-chu* during the time of the short-lived "Taiwan Republic"; see Lamley, "The 1895 Taiwan Republic," pp. 747, 757–58.

37. Translated in Ssu-yu Teng and John K. Fairbank, *China's Response to the West: A Documentary Survey 1839–1923* (Cambridge, 1954), p. 168.

38. *CC,* 202:23b–24. The first of the four points is mentioned in the translated excerpt in Teng and Fairbank, p. 167.

Chapter 3

1. Some of the contributors who first made a name for themselves in its pages were Chang Ping-lin, Mai Meng-hua, Hsü Ch'in, and Ou Ch'ü-chia. For the statistics quoted, see Chang P'eng-yüan, *Liang Ch'i-ch'ao,* pp. 266–67.

2. For a short biography of Wang (1860–1911) to 1898, see T'ang Chih-chün, pp. 90–93. Also *Wang Jang-ch'ing (K'ang-nien) hsien-sheng: chuan-chi, i-wen* [A biography and writings of Wang K'ang-nien], ed. Wang I-nien, in *Chin-tai Chung-kuo shih-liao ts'ung-k'an,* ed. Shen Yün-lung, vol. 5 (Taipei, 1967).

 The article is in *WHPF,* III, 147–49. For the incident, see T'ang Chih-chün, pp. 90–91.

3. T'ang Chih-chün, p. 91.

4. Ibid., pp. 92–93, 256–57.

5. Onogawa Hidemi, pp. 148–49; John Schrecker, "The Pao-Kuo Hui: A Reform Society of 1898," *Papers on China* 14 (1960): 58.

6. T'ang Chih-chün, p. 91.

7. K'ang's autobiography, p. 108. There was a precedent here. On June 28, the Shanghai Translation Bureau (I-shu-chü), first founded by Liang Ch'i-ch'ao, had been nationalized; it was now the I-shu kuan-chü; Kuo T'ing-i, p. 1007.

8. Sun's July memorial translated in Britton, pp. 103–4. K'ang's autobiography, p. 108; Onogawa Hidemi, p. 148. This last move was apparently a maneuver by K'ang's enemies to get him out of Peking, a scheme to which Sun Chia-nai may have been a party.

9. Liang's essay appeared in a September issue of the *Chih-hsin pao* in Macao. Both Wang's and Liang's arguments are reprinted in full in Chang P'eng-yüan, *Liang Ch'i-ch'ao,* pp. 257–60.
10. K'ang's autobiography, p. 113; T'ang Chih-chün, p. 91; *CC,* 156:22b–23b.
11. Lo Jung-pang's note in K'ang's autobiography, pp. 136–37.
12. The best overall account of the Hunan reforms is Onogawa Hidemi, "Bojutsu hempō to Konanshō" [Hunan province and the 1898 reforms], in *Shimmatsu seiji shisō kenkyū,* pp. 181–223. Charlton Lewis has produced the best works in English: "The Reform Movement in Hunan (1896–1898)," *Papers on China* 15 (1961): 62–90; "The Opening of Hunan" (Ph.D. diss., University of California, 1965), chap. 2, pp. 46–86; "The Hunanese Elite and the Reform Movement, 1895–1898," *Journal of Asian Studies* 29.1 (November 1969): 35–42.
13. This last point is made by Lewis, "The Hunanese Elite," p. 37.
14. The text of Chang's announcement, which was printed in the *Hsiang-hsüeh pao* is in *WHPF,* IV, 554–55. Chang had privately telegraphed Chiang Piao and Ch'en Pao-chen to express these concerns; Hsü *nien-p'u,* p. 116.
15. *WHPF,* IV, 555.
16. Onogawa Hidemi, pp. 207–8.
17. Lewis, "The Reform Movement in Hunan," pp. 71–77, and "The Hunanese Elite," pp. 37–38. Huang Tsun-hsien, like K'ang Yu-wei and Liang Ch'i-ch'ao a Cantonese, probably first suggested Liang for this post, as Lewis states. Also see Hao Chang, p. 124.
18. Onogawa Hidemi, pp. 208–9. The articles by Hsü ran from no. 28 through no. 33 (February 21–April 11, 1898).
19. Onogawa Hidemi, pp. 193–200, has a good description here, as does Hao Chang, pp. 125–26.
20. See Lewis, "The Hunanese Elite," pp. 38–39.
21. See Onogawa Hidemi, p. 211. The Hunanese leadership is apparent from the lists in P'i Hsi-jui's biography, *WHPF,* IV, 192–94. I Nai's ideas here seem much like K'ang Yu-wei's vision of the future world utopia, or *ta-t'ung,* as yet unpublished at the time.
22. *WHPF,* IV, 193–95.
23. Wang Erh-min, *Wan-Ch'ing cheng-chih ssu-hsiang shih-lun,* chap. 5; Frederic Wakeman, Jr., "The Price of Autonomy," pp. 57–60; also see the description by Kwang-Ching Liu, "Nineteenth-Century China: The Disintegration of the Old Order and the Impact of the West," in Ping-ti Ho and Tang Tsou, eds., *China in Crisis,* vol. I, book 1 (Chicago, 1968), p. 158.
24. Lewis, "The Hunanese Elite"; this is the major point of his entire article. P'i Hsi-jui, for example, underwent very abusive treatment at the hands of Yeh Te-hui, an arrogant young reactionary; *WHPF,* IV, 195.

25. Lewis contrasts the speech made by Governor Ch'en at the founding of the Shih-wu hsüeh-t'ang, in which he emphasized the need to preserve a solid Confucian foundation in learning, with the iconoclasm which was soon forthcoming; "The Hunanese Elite," p. 37.
26. *WHPF,* II, 609–10.
27. Ibid., p. 609.
28. Onogawa Hidemi, p. 211. A total of twelve of the twenty-four sections of the work were printed in the paper.
29. Ibid., pp. 149–50, 212.
30. T'ang Chih-chün, p. 252; Hu Pin, *Wu-hsü pien-fa* [The reforms of 1898] (Shanghai, 1956), p. 67.
31. Lewis, "The Hunanese Elite," p. 41. Liang Ting-fen is an interesting figure and might make a fascinating study. For a description of the denunciations he directed at K'ang Yu-wei and Liang Ch'i-ch'ao during 1898, see T'ang Chih-chün, pp. 259–60.
32. *WHPF,* IV, 442–44, 588. Unfortunately, little more data on the society, its members and activities seems available. For T'ang Chen's ideas, see Eastman, "Political Reformism in China Before the Sino-Japanese War," p. 703; also Yen-p'ing Hao, "Cheng Kuan-ying: The Comprador as Reformer," *Journal of Asian Studies* 29.1 (November 1969): 19.
33. Hsü *nien-p'u,* p. 113. The publisher of the "authorized" edition was Yüan Ch'ang, later to be one of the anti-Boxer martyrs of 1900, who was now a taotai in Anhui. A complete version of the work, including the introduction, is in *CC, chüan* 202–3. A rough translation is by Samuel I. Woodbridge, *China's Only Hope, An Appeal by Her Greatest Viceroy, Chang Chih-tung* (New York, 1900). A better translation is by Jerome Tobar, *Chang Chih-tung, K'iuen-hio p'ien; exhortations a l'etude* (Shanghai, 1909). Partial translation of five of the twenty-four essays is in Teng and Fairbank, *China's Response to the West,* pp. 166–74.
34. Hsü *nien-p'u,* p. 113.
35. Ayers, p. 148, discusses this. For the preface and a list of supporters of the journal, see *CC,* 213:11b–15b. One of the twelve men listed is Shen Tseng-chih, former close associate of K'ang Yu-wei in Peking in 1895, who now was apparently drifting away from K'ang. Shen would later be an adviser to Liu K'un-i at Nanking in 1900.
36. Ch'en Yen was associated with both of these. See selections on Ch'en in T'ang Chih-chün, p. 161, and *WHPF,* IV, 208. Chang's relationship with another paper, the *Han-pao* in Hankow, which existed from 1893 to 1900, is less clear; Britton, pp. 76–77.
37. Hsü *nien-p'u,* p. 116; T'ang (1857–1917), from an important Chekiang gentry family, was later an adviser to Liu K'un-i, then was a leader of the constitutionalist movement in the last years of the dynasty, and eventually became the first governor of Chekiang after the Revolution of 1911.

38. Ibid., p. 116; see note 36 above. Ch'en (1868–1937), from Foochow, was a friend of Lin Hsü, one of the "six martyrs" of 1898.
39. *WHPF,* IV, 554–55. Lo (1866–1940) was later a famous scholar, archaeologist, and bibliographer, and a supporter of the Japanese puppet state of Manchukuo in the 1930's; Howard Boorman, ed., *Biographical Dictionary of Republican China,* vol. II (New York, 1968), pp. 426–27.
40. Listed in *WHPF,* I, 391–92.
41. *CC,* 48:20b–22b.
42. For Ch'en's memorial, see Ming-Ch'ing tang-an kuan [Office of Ming and Ch'ing archives], ed., *Wu-hsü pien-fa tang-an shih-liao* [Archival historical materials on the 1898 reforms] (Peking, 1958), pp. 160–63. Chang's recommendations are those referred to in notes 40 and 41, above.
43. For an excellent discussion of the *Ch'üan-hsüeh p'ien's* educational system, and the educational reforms of the "100 days," see Ayers, pp. 152–89.
44. Hsü *nien-p'u,* p. 121. Huang Shao-chi's father, Huang T'i-fang, was one of the original *ch'ing-liu* group in the 1880's. After the edict of approval, the popularity of the work soared. One contemporary reported that within ten days after the July 25 edict, three different editions had appeared; Hu Pin, *Wu-hsü pien-fa,* p. 67.
45. T'ang Chih-chün, p. 251. Two minor deletions were stipulated in the edict, both in the essay *"Ming-kang,"* dealing with family relationships; these seem to have been apolitical.
46. Hsü *nien-p'u,* p. 121.
47. *WHPF,* II, 613.
48. Some of the standard sources for the "100 days" of reform and the coup are: K'ang's autobiography; Liang Ch'i-ch'ao, *Wu-hsü cheng-pien chi* [Record of the 1898 coup] (Taipei, 1958), parts of which also appear in *WHPF;* Meribeth E. Cameron, *The Reform Movement in China, 1898–1912* (Stanford, 1931), pp. 23–55; the excellent chronology by Kuo T'ing-i, pp. 1005–24, passim; the chronology in *WHPF,* IV, 557–72; also the recent and perceptive, though brief, account by Kwang-Ching Liu, "Nineteenth-Century China," pp. 161–68.
49. Hao Chang, "Liang Ch'i-ch'ao and Intellectual Changes in the Late Nineteenth Century," *Journal of Asian Studies* 29.1 (November 1969): 24.
50. For differences of emphasis among conservatives see Ch'en Ch'iao, "Wu-hsü cheng-pien-shih fan pien-fa jen-wu chih ssu-hsiang" [Political thought of those opposed to reform at the time of the 1898 coup], *Yen-ching hsüeh-pao* 25 (1939): 59–106.
51. This analysis from T'ang Chih-chün, pp. 49–57.
52. For Yang Jui and Yang Shen-hsiu, see Ayers, pp. 142–43; for Ch'en Yen, *WHPF,* IV, 207–8; for Ch'ien Hsün and Cheng Hsiao-hsü, Kuo

T'ing-i, pp. 1010, 1019, and *WHPF,* II, 614; for Ch'en Pao-ch'en, Hsü *nien-p'u,* pp. 121–22 (Ch'en never did go to Peking before the coup of September 21).

53. T'ang Chih-chün, p. 53.
54. Chang's biographer, after examination of Weng T'ung-ho's diary for this period, concludes that Chang's spring summons was due to the inability of Li Hung-chang and Chang Yin-huan to deal with the latest deluge of foreign demands for concessions; Chang, as usual, had been freely tendering his advice on these matters. Hsü *nien-p'u,* p. 117.

    Although I suspected it for a time, it is highly unlikely that Chang merely used the Sha-shih riot as an excuse to avoid going to Peking. The British consular files make it clear how this incident, occuring as it did at the height of concession grabbing, quickly escalated into demands for the opening of Hunan province, an unrelated and highly explosive issue. Chang truly had his hands full trying to keep the effects of the incident localized. FO 228/1276, Consul Warren to Minister MacDonald, several items May 10–August 16, 1898, passim.
55. Kuo T'ing-i, p. 1023; *WHPF,* II, 614, a telegram to Chang from Ch'ien Hsün in Peking.
56. Hsü *nien-p'u,* p. 122.
57. *WHPF,* II, 614–15, 648.
58. These from *WHPF,* II, 615, 648–49; Ayers, p. 145 n. Chang telegraphed Ch'ü T'ing-shao, the Hupeh judicial commissioner, then in Peking; Sheng Hsüan-huai; and even Jung-lu, the Manchu governor-general of Chihli and commander of all north China troops.
59. T'ang Chih-chün, p. 257.
60. It was here that Liang Ch'i-ch'ao made the crucial conceptual breakthrough to an appreciation of the possibilities of the collectivist-liberal Western style constitutional state. See Hao Chang, *Liang Ch'i-ch'ao and Intellectual Transition in China,* pp. 106–8.

Chapter 4

1. Lo Jung-pang's note in K'ang's autobiography, p. 172 n. 69; Lo gives no references for the total number purged.
2. Kuo T'ing-i, pp. 1027 ff., has the most convenient summary of the edicts of late 1898, culled from the *Shih-lu.*
3. This is also the interpretation of Hsiao Kung-ch'üan, "Weng T'ung-ho and the Reform Movement of 1898," pp. 189–92.
4. Issue of September 23, 1898, in *WHPF,* III, 324–26.
5. *WHPF,* III, 362–63.
6. See the *Shen-pao* of October 27, 1898, in *WHPF,* II, 641–43, and a reader's reaction to Liang's article on p. 645. A long essay by Liang, also dated October, is included in *Nihon Gaikō Bunshō* [Documents on Japanese Foreign Relations], vol. 31, pt. 1, pp. 729–34.

7. The *Shen-pao* review is in *WHPF,* III, 359–62.
8. For the cases of Chang and Huang, see Wang Shu-huai, *Wai-jen yü Wu-hsü pien-fa,* pp. 191–202.
9. Ibid., pp. 212–17.
10. Ibid., pp. 202–12.
11. Kuo T'ing-i, p. 1039; Li Chien-nung, *The Political History of China, 1840–1928,* trans. and ed. Ssu-yu Teng and Jeremy Ingalls (Princeton, 1956), pp. 170–71.
12. Wang Shu-huai, pp. 217–19; Li Chien-nung, pp. 171–72. Establishment of an heir apparent to Kuang-hsü's predecessor was an obvious step in his possible replacement, but it let the court gauge foreign reaction before proceeding further.
13. Hsü *nien-p'u,* p. 122. The consul general was Odagiri Masunosuke, with whom Chang had extensive communications in the last few months of 1898. His report of December 21, 1898, in *Nihon Gaikō Bunshō,* vol. 31, pt. 1, p. 725.
14. Hsü *nien-p'u,* p. 122; Kuo T'ing-i, pp. 1027–28; *WHPF,* II, 615–16. Chang let the police bureau survive, however, by changing its name to the traditional *pao-chia.*
15. This assertion is in Boorman, I, 227.
16. T'ang Ts'ai-chih, "T'ang Ts'ai-ch'ang ho Shih-wu hsüeh-t'ang" [T'ang Ts'ai-ch'ang and the academy of current affairs], *Hu-nan li-shih tzu-liao* [Historical materials on Hunan], 1958, no. 3, p. 106.
17. Observations of Japanese Consul General Odagiri, December 21, 1898, *Nihon Gaikō Bunshō,* vol. 31, pt. 1, p. 726.
18. Wang Shu-huai, p. 204, mistakenly identifies a telegram from Sheng to Chang as one from Chang to the throne, and on this basis includes Chang among the protesting officials.
19. FO 228/1276, Warren to MacDonald, September 30, 1898.
20. Wang Shu-huai, pp. 217–18.
21. See Schiffrin, pp. 166–67, 189, the latter for Li Hung-chang's "unre lenting hostility" toward the reformers when he was stationed in Canton in early 1900.
22. This was Chang Ssu-hsün. See Wang Shu-huai, pp. 225–26. I myself am doubtful of the truth of this rumor.
23. See Ayers, pp. 134–35, for a more complete description. Also Hsü *nien-p'u,* pp. 110, 112–13, 122.
24. Shih Ching, *Chung-kuo hsien-tai-hua yün-tung yü Ch'ing-mo liu-jih hsüeh-sheng* [China's modernization movement and students studying in Japan at the end of the Ch'ing] (Taipei, 1967), p. 16.
25. For a general account, see Wang Shu-huai, pp. 231–33. Segawa's telegram in *Nihon Gaikō Bunshō,* vol. 31, pt. 1, pp. 723–24.
26. Wang Shu-huai, p. 233.
27. Aoki's telegram in *Nihon Gaikō Bunshō,* vol. 31, pt. 1, p. 724; Wang Shu-huai, p. 232; Chang's memorial from *WHPF,* II, 618–19.

28. Wang Shu-huai, p. 234. Wang says he left March 12. Lo Jung-pang, in *K'ang Yu-wei: A Biography and A Symposium,* p. 179, mentions nothing of the circumstances of K'ang's departure.
29. Powell, *The Rise of Chinese Military Power 1895–1912,* pp. 120–21.
30. Kuo T'ing-i, pp. 1051–53; Shih Ching, p. 16. The total of 27 is compiled from the tables in Fang Chao-ying, *Ch'ing-mo min-ch'u yang-hsüeh hsüeh-sheng t'i-ming lu, ch'u-chi* [Name registers of students abroad in the late Ch'ing and early Republic, first collection] (Taipei, 1962).
31. Wang Shu-huai, p. 235.
32. Ibid., p. 239.
33. Ibid., pp. 240–41; *WHPF,* II, 619–20.
34. For the best brief description of Liang in 1899, see Schiffrin, pp. 161–65. More extended treatment is in Chang P'eng-yüan, *Liang Ch'i-ch'ao.*
35. For the commercial newspaper, Hsü *nien-p'u,* p. 128, *WHPF,* IV, 208. For military affairs, Hsü *nien-p'u,* pp. 126, 128, and Powell, p. 120. For education, Hsü *nien-p'u,* pp. 125–26, and *CC,* 102:27b–30.
36. See Wang Shu-huai, pp. 218–19.
37. Wang Shu-huai, pp. 220–21. A special message emphasizing the poorness of the emperor's health accompanied the delivery of the decree to each foreign embassy.
38. Ibid., p. 219; Kuo T'ing-i, pp. 1059–60.
39. Wang Shu-huai, p. 219.
40. Ibid. For a contemporary Chinese newspaper account of the mass telegram incident, see *WHPF,* III, 474. Ching Yüan-shan had to flee for his life to Macao, where he was arrested, though he eventually was freed due to British pressure on his behalf; Albert Feuerwerker, *China's Early Industrialization: Sheng Hsüan-huai and Mandarin Enterprise* (Cambridge, 1958), pp. 190–91, and Wang Shu-huai, pp. 221–23.
41. For the assertions in this paragraph, see Li Shou-k'ung, "T'ang Ts'ai-ch'ang yü Tzu-li chün" [T'ang Ts'ai-ch'ang and the independence army], in Wu Hsiang-hsiang, ed., *Chung-kuo hsien-tai shih ts'ung-k'an* [Selected articles on the contemporary history of China] 6 (1964): 41–159.
42. See quotes from a letter by Liang to Wang in the spring of 1900 in *Wang Jang-ch'ing (K'ang-nien) hsien-sheng: chuan-chi, i-wen,* pp. 108–10.
43. See Hsü *nien-p'u,* pp. 126–27, for long quotes from a memorial of 1899 in which Chang pointed out the difficulties and dangers in the court's policy of trying to use local militia (*t'uan-lien*).
44. Wang Shu-huai, p. 241.
45. This version is from the Macao *Jih-chih hsin-pao,* February 14, 1900, in *WHPF,* III, 474–75.

46. Ts'en was the younger brother of Ts'en Ch'un-hsüan, an important governor-general in the last years of the dynasty. Cheng was a longtime member of Chang Chih-tung's *mu-fu*.
47. There were definitely rumors of a group of fifty "officials" who set off from Wuchang to lodge a protest in Peking on the issue. But they seem to have been ephemeral, for British Consul General Fraser in Hankow reported that if they existed, they had never been heard of again. FO 228/1361, Fraser's quarterly intelligence report, April 4, 1900.
48. *WHPF,* II, 620.
49. FO 228/1361, Fraser's quarterly intelligence report, April 4, 1900. In his appeal, Chang reminded the consuls that he had more than once suppressed libels against foreigners, and they now owed him like consideration. Fraser allowed Chang's point, but observed that the other consuls did not seem very sympathetic to the idea.
50. *WHPF,* II, 621–22.
51. Kuo T'ing-i, pp. 1064–65.
52. Wang Shu-huai, p. 241.
53. Liang was in Hawaii at this time. The editorial was dated March 25, and appeared in issue no. 42, April 20, 1900, pp. 2729–34 (reprint edition).
54. Hao Yen-p'ing, "The Abortive Cooperation Between Reformers and Revolutionaries," *Papers on China* 15 (1961): 91–114; Chang P'eng-yüan, *Liang Ch'i-ch'ao,* pp. 119–36.
55. See Schiffrin, pp. 161–67, for an excellent description here.
56. Ibid., pp. 186–88. For the text of many of these letters, see Ting Wen-chiang, *Liang Jen-kung hsien-sheng nien-p'u ch'ang-pien ch'u-kao* [Preliminary draft of sources for a chronological biography of Liang Ch'i-ch'ao] (Taipei, 1962), vol. I, pp. 101–38. The account of these preparations by Chang P'eng-yüan, pp. 139–57, is based almost entirely on these letters collected by Ting Wen-chiang.

Chapter 5

1. The best account is Chester Tan, *The Boxer Catastrophe* (New York, 1955), pp. 76–80.
2. For an excellent account from the British documents, see L. K. Young, *British Policy in China 1895–1902* (London, 1970), pp. 161–64. Tan's account gives the impression that the initiative was all on the Chinese side. Young shows an equal amount on the British side.
3. Tan, pp. 80–82; L. K. Young, pp. 165–67.
4. L. K. Young, pp. 165–67. Warren was always hoping for a larger British role in patrolling and occupying the lower Yangtze; thus he was less enthusiastic than Salisbury in London.
5. See Marilyn Blatt Young, *The Rhetoric of Empire: American China*

Policy 1895–1901 (Cambridge, 1968), pp. 161–67. The United States government also consciously refrained from any acts which would imply lack of confidence in the word of the governors-general.

6. L. K. Young, pp. 167–68. In this he cooperated with the local British consul general Fraser. Also see below, on Chang's precautions against unrest.
7. Tan, pp. 83–91, describes in some detail the various efforts of Chang and other officials, including Sheng Hsüan-huai, Liu K'un-i, and Li Hung-chang, now governor-general in Canton.
8. Tan, p. 80; *CC,* 51:8–9b. Roger V. Des Forges, *Hsi-liang and the Chinese National Revolution* (New Haven, 1973), p. 16, asserts that Chang gave Hsi-liang, then Hunan judicial commissioner, who was leading these forces north, his best troops and pick of officers. In view of Chang's worries over keeping the peace along the Yangtze, I doubt this.
9. L. K. Young, pp. 174–78.
10. Tan, pp. 104–9.
11. L. K. Young, pp. 178–79.
12. Ibid., pp. 180–81.
13. For some relevant ideas on the neglected subject of secret societies, especially the Ko-lao hui, the dominant society in the Yangtze Valley during these years, see the essays by Jean Chesneaux, Charlton M. Lewis, and Guy Puyraimond in *Popular Movements and Secret Societies in China 1840–1950,* ed. Jean Chesneaux (Stanford, 1972). Kuhn, *Rebellion and Its Enemies,* pp. 167–75, also has some illuminating comments on the organization and activities of secret societies and how they related to general banditry.
14. For an impression in the late 1880's, from the point of view of British diplomats and missionaries, of the increasing danger of rowdy mobs and riots in the Wuhan cities, as well as of rural incidents, see FO 228/878, Consul Allen's reports to Walsham; also letters from Hupeh in the late 1880's in the archives of the London Missionary Society and the Wesleyan Methodist Missionary Society.
15. See Roberto M. Paterno, "The Yangtze Valley Anti-Missionary Riots of 1891" (Ph.D. diss., Harvard University, 1967). Also Edmund S. Wehrle, *Britain, China, and the Antimissionary Riots 1891–1900* (Minneapolis, 1966), chap. 2.
16. Paterno, pp. 579–618. *CC,* 31:1–11; 32:13–19, 27–35.
17. In May, 1898, for example, an inflammatory placard posted on the wall of the Wuchang examination hall denounced Chang for being proforeign and called upon the populace to rise on a certain date to kill him and all foreigners. FO 228/1276, Warren to MacDonald, June 2, 1898.
18. The British consular papers from Hankow for the 1890's are dominated by this issue, especially for the first half of the decade. See FO

228/1065 (1891), 1085 (1892), 1118 (1893), 1156 (1894), 1189 (1895), 1226 (1896), 1257 (1897), 1276 (1898), 1325 (1899).

19. Wehrle, passim; FO 228/1276, as cited above in chapter 3, for how the Sha-shih (Hupeh) riot of May, 1898, became entangled with the issue of the opening of Hunan, despite Chang Chih-tung's best efforts to keep the two issues separate.
20. British consular records cited in note 18 above. Also see Lü Shih-ch'iang, "Chou Han fan-chiao an" [Chou Han's anti-missionary activities], *Chung-yang yen-chiu yüan chin-tai shih yen-chiu so chi-k'an* [Bulletin of the Institute of Modern History, Academia Sinica], 2 (June 1971): 417–61.
21. FO 228/878, reports of 1889. These workers were reportedly also heavily recruited by the Ko-lao hui.
22. Ibid.
23. FO 228/1189, Warren to O'Connor, May 20, September 13, 1895. FO 228/1257, Warren to MacDonald, July 17, 1897.
24. As early as 1895, when a small group of Hunanese proposed opening the city of Yüeh-chou (Yochow) in northern Hunan as a treaty port, part of their scheme was the formation of a modern police force to handle the unruly elements which they acknowledged would inevitably be attracted. FO 228/1226, January 2, 1896. Chang established a force in Wuchang in 1902; *CC,* 56:5b–8.
25. FO 228/878, passim.
26. FO 228/1118, passim.
27. See Kuo T'ing-i, pp. 844–61, 1032–39; also Hsü *nien-p'u,* pp. 123–25.
28. Ayers, pp. 178–79; Hsü *nien-p'u,* pp. 126–27.
29. This was Cheng Hsiao-hsü. Hsü *nien-p'u,* pp. 131–32.
30. The major items here are E. Joan Smythe, "The Tzu-li hui: Some Chinese and Their Rebellion," *Papers on China* 12 (1958): 51–68; Charlton Miner Lewis, "The Opening of Hunan," chap. 3, pp. 87–110; Li Shou-k'ung, "T'ang Ts'ai-ch'ang yü Tzu-li chün"; Edmund S. K. Fung, "The T'ang Ts'ai-ch'ang Revolt," *Papers on Far Eastern History* 1 (1970): 70–114; Chang P'eng-yüan, *Liang Ch'i-ch'ao yü Ch'ing-chi ko-ming,* pp. 139–57, which deals with Liang's role in the revolt.

    The best of these by far is Li Shou-k'ung, with the chapter by Lewis the best in English. These two are largely the basis of this section of the chapter.
31. Lewis, "The Opening of Hunan," p. 88.
32. Lo Jung-pang, p. 186. In the recriminations which K'ang directed at Chang Chih-tung in late 1900 (see below, p. 99), there is also frequent reference to this analogy.
33. This is apparent from their correspondence of the time. K'ang seems more reluctant than Liang; see a quote from one of his letters in Lo Jung-pang, p. 186.

34. The Cheng-ch'i hui was preceded by the Tōbun Gakkai, founded with a Japanese collaborator.
35. Li Shou-k'ung, p. 96.
36. Lo Jung-pang, p. 186.
37. Lewis, p. 100, claims an attendance of several hundred at the first meeting. But Li Shou-k'ung, p. 98, and Kuo T'ing-i, p. 1090, agree that about eighty came to the first meeting, and over sixty to the second.
38. Li Shou-k'ung, pp. 96–97.
39. FO 405/96, pt. 16, p. 4.
40. Li Shou-k'ung, p. 100.
41. Ibid., pp. 96–97.
42. *HHKM,* I, 292.
43. Schiffrin, p. 291 n. 21.
44. Lo Jung-pang, p. 186; Li Shou-k'ung, p. 114.
45. Feng Tzu-yu, *Chung-hua min-kuo k'ai-kuo ch'ien ko-ming shih* [History of the Chinese revolution before 1911] (Taipei, 1954), I, 76; *HHKM,* I, 291.
46. I am indebted for this speculation to Schiffrin, pp. 220–21.
47. Feng Tzu-yu, *Chung-hua min-kuo k'ai-kuo ch'ien ko-ming shih,* I, 76; *HHKM,* I, 291.
48. Hsiao Ju-lin, *Liu-yang lieh-shih chuan* [Biographies of martyrs of Liu-yang, Hunan] (n.p., 1913), pp. 11–12. Joseph Esherick made available to me his copy of this source. Li Shou-k'ung, p. 126, has the account of the August 17 visit to T'ang by Li P'eng-sheng, an employee of Chang's Bureau of Foreign Matters (Yang-wu chü).
49. Hsiao Ju-lin, p. 12. One of the other officials was Feng Ch'i-chün, of Hsia-k'ou department.
50. Li Shou-k'ung, pp. 114–15, 131; Hsü *nien-p'u,* p. 137; *CC,* 103:22–35b.
51. Li Shou-k'ung, p. 115; FO 405/96, pt. 16, pp. 97–101.
52. FO 405/96, pt. 16, p. 104.
53. Hsü *nien-p'u,* pp. 139, 163. See Chang's telegram to Governor Yü of Hunan in *CC,* 167:14–14b. Also see Li Shou-k'ung, p. 126, and Hsiao Ju-lin, p. 12.
54. The following is taken from Li Shou-k'ung, pp. 124–25. This in turn quotes from Liu Hou-sheng's biography of Chang Chien. Liu supposedly heard the story from Cheng Hsiao-hsü himself.
55. Feng Tzu-yu, *Chung-hua min-kuo k'ai-kuo ch'ien ko-ming shih,* I, 77.
56. Schiffrin, p. 255, claims that "over twenty of Chang's Hunan-Hupeh students returned to join T'ang Ts'ai-ch'ang's Hankow plot." Y. C. Wang, *Chinese Intellectuals and the West: 1872–1949* (Chapel Hill, 1966), pp. 230–31, says that over ten of Chang's students died at his hand.
57. Feng Tzu-yu, *Chung-hua min-kuo k'ai-kuo ch'ien ko-ming shih,* I, 66–67.

58. For a brief biography of Fu, see Chang Nan-hsien, *Hu-pei ko-ming chih-chih lu* [An account of the revolution in Hupeh] (Shanghai, 1947), pp. 25–26.
59. Feng Tzu-yu, *Ko-ming i-shih* [Reminiscences of the revolution] (Taipei, 1969), III, 43–46, 51–55. To cross-check these names, the following lists of those captured are helpful: that of Chang Nan-hsien, in *WHPF,* IV, 296–97; and that of Huang Chung-huang (Chang Shih-chao), *HHKM,* I, 292–93.
60. Li Shou-k'ung, p. 100. Wu would always be called a "veteran" of the uprising in the future, however.
61. They are listed for January, 1899, in the student rosters compiled by Fang Chao-ying, p. 47, where their *tzu* and given names are reversed.
62. For the text of these, see Feng Tzu-yu, *Chung-hua min-kuo k'ai-kuo ch'ien ko-ming shih,* I, 70–71.
63. Li Shou-k'ung, p. 123.
64. Hsü *nien-p'u,* p. 138; Li Shou-k'ung, pp. 127–29.
65. *CC,* 103:22–35b. On September 23, Chang requested the dismissal of a garrison commander who had been lax about weeding out *fu-yu p'iao* adherents among his own troops; *CC,* 51:17b–18b.
66. FO 405/96, pt. 16, p. 103.
67. *WHPF,* II, 628.
68. FO 405/96, pt. 16, pp. 103–4.
69. Li Shou-k'ung, pp. 142–44, has the best account here. Also see Charlton Lewis, "The Opening of Hunan," pp. 106–7, and Feng Tzu-yu, *Chung-hua min-kuo k'ai-kuo ch'ien ko-ming shih,* I, 77–79.
70. Roswell S. Britton, *The Chinese Periodical Press, 1800–1912,* pp. 76–77; *Ch'ing-i pao,* no. 66, December 12, 1900, p. 4233.
71. See letters from the Shanghai *North China Herald,* quoted by Lewis, "The Opening of Hunan," pp. 109–10. Also see FO 405/96, pt. 16, pp. 97–98.
72. Li Shou-k'ung, pp. 143–44.
73. From *CC,* 51:9b–17b, and *HHKM,* I, 264–69 (where the date is incorrectly given as September 13). For previous reports on their areas by Hunan Governor Yü Lien-san and a joint one by Anhui Governor Wang Chih-ch'un and Liu K'un-i, see *HHKM,* I, 258–60 and 260–64, respectively.
74. *WHPF,* II, 625.
75. *HHKM,* I, 274–75; *WHPF,* II, 478–80. Also see Li Shou-k'ung, pp. 142–43.
76. FO 405/96, pt. 16, p. 97.
77. *CC,* 103:29b–32b, 35b–38b; 104:11b–14. Li Shou-k'ung, pp. 144–46. FO 228/1361, Fraser to Satow, November 16, 1900.
78. *CC,* 121:7b–12.
79. *WHPF,* II, 627–628; *CC,* 104:9–11b.

80. *WHPF,* II, 630. For long quotes from this pamphlet, see Li Shou-k'ung, p. 145.
81. Li Shou-k'ung, pp. 148–49.
82. Shih Ching, p. 24; *WHPF,* II, 625–26.
83. See Chang's telegram of October 9 to Ch'ien Hsün in Tokyo, in *WHPF,* II, 626–27.
84. "Ch'üan-chieh Shang-hai Kuo-hui chi ch'u-yang hsüeh-sheng wen." *CC,* 104:1–9.
85. Hsü *nien-p'u,* p. 163. The other two were T'ien Wu-chao and Lu Ching-yüan, both of whom he recommended for the special *ching-chi t'e-k'o* examination in 1902.
86. Feng Tzu-yu, *Ko-ming i-shih,* I, 121.
87. "Fu Chang Chih-tung shu," in Chang Nan and Wang Jen-chih, eds., *Hsin-hai ko-ming ch'ien shih-nien chien shih-lun hsüan-chi* [Selected articles on current events during the decade preceding the 1911 Revolution], vol. I, pt. 2 (Peking, 1960), pp. 764–75.
88. Feng Tzu-yu, *Ko-ming i-shih,* I, 121–22.
89. Ibid.
90. Lewis, "The Opening of Hunan," p. 110.
91. Shih Ching, p. 115; Schiffrin, p. 223.
92. See Ernest P. Young, "The Reformer as a Conspirator: Liang Ch'i-ch'ao and the 1911 Revolution," in Albert Feuerwerker et al., eds., *Approaches to Modern Chinese History* (Berkeley and Los Angeles, 1967), pp. 239–67.
93. Schiffrin, p. 224; Chang P'eng-yüan, pp. 156–57.
94. The diary of Sun Chung-yü, quoted in Li Shou-k'ung, p. 148.
95. No. 58, pp. 3735–39; no. 59, pp. 3797–3802; no. 60, pp. 3859–65; no. 63, pp. 4045–49; no. 66, pp. 4231–38.
96. No. 66, December 12, 1900.
97. No. 60, October 14, 1900.
98. This appeared in two parts: *Ch'ing-i pao,* no. 64, November 22, 1900, pp. 4113–16, and no. 65, December 2, pp. 4169–75. A punctuated version is in *WHPF,* II, 522–29.
99. "Po hou-tang Chang Chih-tung Yü Yin-lin wei-shih," *Ch'ing-i pao,* no. 66, December 12, 1900, pp. 4265–76. Also in *WHPF,* I, 424–33.

Chapter 6

1. Tan, pp. 133–34. Sheng was also wary of such an honor, and declined.
2. Kuo T'ing-i, p. 1101; FO 405/96, pt. 16, p. 26.
3. Hsü *nien-p'u,* p. 154.
4. Tan, pp. 136–37.
5. Bays, "The Nature of Provincial Political Authority," p. 334; FO 228/1118, Warren's intelligence report of November 3, 1893.
6. FO 228/1276, Warren to MacDonald, July 18, 1898.

7. FO 228/1361, Fraser's intelligence report of April 4, 1900.
8. Liang, who was a member of Yung Wing's educational mission to the United States in the 1870's, was later Minister of Foreign Affairs under both the dynasty and the early Republic.
9. First quote from FO 405/96, pt. 16, p. 10, the second from PRO 30/33/8/10, Fraser personal note to MacDonald, September 26, 1900. Other laudatory statements are in FO 405/97, pt. 17, pp. 29, 31. For an admiring American view, see Marilyn Young, *The Rhetoric of Empire,* p. 201, quoting from an October 16 message from Rockhill to Hay: "The great viceroys . . . have been standing by us splendidly for the last four months." Sir Ernest Satow, who replaced Claude MacDonald as British minister to China in the fall of 1900 and remained in that post until 1906, had occasion to have several personal interviews with Chang during his tenure in China, and also developed considerable respect for Chang's character and abilities. See, for example, PRO 30/33/16/4, Satow's journal of November 25, 1901.
10. FO 405/96, pt. 16, p. 125, and 405/97, pt. 17, pp. 173–74.
11. FO 405/96, pt. 16, pp. 125–26, 141, 165, 167, 174.
12. Tan, p. 143.
13. Tan, p. 139; Hsü *nien-p'u,* pp. 140–41; Marilyn Young, *The Rhetoric of Empire,* pp. 199–200.
14. Hsü *nien-p'u,* p. 141; Wu Yung's own account is in Wu Yung, *Flight of an Empress,* trans. Ida Pruitt (New Haven, 1936), pp. 135–40. Chester Tan, pp. 117–18 n. 8, strongly doubts Wu Yung's claim of passing on Chang's views to the empress dowager in 1901, but since the account of Chang's original interview with Wu also appears in the *nien-p'u,* above, it seems fairly credible.
15. *CC,* 169:29–30, 34–34b. Lu had been appointed to the Grand Council on September 25; Ts'en's younger brother, Ch'un-ming, had served under Chang in Hupeh.
16. PRO 30/33/8/10, Fraser private letters to Satow, October 26, November 29, 1901; FO 228/1387, Fraser to Satow, December 11, 1901. Those he denounced were I-ku, Wang Lung-wen, Lien Wen-ch'ung, Tseng Lien, and Huang Kuei-chün.
17. Chang was especially interested in lifting the proposed suspension of examination quotas for all of Chihli province, at least for some parts of it, including his home district of Nan-p'i. FO 228/1361, Fraser to Satow, December 10, 1900.
18. Development of this topic might make a fascinating monograph. The best general treatment of the period at present is in Tan, especially pp. 153–56, 170–214. Also see L. K. Young, p. 181; Marilyn Young, pp. 208–11; Kosaka Masakata, "Ch'ing Policy over Manchuria (1900–1903)," *Papers on China* 16 (1962): 126–53.
19. See *CC, chüan* 170–72, for Chang's hundreds of telegrams of early 1901.

20. Chang variously accused Li Hung-chang and pro-K'ang Yu-wei Shanghai newspapers of making false insinuations of antiforeignism against Lu. See FO 405/106, pt. 23, pp. 62–63, and FO 228/1387, Fraser to Satow, March 12, 1901. Chester Tan's characterization of Lu, p. 135, seems too harsh.
21. Hsü Wan-ch'eng, ed., *Chang Chih-tung chih Liang Ting-fen lun hsüeh-wu shou-cha* [Handwritten letters of Chang Chih-tung to Liang Ting-fen concerning educational affairs] (Hong Kong, 1968), introduction.
22. Kuo T'ing-i, pp. 1114, 1119.
23. See Ayers, pp. 201–2, and *CC,* 171:30b–32.
24. Kuo T'ing-i, p. 1136.
25. See Lo Jung-pang, pp. 157–58. K'ang's "Bureau of Institutions" was in turn explicitly modeled on the Japanese "Bureau for the Investigation of Constitutional Systems" of 1884–85, which paved the way for the Japanese Constitution of 1889.
26. FO 228/1387, Fraser to Satow, March 5 and March 13, 1901.
27. FO 228/1387, Fraser to Satow, April–May, 1901, passim. Hsü *nien-p'u,* p. 144, describes the British interference in these appointments, but gives no hint that Chang requested it. Des Forges, *Hsi-liang,* p. 26, claims that foreign opposition and Li Lien-ying's machinations deprived Hsi-liang of this post, and gives no indication of awareness that Chang had a major hand in it.
28. Governor Yü was more conservative than Chang, and rather antiforeign (he posted the antiforeign edicts which Chang suppressed in the summer of 1900), but Chang had a good working relationship with him, and warned Fraser that his replacement would likely be far worse. FO 228/1387, Fraser to Satow, April 7, 1901.
29. *CC,* 52:9b–54:36; also Hsü *nien-p'u,* pp. 149–50. The first memorial, on education, is examined in great detail by Ayers, pp. 205–15. The second is summarized in Teng and Fairbank, pp. 199–200, and the third is more extensively translated in Teng and Fairbank, pp. 200–205.
30. Translated in Teng and Fairbank, pp. 199–200.
31. Ibid., p. 205.
32. Mary Backus Rankin, "The Manchurian Crisis and Radical Student Nationalism, 1903," *Ch'ing-shih wen-t'i* 2.1 (October 1969): 88; Tan, pp. 198–99.
33. For example, Chang was very distrustful of the anti-Russian demonstrations in Shanghai in March and April, 1901, fearful that they were a front for the continuing activities of Tzu-li hui sympathizers. *CC,* 172:2–2b.
34. Hsü *nien-p'u,* pp. 149–50.
35. For example, the contributions of Yüan Shih-k'ai and of T'ao Mo, governor-general at Canton, are noted by Wolfgang Franke, *The Re-*

form and Abolition of the Traditional Chinese Examination System (Cambridge, 1960), pp. 48–54.

36. Ayers, pp. 215–16; Franke, p. 55; Kuo T'ing-i, pp. 1146–47, 1153; Hsü *nien-p'u,* p. 152.
37. E.g., a new Ministry of Foreign Affairs replaced the Tsungli yamen in July; the sale of office was terminated in August; a large reduction in the size of the useless Army of the Green Standard was decreed in August. A convenient listing of the major reform measures between 1901 and 1905 is in Immanuel C. Y. Hsü, *The Rise of Modern China* (New York and London, 1970), pp. 490–92.
38. Kuo T'ing-i, p. 1148.
39. *CC,* 55:1–2.
40. Citations from note 16 above, chapter 6. Satow also did not press very hard, I think. I-ku, a board vice-president, eventually was sent on a provincial inspection mission but was not demoted in rank.
41. Hsü *nien-p'u,* pp. 152–53; Kuo T'ing-i, pp. 1152–53; *CC*, 175:13b–14, 21b–22. Chang also obtained the appointment of Liang Ting-fen, his close associate, as prefect in the Wuhan area by working through Lu Ch'uan-lin in the fall of 1901; Hsü *nien-p'u,* pp. 147–48.
42. FO 228/1387, Fraser to Satow, December 7, 11, and 30, 1901.
43. *CC,* 55:17–20b.
44. FO 228/1457, Fraser to Satow, January–February, 1901, passim; PRO 30/33/16/5, Satow's journal; PRO 30/33/8/10, Fraser private letters to Satow, January–February, 1901. Chang's best Chinese biographer, Hsü T'ung-hsin, claims that the intention of the empress dowager's summons was to reward Chang and patch up any hard feelings that might remain because of past events; Hsü *nien-p'u,* p. 154. This sounds too ingenuous, but should be considered.
45. FO 228/1457, items of May 28, May 30, June 4, 1902; PRO 30/33/16/5, Satow's journal, June 4, 1902.
46. This was the *Huang-ch'ao hsü-ai wen-pien,* a collection edited by Yü Pao-hsien in eighty *chüan,* similar in format to the various *Ching-shih wen-pien* collections published between 1895 and 1898. It was printed in 1902 in Shanghai (reprinted Taipei, 1965, 8 vols.). Besides Chang, a certain Sung Yü-jen (no relationship to the later revolutionary Sung Chiao-jen) also wrote a preface. In addition to translations from foreign works, and essays by reformers from Wang T'ao to Chang Chih-tung himself, it included K'ang's "Fifth Memorial to the Emperor" from early 1898, his first speech before the Peking Pao-kuo hui in the spring of that year, and Liang Ch'i-ch'ao's letters to Hunan Governor Ch'en Pao-chen in 1897–98. Chang's willingness to write a preface for such a collection is interesting, given his bitter feelings toward K'ang and Liang in 1900.
47. *CC,* 57:29b–39b. Chang set up the police bureau in June and reported it in July. *CC,* 56:5b–8; Hsü *nien-p'u,* p. 157.

48. Yüan reported his Pao-ting police bureau in August, 1902, and an October edict recommended that all provincial officials follow suit. Kuo T'ing-i, pp. 1166, 1170.
49. This paragraph is taken from Ayers, pp. 218–24, who treats the subject in considerable detail.
50. Ibid. These were: Liang Ting-fen, director of civil schools for the entire province and supervisor of the Wuchang Normal School; Huang Shao-chi, chief editor of the joint Kiangsu-Hupeh Translation Bureau; Miao Ch'üan-sun, an assistant editor of the Translation Bureau; Lo Chen-yü, also an assistant editor of the Translation Bureau and general manager of the School of Agriculture in Wuchang; Huang Shao-ti (Shao-chi's younger brother), supervisor of the Civil Middle School; Chi Chü-wei, assistant supervisor of the Civil High School; Wang Ping-en, director of the Civil High School; Wang Feng-ying, director of the School of Agriculture; Liang Tun-yen, director of the Industrial School.
51. See Chang's recommendation list in *CC,* 56:18b–24. There were Liu Pang-chi, Ch'en Wen-hsien, T'ien Wu-chao, Lu Ching-yüan, and Wan T'ing-hsien. Other individuals named in this document may also have been instructors in Chang's schools, but this is not specifically stated.
52. See Ayers, pp. 207 and 220, respectively.
53. Ayers, p. 225, deals well with Chang's growing realization of the importance of primary schools, and thus of normal schools.
54. Ayers, pp. 229, 233–35.
55. PRO 30/33/8/10, Fraser private letter to Satow, September 27, 1902.
56. FO 228/1457, 228/1458, October, 1902, passim. These demands, the latter of which was quite out of the question, reduced Satow to exasperation. In a letter to Lord Lansdowne, the foreign secretary, on October 9, Satow complained, "Chang is a difficult person to manage, for he varies from one moment to another . . . he is as exigeant as a pretty woman." PRO 30/33/14/13.
57. Both of these requests were granted. PRO 30/33/16/6, Satow's journal, November 27, 1902.
58. Liang Tun-yen, who had accompanied Chang to Nanking, kept Fraser back in Hankow well informed of Chang's purported intentions by frequent letters. FO 228/1502, Fraser to Townley, February, 1902, passim; *CC,* 58:14b–15b.
59. FO 228/1502.
60. FO 228/1502, Fraser to Townley, April 14 and April 20, 1903. In his despatch of the latter date, Fraser remarked of Chang, "I have rarely seen him so depressed over public affairs, even in 1900."
61. Hsü *nien-p'u,* pp. 165–71. For Chang's actions regarding the arsenal, see Thomas L. Kennedy, "The Kiangnan Arsenal in the Era of Reform, 1895–1911," *Chung-yang yen-chiu yüan chin-tai shih yen-chiu so chi-k'an* 3.1 (July 1972): 300–304.

62. Translated in Teng and Fairbank, p. 207. Franke, p. 56, notes that Chao Erh-sun, governor of Shansi, also proposed a limited transfer of degrees to the new school system in early 1903.
63. Franke, p. 57.
64. *CC,* 186:29–29b. Discussed in Ayers, pp. 239–40.
65. Hsü *nien-p'u,* p. 178, claims that it was his original intention to remain only a month in Peking.
66. He was also received on May 20 and 21, and then somewhat less frequently over the next few weeks. Hsü *nien-p'u,* pp. 172 ff.
67. Some indication that this is so is provided by the fact that Chang suddenly stopped asking the British for protection and favors; he saw Satow very seldom, for example, after the latter's return from leave in the summer of 1903, and then only on mundane matters.
68. Hsü *nien-p'u,* p. 180. For his poems from the summer of 1903, see *CC, chüan* 224.
69. Hsü *nien-p'u,* p. 175.
70. *CC,* 187:22–22b.
71. Hsü *nien-p'u,* p. 173; Kuo T'ing-i, pp. 1182–83.
72. The story of the *ching-chi t'e-k'o* is told in some detail in Hsü *nien-p'u,* pp. 174–75, and in Fang Tu Lien-che, "Ching-chi t'e-k'o" [The special examination in political economy], in Wu Hsiang-hsiang, ed., *Chung-kuo hsien-tai shih ts'ung-k'an,* 3 (1961): 1–44.
73. *CC,* 56:18b–24; 58:3–8b. Of the thirty from Liang-chiang, at least two, Miao Ch'üan-sun and Lo Chen-yü, were administrators of the joint Kiangsu-Hupeh Translation Bureau which Chang had helped to set up in Nanking. Several others had been associated with Chang in the past, either as employees in his secretariat or as those recommended.
74. Hsü *nien-p'u,* p. 174, says that of the 370 recommended for the exam, only about 130 actually took it. If so, then almost all "passed." For basic biographical data on Liang Shih-i, see Boorman, III, 354–57; for Yang Tu, see Boorman, IV, 13–16.
75. There are several good accounts of the famous Su-pao case. See Schiffrin, pp. 265–74; also Y. C. Wang, "The Su-Pao Case: A Study of Foreign Pressure, Intellectual Fermentation, and Dynastic Decline," *Monumenta Serica,* 24 (1965): 84–129; and Mary Backus Rankin, *Early Chinese Revolutionaries: Radical Intellectuals in Shanghai and Chekiang, 1902–1911* (Cambridge, 1971), pp. 69–95.
76. *CC,* 188:1. Chang failed in an attempt to counter the bad effects of the Su-pao case during the late summer, as well. He kept up on developments almost on a day-to-day basis (Tuan-fang sent Chang almost twenty telegraphed reports on the case in July alone; *HHKM,* I, 443–80, passim; none of these are in *CC*), and tried indirectly to influence the British to turn over the arrested parties to the Chinese authorities in Shanghai (their failure to do so, and the ensuing publicity given the

defendants in the trial before the British-run Mixed Court, was an unpleasant humiliation for the central government). For example, Chang paid a private visit to Sir Ernest Satow on the subject in late August, 1903, after which Satow warned Chang, in a friendly way, not to get involved in the case, because he could not influence the outcome; PRO 30/33/16/6, Satow's journal, August 31 and September 3, 1903.

77. The remaining members were Prince Ch'ing, Wang Wen-shao, Lu Ch'uan-lin, and Ch'ü Hung-chi. These changes are pointed out by Franke, pp. 57–58.
78. Franke, p. 58.
79. Ibid. Only those of Chihli, Kansu, Fukien, Kwangtung, Kwangsi, and Yunnan survived the purge.
80. The two major memorials (*che*) and three minor ones (*p'ien*) are in *CC,* 61:15b–29.
81. This memorial is fully translated by Franke, pp. 59–64.
82. The language of her edict is noted in Franke, p. 64.
83. For a concise description of Chang's Hupeh activities in the field of education in 1904 and after, see Ayers, pp. 231–36.
84. Hsü *nien-p'u,* pp. 184–85. For a British military intelligence report on Chang's troops in the fall of 1904, see FO 17/1567, report by Captain Light, November 3, 1904. Also see Powell, *The Rise of Chinese Military Power, 1895–1912,* pp. 219 ff., and Yoshihiro Hatano, "The New Armies," in Mary C. Wright, ed., *China in Revolution: The First Phase, 1900–1913* (New Haven, 1968), pp. 378–79.
85. Chang Ts'un-wu, *Kuang-hsü san-shih-i nien Chung-Mei kung-yüeh feng-ch'ao* [The protest movement over the Sino-American treaty of 1905] (Nankang, Taiwan, 1966). Akira Iriye, "Public Opinion and Foreign Policy: The Case of Late Ch'ing China," in Feuerwerker, Murphey, and Wright eds., *Approaches to Modern Chinese History,* pp. 216–38. Also Margaret Field, "The Chinese Boycott of 1905," *Papers on China* 11 (1957): 63–98, and Edward J. M. Rhoads, "Nationalism and Xenophobia in Kwangtung (1905–1906): The Canton Anti-American Boycott and the Lienchow Anti-Missionary Uprising," *Papers on China* 16 (1962): 154–97.
86. Schiffrin, chap. 12, pp. 344–66.
87. For a brief summary, see Ayers, pp. 243–44. The five other memorialists were Yüan Shih-k'ai, governor-general of Chihli; Chao Erh-sun, military governor at Mukden; Chou Fu, acting governor-general of Liang-chiang; Ts'en Ch'un-hsüan, governor-general of Liang-kuang; and Tuan-fang, governor of Hunan.
88. Chang went to Nanking in May, 1904, to confer with Governor-General Wei Kuang-tao about the fate of the Kiangnan Arsenal. While there, he saw Chang Chien, who later claimed that Wei and Chang had asked him to write a draft memorial for them recommending a

constitutional system. Liu Hou-sheng, *Chang Chien ch'uan-chi* [Biography of Chang Chien] (Shanghai, 1958), p. 516, based on Chang Chien's chronological autobiography; also Chang Yu-fa, *Ch'ing-chi te li-hsien t'uan-t'i* [Constitutionalists of the Ch'ing period] (Nankang, Taiwan, 1971), p. 307. Samuel C. Chu, *Reformer in Modern China: Chang Chien, 1853–1926* (New York, 1965), pp. 60—61, claims that Chang Chih-tung and Wei Kuang-tao actually submitted the memorial. This, I am sure, did not occur.

For a description of some important officials, including Yüan Shih-k'ai, Tuan-fang, and Minister to France Sun Pao-ch'i, among others, who began to advocate constitutionalism, see Chang Yu-fa, pp. 307–12, and Samuel C. Chu, pp. 61–62.

89. Kuo T'ing-i, p. 1231; Hsiao I-shan, *Ch'ing-tai t'ung-shih* [A general history of the Ch'ing period] (Taipei, 1963), IV, 2394–95; *Tung-fang tsa-chih* [The Eastern Miscellany], 2.7 (1905): 58.
90. *NCH,* July 7, 1905, p. 24. The third memorialist is noted as Ts'en Ch'un-hsüan, governor-general at Canton, not Chou Fu.
91. Hsiao I-shan, IV, 2394–95, says that their memorial was the decisive factor leading to the edict of July 16. The four commissioners were Tsai-tse, Tai Hung-tz'u, Hsü Shih-ch'ang, and Tuan-fang. On July 27, Shao-ying was added as the fifth commissioner. Kuo T'ing-i, pp. 1231–32.
92. See, for example, Li Chien-nung, *The Political History of China, 1840–1928,* pp. 194–99, and Immanuel C. Y. Hsü, *The Rise of Modern China,* pp. 488–500.
93. See Mary C. Wright, "Introduction: The Rising Tide of Change," in Wright, ed., *China in Revolution,* pp. 1–63; Ernest P. Young, "Nationalism, Reform and Republican Revolution: China in the Early Twentieth Century," in James B. Crowley, ed., *Modern East Asia: Essays in Interpretation* (New York, 1970), pp. 151–65; En-han Lee, "China's Response to Foreign Investment in her Mining Industry (1902–1911)," *Journal of Asian Studies* 28.1 (1968): 55–76; John Schrecker, *Imperialism and Chinese Nationalism: Germany in Shantung* (Cambridge, 1971).
94. Obvious candidates here are Yüan Shih-k'ai, Ts'en Ch'un-hsüan, Tuan-fang, Chou Fu, and Hsü Shih-ch'ang, to name only a few. Des Forges, *Hsi-liang and the Chinese National Revolution,* adds to our knowledge of this generation of officials, as does Michael H. Hunt, *Frontier Defense and the Open Door* (New Haven, 1973). Recent dissertations which are relevant include Stephen R. MacKinnon, "Yüan Shih-k'ai in Tientsin and Peking: The Sources and Structure of his Power, 1901–1908" (Ph.D. diss., University of California, Davis, 1971), and Louis T. Sigel, "T'ang Shao-yi (1860–1938): The Diplomacy of Chinese Nationalism" (Ph.D. diss., Harvard University, 1973).

Chapter 7

1. This is the estimate of Shih Ching, *Chung-kuo hsien-tai-hua yün-tung yü Ch'ing-mo liu-jih hsüeh-sheng,* p. 165.
2. The figures cited in this paragraph come from Shih Ching, pp. 141–42. Shih's figures differ only slightly from those in the other major source for this subject, Sanetō Keishū, *Chūgokujin Nihon ryūgaku shi* [A history of Chinese students in Japan] (Tokyo, 1960), p. 544. Roger F. Hackett, "Chinese Students in Japan, 1900–1910," *Papers on China* 3 (1949): 134–69, estimates as many as 15,000 at the peak; this seems too large a figure.
3. Sanetō Keishū, p. 544, and Shih Ching, pp. 141–42, agree on this figure. Also see Huang Fu-ch'ing, "Ch'ing-mo te liu-Jih cheng-ts'e" [Policy on study in Japan in the late Ch'ing period], *Chung-yang yen-chiu yüan chin-tai shih yen-chiu so chi-k'an* 2 (June 1971): 47–95.
4. These schools are individually described very well by Shih Ching, pp. 159–62.
5. Ibid., p. 159. This included both public and private schools.
6. Ibid., p. 164, and Y. C. Wang, *Chinese Intellectuals and the West,* p. 68.
7. Schiffrin, pp. 256–60, and 274–76, for pre-1903 organizations and publications, respectively; also Paula S. Harrell, "The Years of the Young Radicals: The Chinese Students in Japan, 1900–1905" (Ph.D. diss., Columbia University, 1970).
8. Schiffrin, chap. 10, pp. 283–97, has the most perceptive treatment of this subject I have seen. Also see Harrell, passim; Robert Scalapino, "Prelude to Marxism: The Chinese Student Movement in Japan, 1900–1910," in Feuerwerker, Murphey, and Wright, eds., *Approaches to Modern Chinese History,* pp. 190–215; and Michael Gasster, *Chinese Intellectuals and the Revolution of 1911* (Seattle, 1969), pp. 65–106.
9. The most detailed account of the fracas at Minister Ts'ai Chün's office is in Sanetō Keishū, pp. 424–60. Also see Harrell, pp. 64–88.
10. Schiffrin, p. 259, says the Ch'ing-nien hui was established in later 1902; Shelley Cheng, "The T'ung Meng Hui: Its Organization, Leadership and Finances: 1905–1912" (Ph.D. diss., University of Washington, 1962), p. 68, says it was early 1903.
11. The 1900 veterans were Ch'in Li-shan, Chi I-hui, and Shen Hsiang-yün. Wu Lu-chen, though not a participant in the actual revolt of 1900, could still be included in this group.
12. Shih Ching, pp. 56–57. Hu Han-min later remarked along the same lines: Paula Harrell, p. 32 n. 67.
13. Shih Ching, pp. 68, 70–71; Harrell, pp. 33–36; Shelley Cheng, p. 69.
14. Sun was in Yokohama most of the time from late 1900 to the end of 1902. Schiffrin, pp. 300–302; Shelley Cheng, pp. 36–37 and p. 62 n. 139.

15. Ts'ai Chün, due to his arrogance and venality, had already by this time won the contempt of many of the students. Harrell, pp. 57–58.
16. For Tsai-chen's report, see *KKWH,* series 1, vol. 8, pp. 273–75. Also see Harrell, pp. 89–93.
17. Shih Ching, pp. 25–26. Though they were more fair, the rules also tried to provide for more control of the students by requiring them to be guaranteed by two Japanese residents before admission to any Japanese state school.
18. Yang had a heavy burden with his dual responsibilities, and already before the end of 1904 he was asking for more personnel to help with the task of keeping track of the students. *KKWH,* series 1, vol. 8, p. 277. Harrell, p. 93, incorrectly states that Ts'ai Chün retained his post until October, 1903.
19. *CC,* 203:7.
20. He also continued the use of Japanese as instructors in his own Hupeh schools, begun in 1898. As of December, 1901, there were at least fourteen Japanese instructors or interpreters employed in the Wuchang schools. Imperial Maritime Customs, *Decennial Reports,* Second issue (1892–1901), vol. 1, pp. 315–16.
21. Chi I-ch'iao, "Hsien-hsien Wen-hsiang-kung shih-chi t'an" [Talking about the life of the former worthy Chang Chih-tung], *Hu-pei wen-hsien* [Documents on Hupeh], 2 (1967): 20. An example of formal recommendation of his students was his attempt to get several of them better jobs through the *ching-chi t'e-k'o* special examination in the summer of 1903, dealt with in the previous chapter.
22. *CC,* 228:17b.
23. See Ayers, pp. 190–91, for several examples here.
24. Hsü *nien-p'u,* p. 128.
25. *CC,* 104:36b–37.
26. *CC,* 185:19–19b; Ayers, p. 193. This admonition was ineffective; the journal appeared anyway in early 1903.
27. *CC,* 186:13b–14.
28. *CC,* 61:1–10. Though these rules applied to students in all foreign countries, it is quite clear that they were devised especially to meet the requirements of the Japanese case.
29. *CC,* 61:1–2.
30. *CC,* 61:3–5, 7b–10. Ayers, pp. 193–95, describes the more important of the control measures. The final seven articles, on pp. 7b–10, were suggested by the Japanese authorities after Chang showed them the first twenty. These, which like the first ten articles aimed at control and discipline, seem to be what Hsü *nien-p'u,* pp. 175–76, is referring to. There is no evidence that, as Ayers claims (p. 195), the rules for rewarding the students, discussed in the next paragraph, were inserted at the suggestion of the Japanese. These were Chang's ideas from the start and were quite consistent with his general policy of giving his students recognition and rewards for their efforts.

31. *CC,* 61:5b–7b.
32. Y. C. Wang, *Chinese Intellectuals and the West,* pp. 62–64.
33. This is discussed in Shih Ching, pp. 28–29.
34. Shih Ching, p. 29.
35. The best guide to these journals, as well as to several others between 1900 and 1911, is P. K. Yu et al., comps, *The Revolutionary Movement During the Late Ch'ing: A Guide to Chinese Periodicals* (Washington, D.C., 1970); this contains the inaugural manifestos and full tables of contents of all issues. The journals have been reprinted in their entirety in Lo Chia-lun, ed., *Chung-hua min-kuo shih-liao ts'ung-pien* [Compendium of historical materials on the Republic of China], series A (Taipei, 1968). Also see Shelley Cheng, pp. 68–69, and Harrell, pp. 36–50.
36. Li Lien-fang, *Hsin-hai Wu-ch'ang shou-i chi* [A record of the 1911 Revolution in Wuchang] (Wuchang, 1947), pp. 2b–3. Li was an early contributor to the journal before returning to Hupeh, and he understandably claims a seminal revolutionary role for the publication. Also P. K. Yu, *A Guide to Chinese Periodicals,* introduction, p. xii.
37. Harrell, pp. 100–105.
38. Schiffrin, p. 260; Harrell, p. 105; Rankin, *Early Chinese Revolutionaries,* pp. 74–75.
39. Most accounts (Shelley Cheng, p. 70, Shih Ching, p. 116) agree on the figure of 500 who attended. If true, this would include very nearly half of all the Chinese students, who probably numbered between 1,000 and 1,300 in early 1903. Schiffrin, p. 260, notes that, with the recent Anglo-Japanese Alliance, Japanese nationalists were "beating the drums for war with Russia." A misquotation attributed to the Russian minister in Peking by the rabid Tokyo press on April 28 gave the Chinese students the impression that Russia was openly trying to annex Manchuria, and precipitated the meeting. The students' excitement may well have been intensified by the Japanese atmosphere around them. Harrell, pp. 109–10, also notes this as a factor exciting the students.

    The description of events until mid-May is taken from Shih Ching, pp. 116–23, and Harrell, chap. 3.
40. For the charter and regulations of the Hsüeh-sheng chün, see Feng Tzu-yu, *Ko-ming i-shih,* I, 156–57. A similar student volunteer corps was formed in Shanghai in early May; Rankin, *Early Chinese Revolutionaries,* pp. 76–77.
41. A basic account, Feng Tzu-yu, *Ko-ming i-shih,* I, 157, claims that the Chinese government was warned of the group's revolutionary tendencies almost from the first, and already in early May requested the Japanese government to suppress it. Major works such as Schiffrin and Hsüeh Chün-tu, *Huang Hsing and the Chinese Revolution* (Stanford, 1961), have accepted this. But all the evidence points to the Chinese government's suspicions not being aroused until later in May.

42. All three of these items were printed in the *Su-pao,* on May 15, 19, and 21, respectively. I have taken them from *KKWH,* series 1, vol. 10, pp. 705–10.
43. See Kosaka Masakata, "Ch'ing Policy over Manchuria (1900–1903)," especially pp. 142–45.
44. Shelley Cheng, p. 72. Feng Tzu-yu's account, and therefore those of Schiffrin and Hsüeh, give the impression that a detailed revolutionary charter was already written by the time of the founding of the Educational Association for a Militant Citizenry on May 11, and that this was a highly secret group from the beginning. Shih Ching's work, and that of Paula Harrell as well, both based more on contemporary newspapers than on Feng Tzu-yu's recollections, have led me to conclude that the radical leadership of the Educational Association was committed to revolutionary action from this time on, but did not come up with a real statement of revolutionary purpose until July.
45. Tuan-fang's telegram of May 27 appeared in the *Su-pao* on June 6, and the imperial edict was printed on June 5; Shih Ching, p. 124, and *KKWH,* series 1, vol. 10, p. 134.
46. Mary Backus Rankin, "The Manchurian Crisis and Radical Student Nationalism, 1903," especially emphasizes the bad image the government acquired by its heavy-handed reaction. For the radicalization of one Hunanese student, see Ernest P. Young, "Problems of a Late Ch'ing Revolutionary: Ch'en T'ien-hua," in Hsüeh Chün-tu, ed., *Revolutionary Leaders of Modern China* (New York, 1971), pp. 213–14.
47. This statement, or *i-chien shu,* from Feng Tzu-yu, *Ko-ming i-shih,* I, 162–65, is translated in Hsüeh Chün-tu, *Huang Hsing,* pp. 10–11. Hsüeh gives the impression that this document dates from the founding of the Educational Association in early May. As I have mentioned (note 44), this is doubtful.
48. The *Che-chiang ch'ao* claimed that only eleven quit; Chinese student supervisor Wang estimated over a hundred; Shelley Cheng, p. 72. Again, the student movement in Shanghai paralleled this development; in June, there was a split in the group around the *Su-pao,* partly over how radical a stance to assume toward the government. Rankin, *Early Chinese Revolutionaries,* pp. 81–83.
49. Kuo T'ing-i, p. 1185.
50. *Ko-ming i-shih,* I, 165–66.
51. Kuo T'ing-i, p. 1181; Hsüeh Chün-tu, *Huang Hsing,* p. 12.
52. *HHKM,* I, 470–71. One possible reason for the calmer tone of this report was the absence of Minister Ts'ai Chün, who had been recalled on June 15. Ts'ai seems to have been much more alarmist than Wang; the failure of the threat to match his urgent warnings of May, combined with the memory of his altercation with the students in 1902, might have been sufficient to cost him his job.
53. *HHKM,* I, 470–71.

54. Shelley Cheng, p. 98 n. 53; Hsüeh Chün-tu, *Huang Hsing,* p. 7; Schiffrin, p. 258.
55. Chu Ho-chung, "Ou-chou T'ung-meng hui chi-shih" [A record of the T'ung-meng hui in Europe], *Ko-ming wen-hsien* [Documents on the Revolution], 2 (1953): 253–54.
56. Chu Yen-chia, "Wu Lu-chen yü Chung-kuo ko-ming" [Wu Lu-chen and the Chinese revolution], in *Chung-kuo hsien-tai shih ts'ung-k'an* [Selected articles on the contemporary history of China], ed. Wu Hsiang-hsiang, 6 (1964): 166–67.
57. By 1911, Wu was commander of the Sixth Division of the Peiyang Army, and his role in the 1911 Revolution in the north, once thought to be unequivocably revolutionary, has recently been shown to be rather ambiguous. Ernest P. Young, "The Reformer as a Conspirator: Liang Ch'i-ch'ao and the 1911 Revolution," pp. 251–54.
58. Shen Hung-lieh, "Ssu chia-hsiang nien Nan-p'i" [Recalling home and Chang Chih-tung], *Hu-pei wen-hsien,* 1 (1966): 37; Chi I-ch'iao, "Hsien-hsien Wen-hsiang-kung shih-chi t'an," pp. 19–21.
59. This paragraph from Chu Ho-chung, p. 253; Shelley Cheng, p. 87; Chang Nan-hsien, *Hu-pei ko-ming chih-chih lu,* pp. 29–30.
60. It seems possible that Chu Ho-chung's story of intellectuals enlisting in the army is simply misdated. After Chu was shipped off to Europe, this did occur in 1904, in connection with the Science Study Center (note 63).
61. Chang Nan-hsien, p. 30. Chu Yen-chia, p. 168, says that when he left Hupeh, Wu Lu-chen went to Changsha, Hunan, to help in the organization of Huang Hsing's Hua-hsing hui revolt of 1904. But since Chu seems to have misplaced several other events of the 1903–4 period in his account, I am inclined to follow Chang Nan-hsien and to credit Wu with only a brief visit to Hunan, if any at all, before going to his new job in Peking. Liu K'uei-i's major biography of Huang Hsing, however, does list Wu as an initial member of the Hua-hsing hui; Hsüeh Chün-tu, *Huang Hsing,* p. 193 n. 23.
62. See Chu Ho-chung, p. 254, for his account of receiving in the middle of the night an order to see Tuan-fang the next morning, and finding himself on a boat to Shanghai by 4 P.M. of the same day. On January 28, 1904, 25 Hupeh students, with a supervisor, arrived in Belgium; Kuo T'ing-i, p. 1196.
63. Both Chang Nan-hsien and Li Lien-fang seem to refer to the radicals' enlistment as common soldiers at this time as something new and surprising, which leads me to suspect even more Chu Ho-chung's assertion that the same thing happened in 1903 (see note 60).
64. Lü Ta-sen was president; Hu Ying, executive secretary; Ts'ao Ya-p'o, propaganda; Shih Kung-pi, treasurer; Sung Chiao-jen, recording secretary; K'ang Chien-t'ang, general affairs. Also active in the group, and important in the Hupeh revolutionary movement in later years,

were Liu Ching-an and Chang Nan-hsien. Chang Nan-hsien, pp. 56–57, lists 48 men as members of the Science Study Center.

65. Hsüeh Chün-tu, *Huang Hsing,* p. 16.
66. Basic accounts of events in the last two paragraphs are Li Lien-fang, pp. 2b, 4–5, and Chang Nan-hsien, pp. 55–56. Hsüeh Chün-tu, *Huang Hsing,* chap. 2, covers other aspects of the Hua-hsing hui and the abortive Hunan revolt.
67. Chang Nan-hsien, p. 56. Ou-yang Jui-hua himself confirms this in *HHKM,* I, 554.
68. See the overall description by Joseph W. Esherick, "Reform, Revolution and Reaction: The 1911 Revolution in Hunan and Hupei" (Ph.D. diss., University of California, Berkeley, 1971), pp. 86–92.
69. This general description of the P'ing-Liu-Li uprising is taken from Charlton Lewis, "The Opening of Hunan," chap. 7, and especially from Esherick, "Reform, Revolution and Reaction," chap. 3.
70. For Chang's rapid sending of troops to help quell the revolt, and his communications with other principals from December 9, 1906, to January 24, 1907, see *CC,* 85:33–34b, 197:15b–19, 197:31b.
71. Vidya Prakash Dutt, "The First Week of Revolution: The Wuchang Uprising," in Wright, ed., *China in Revolution,* pp. 386–87. There were also some interesting links between this society and the U.S. Episcopal mission in Wuchang.
72. FO 228/1664, Fraser to Jordan, January 19 and January 22, 1907. Fraser's own fear of secret societies was also aroused. Early in January, 1907, he ordered the concession police to cooperate with the Chinese authorities in arresting suspects taking refuge in the concession even without a warrant from himself, which normally was required.
73. *CC,* 107:1–2.
74. See Sanetō Keishū, pp. 153–54. He relies upon the diary of Huang Tsun-san, published under the title *San-shih nien jih-chi* [A diary of thirty years].
75. Recovery of the Canton-Hankow railway rights is dealt with in the next chapter. For a description of the fight to prevent further inroads in Shantung, which was led largely by provincial officials and was already showing results by the end of 1905, see John Schrecker, *Imperialism and Chinese Nationalism,* pp. 149–209, passim.
76. Hsüeh Chün-tu, *Huang Hsing,* p. 44. Schiffrin, p. 362, uses the figure of 15,000, but I am convinced of the relative accuracy of Shih Ching and Sanetō Keishū, who agree on 8,000.
77. Harrell, pp. 207–8.
78. The rules are listed in *KKWH,* series 1, vol. 8, pp. 286–88.
79. General accounts of the strike are in Sanetō Keishū, pp. 461–94, and Shih Ching, pp. 127–35. Minister Yang Shu has a detailed and fairly dispassionate description in his later memorial of January 17, 1906, in *KKWH,* series 1, vol. 8, pp. 285–86.

80. The Japanese language papers were most offensive here, but even the English language *Japan Weekly Mail* opined that "the real cause of anger is the regulation subjecting them to supervision and restraint in the afteracademical hours . . . many of the students having fallen into dissipation such as not only ruins their own prospects but constitutes a contaminating influence" (December 16, 1905, p. 651).
81. Ernest P. Young, "Ch'en T'ien-hua," pp. 243–44.
82. *CC,* 195:11–11b, 16–16b; Ayers, pp. 246–47, also has a description of Chang's reactions. It was reported that Yüan Shih-k'ai was also totally unsympathetic to the protesting students, and wanted to arrest all of those who returned to China. *Japan Weekly Mail,* December 23, 1905, p. 677.
83. Sanetō Keishū, pp. 487–90, has the most detailed account of the struggle between the two factions.
84. Estimates of the number who returned to China vary from 400 (Hsü *nien-p'u,* p. 196), to 1,000 (*Japan Weekly Mail,* January 6, 1906, p. 5), to 2,000 (Ernest P. Young, "Ch'en T'ien-hua," p. 244). Y. C. Wang, *Chinese Intellectuals and the West,* p. 62, says that most returned to Japan. Those who remained in Shanghai formed the Chinese Public Institute (Chung-kuo kung-hsüeh) early in 1906, though they had difficulty in finding sufficient students and funds; Mary Backus Rankin, *Early Chinese Revolutionaries,* pp. 113–15.
85. *KKWH,* series 1, vol. 8, p. 286.
86. Hsü *nien-p'u,* p. 196; *Japan Weekly Mail,* January 6, 1906, p. 5.
87. *CC,* 195:19b; *KKWH,* series 1, vol. 8, p. 286.
88. *KKWH,* series 1, vol. 8, p. 286; Sanetō Keishū, p. 488; Noriko Tamada, "Sung Chiao-jen and the 1911 Revolution," *Papers on China* 21 (1968): 191–92. Also see K. S. Liew, *Struggle for Democracy: Sung Chiao-jen and the 1911 Chinese Revolution* (Berkeley, 1971), pp. 52–58, who speculates as to a further regional split among the participants, with Sung and Hu Ying representing central China, and Wang Ching-wei and Hu Han-min a Cantonese faction.
89. In addition to the government's making the qualifications for study abroad more stringent after 1905, Minister Yang Shu in Tokyo continued to keep an eye out for troublemakers and managed to nip future student movements in the bud. In late January, 1907, for example, he conducted an investigation of the Chinese students, and at his request the Japanese government deported 39 of them on February 17, 1907. Kuo T'ing-i, p. 1269. In the following month, Sun Yat-sen was also deported.
90. For some excellent comments on this point, see Mary Backus Rankin, *Early Chinese Revolutionaries,* pp. 5–11, 231.
91. Shih Ching, pp. 40–49, gives many cases here; also Y. C. Wang, *Chinese Intellectuals and the West,* pp. 68–70.
92. Huang Fu-ch'ing, "Ch'ing-mo te liu-Jih cheng-ts'e," pp. 88–94; Y. C.

Wang, *Chinese Intellectuals and the West,* pp. 64–65; Shih Ching, pp. 145–46.

93. *KKWH,* series 1, vol. 8, pp. 283–85.
94. For Ts'ai, Ts'ao, Liu, and Ch'ien, see Boorman: III, 297; III, 287; II, 411–12; I, 367–68, respectively.
95. This conclusion is rather at variance with that of Harrell, "The Years of the Young Radicals."

Chapter 8

1. For the best account here, see Li Kuo-chi, *Chung-kuo tsao-ch'i te t'ieh-lu ching-ying,* pp. 148–78.
2. Li En-han, "Chung-Mei shou-hui Yüeh-Han lu-ch'üan chiao-she: wan-Ch'ing shou-hui t'ieh-lu li-ch'üan yün-tung te yen-chiu chih i" [The Sino-American negotiations for the recovery of the Canton-Hankow railway rights: The late Ch'ing movement for recovery of railway rights, part 1], *Chung-yang yen-chiu-yüan chin-tai shih yen-chiu so chi-k'an,* 1 (August 1969): 149–54. The amount was increased due to a more realistic estimate of the costs after the line was surveyed in late 1898 and 1899. For a fascinating account of the surveying expedition by the chief engineer, see Wm. Barclay Parson, *An American Engineer in China* (New York, 1900).
3. Li En-han, p. 161; William R. Braisted, "The United States and the American China Development Company, 1895–1911," *Far Eastern Quarterly* 11.2 (February 1952): 153–55.
4. Li En-han, pp. 161–62.
5. Ibid., pp. 162–65; Braisted, pp. 155–56.
6. Hsü *nien-p'u,* p. 181; Li En-han, p. 164.
7. *CC,* 189:23–24. While he was acting governor-general in Nanking early in 1903, Chang had worked jointly with Sheng in trying to improve the terms of the British concession and loan on the Shanghai-Nanking railway line, but they had largely failed. E-tu Zen Sun, *Chinese Railways and British Interests 1898–1911* (New York, 1954), pp. 50–53. This may have been partially responsible for Sheng's reluctance.
8. The term "national elite," used here, as in the introduction, to distinguish gentry with national connections from those with a more limited provincial or local outlook and radius of influence, is still not sufficiently precise; neither are other terms such as "provincial elite" or "public opinion." I agree with the general observations made by Philip A. Kuhn on the need to differentiate between the national, provincial, and local levels of the gentry class; *Rebellion and Its Enemies in Late Imperial China,* pp. 183–88, and p. 217 n. 44. The difficulty is in deciding on what basis to do so. We are still far from an adequate understanding of the different subdivisions of the post-1900

elite, in terms of traditional and modern status criteria, generational and urban-rural gaps, national and sub-national identification, etc.

In a broad sense, all those to whom I refer as "gentry," or "elite," including the students in Japan and those in modern schools in China as well, are members of the same general social-economic-political class, although that class was in motion after 1900. Yet divisions certainly seem in order. One the most stimulating efforts to approach this problem is made by Joseph W. Esherick, who detects a shift in dominance within the gentry class in Hunan and Hupeh between 1900 and 1911 from the "conservative gentry" (the "national elite" I have referred to above) to a younger, progressive, urban-oriented "reformist elite"; "Reform, Revolution and Reaction," chap. 4.

9. It is possible, of course, that another reason for this was that Chang's position at court was now quite secure, or that he was even more afraid of other people using his British support against him than he was in 1901 and 1902.
10. FO 228/1595, Fraser to Satow, July 11, 1905; FO 228/1632, Fraser's report of July 6, 1906.
11. For example, FO 228/1664, Fraser's report of January 9, 1907, and Fraser to Jordan, April 16, 1907. The departure in the fall of 1904 of the talented Liang Tun-yen, for years Chang's chief link with Fraser and other diplomats, may also have contributed to the chill in relations. Liang, one of Chang's most trusted advisers, went to Tientsin as taotai, and soon rose rapidly within the bureaucracy of the Ministry of Foreign Affairs. Chang certainly missed Liang's services, as he often let it be known. FO 228/1554, Fraser to Satow, October 8, 1904; FO 228/1595, Fraser to Satow, January 4, 1905.
12. *CC,* 189:17b.
13. Li En-han, pp. 165–67. The dissertations by Charlton M. Lewis and Joseph W. Esherick both have considerable biographic data on some of the leading Hunan gentry members mentioned in this paragraph.
14. FO 17/1762, Satow to Lansdowne, July 27, 1904, enclosed translation from the Shanghai *Chung-wai jih-pao* of July 10. In 1902, when this same group of gentry, led by Wang Hsien-ch'ien, moved to set up a province-wide mining company for the same purpose of preempting foreigners, they also expressed a willingness to borrow abroad if they could not raise the entire capitalization of two million taels. Esherick, p. 137.
15. Li En-han, p. 167.
16. Quotations from all four publications mentioned in this paragraph are to be found in ibid., pp. 172–74.
17. Quoted in ibid., p. 175.
18. Ibid., pp. 176–78. Yang Tu, it will be remembered, was one of the two students to whom Chang Chih-tung had awarded highest honors in the

special examination in Peking in the summer of 1903, before his choices had been eliminated in the second round.

19. United States National Archives, *Despatches from United States Consuls in Shanghai,* FM-112, roll 50, enclosure of June 22, 1904.
20. Li En-han, p. 168; E-tu Zen Sun, p. 77.
21. Li En-han, pp. 168–69; Hsü *nien-p'u,* pp. 183–84.
22. *CC,* 191:15b.
23. See the comments of Li En-han, pp. 169, 179.
24. Ibid., pp. 179–80.
25. Braisted, pp. 156–58.
26. Li En-han, p. 182.
27. Quoted in ibid., pp. 182–83.
28. Ibid., pp. 183–84; E-tu Zen Sun, p. 78.
29. Li En-han, pp. 184–85.
30. Ibid., pp. 185–86.
31. Braisted, pp. 160–63; Li En-han, pp. 187–90.
32. E-tu Zen Sun, pp. 77–80.
33. Ibid., pp. 80–83.
34. A Hankow newspaper in 1906 remarked that after the redemption, "the gentry and people of Hupeh . . . extolled Chang Chih-tung . . . [and] those of other provinces were loud in his praise." Translation in FO 228/1632, Fraser's report of May 12, 1906.
35. Li En-han, pp. 192–95.
36. This distinction between "modern provincial elite" and "national elite" is tenuous, because both groups, after all, were part of what up until 1900 and even after was the same general class of "gentry." This distinction corresponds more or less to Joseph Esherick's distinction between "reformist elite" and "conservative gentry"; the very attempt to make such an analytical differentiation in this case is heavily indebted to the detailed research and lucid exposition presented in his dissertation. I will continue to use the generic "gentry" or "provincial gentry" when both of these groups seem to be involved, or are obviously acting together.
37. FO 405/156, p. 88, Satow to Lansdowne, September 15, 1905.
38. Li En-han, pp. 193–94.
39. FO 405/157, pp. 116–17, Fraser to Satow, October 31, 1905.
40. FO 405/157, p. 43, Satow to Lansdowne, October 31, 1905.
41. Ibid.
42. For Chang's telegrams to Ch'ü and the Ministry of Foreign Affairs, see *CC,* 194:28–29b, 195:1b–4. Fraser's report is in FO 405/157, p. 117.
43. The quote is in a summary of an interview between Mr. C. W. Campbell of the British legation staff and Yüan Shih-k'ai, dated November 7, enclosure in FO 405/165, p. 20, Satow to Lansdowne, November 13, 1905.
44. *CC,* 194:29b–30b.

45. Li En-han, pp. 193–94.
46. *CC,* 65:21b–35, 66:1–18.
47. FO 228/1595, Fraser to Satow, November 23, 1905.
48. FO 228/1595, Fraser to Satow, December 26, 1905.
49. For the Shanghai-Nanking line, see E-tu Zen Sun, pp. 53–61. For the Shanghai-Hangchow line, see Sun, pp. 61–68; En-han Lee, "The Chekiang Gentry-Merchants Vs. the Peking Court Officials: China's Struggle for Recovery of the British Soochow-Hangchow-Ningpo Railway Concession, 1905–1911," *Chung-yang yen-chiu-yüan chin-tai shih yen-chiu so chi-k'an* 3.1 (July 1972): 223–68; and especially Madeleine Chi, "Shanghai-Hangchow-Ningpo Railway Loan: A Case Study of the Rights Recovery Movement," *Modern Asian Studies* 7.1 (1973): 85–106. Chi's article is superior in that she follows the fate of the issue after 1908, showing that the Chinese company, which had dramatically pledged not to use the forced British loan, eventually did precisely that.
50. En-han Lee, "China's Response to Foreign Investment in Her Mining Industry (1902–1911)," *Journal of Asian Studies* 28.1 (November 1968): 68–72. For mining rights recovery in Shantung province, see Schrecker, *Imperialism and Chinese Nationalism,* pp. 179–91.
51. The late Mary C. Wright, in her last major work ("Introduction: The Rising Tide of Change," in *China in Revolution*), has helped to redirect our attention to the contemporary writings of some of these foreign observers and residents. Satow's comment in FO 405/165, p. 120. One of many journalists' accounts is Thomas F. Millard, *The New Far East* (New York, 1906).
52. "Reform, Revolution and Reaction," chap. 4. He sees this as an example of diverging interests between the old elite and the new "reformist elite" (or the "modern provincial elite," as I have called it).
53. Hsü *nien-p'u,* p. 195.
54. FO 405/157, pp. 87–88.
55. For a brief account of how the Kwangtung redemption coalition already broke down into competing interest groups in early 1906, see Edward J. M. Rhoads, *China's Republican Revolution: The Case of Kwangtung, 1895–1913* (Cambridge, 1975), pp. 91–92.
56. See Madeleine Chi, "Shanghai-Hangchow-Ningpo Railway Loan," and Esherick, chap. 4, for some examples.

Chapter 9

1. Hsü *nien-p'u,* p. 206.
2. Ibid., pp. 196–201, passim, and E-tu Zen Sun, pp. 91–96.
3. For the basic facts on this line, see Hsü *nien-p'u,* p. 202, and E-tu Zen Sun, pp. 131–33.
4. FO 228/1664, Fraser's report of April 8, 1907; FO 405/175, p. 244; *NCH,* May 11, 1908, p. 353.

5. FO 228/1644, Fraser's report of April 8, 1907.
6. See, for example, Fraser's 1907 report in ibid., and his report of a 1906 conversation with Liang Tun-yen in PRO 30/33/8/11, a private letter to Satow, March 17, 1906.
7. Fraser's report on a conversation with Liang Tun-yen in PRO 30/33/8/11, private letter to Satow, March 17, 1906; FO 228/1632, Fraser's intelligence report dated April 7, 1906.
8. PRO 30/33/8/11, Fraser to Satow, March 17, 1906.
9. An excellent description of this power struggle is to be found in Stephen S. MacKinnon, "Yüan Shih-k'ai in Tientsin and Peking," pp. 105–19. Another casualty was Chang Chih-tung's old associate Wang K'ang-nien, whose Peking newspaper had allied itself with Ch'ü Hung-chi in the struggle and was closed down a few weeks after Ch'ü's fall.
10. FO 350/4, Jordan personal letters to F. Campbell at the Foreign Office, July 11, August 8, September 4, 1907. FO 405/175, Jordan to Grey, August 21, 1907.
11. The narrative which follows in this and the next paragraph derives from Kuo T'ing-i, pp. 1278–87, and Hsü *nien-p'u,* pp. 203–4, 206.
12. The assertion that Chang telegraphed Lu on August 6 appears only in Hsü *nien-p'u,* p. 206, and the telegram is not in *CC,* but I am inclined to accept it as valid. Suspicion that Chang's request for sick leave was political in nature is enhanced by Fraser's observation a month before that Chang "looks very well and is more garrulous than ever when we meet." FO 228/1664, Fraser's intelligence report of July 8, 1907.
13. It is possible that Yüan Shih-k'ai was doing the same sort of thing when on July 28, in the midst of rumors as to his future and having given himself an escape route by his previous request for sick leave, he memorialized recommending faster moves toward a constitutional system.
14. This telegram is in *CC,* 200:14b–15.
15. Li Chien-nung, *The Political History of China, 1840–1928,* pp. 211–12; Immanuel C. Y. Hsü, *The Rise of Modern China,* p. 497.
16. FO 405/175, Jordan to Grey, August 21, 1907; FO 350/4, Jordan to Campbell, September 4, 1907.
17. Hsü *nien-p'u,* pp. 206–7.
18. Ibid., pp. 197–200, passim.
19. *NCH,* September 20, 1907. It is, of course, possible that Chang was in fact ill, or weak from his journey. On September 27, he wired his old associates Liang Ting-fen and Huang Shao-chi back in Wuchang that since his arrival in Peking, his old asthma had flared up again. *CC,* 201:1.
20. This account appeared in the *Hupeh News* (*O-pao?*) on October 7; a translation is included in Fraser's compilation of local press extracts, FO 228/1644, Fraser to Jordan, October 12, 1907. It is always possible that the account is spurious.

21. Kuo T'ing-i, p. 1288.
22. MacKinnon, "Yüan Shih-k'ai in Tientsin and Peking," chap. 5.
23. Ibid., charts pp. 198–200.
24. Liang's remarks reported by Fraser to Satow, March 17, 1906. PRO 30/33/8/11.
25. FO 228/1632, Fraser's intelligence report, April 7, 1906, reporting a conversation with Liang Tun-yen.
26. FO 350/4, Jordan to Campbell, September 4, 1907. FO 405/175, Jordan to Grey, September 18, 1907. Again on November 11 Jordan reported to Grey that Chang Chih-tung's activities were being utilized as a "counterpoise to the progressive tendencies of his younger rival Yüan Shih-k'ai."
27. Hsü *nien-p'u,* p. 209.
28. See Hsiao I-shan, *Ch'ing-tai t'ung-shih,* IV, 2462–63. Also Chang Ping-to, *Chang Chih-tung p'ing-chuan,* pp. 270–71, 284. Both of these sources are quite hostile to Yüan, Chang Ping-to immensely so.
29. E-tu Zen Sun, pp. 131–36, and further elaboration below.
30. *NCH,* September 20, 1907, p. 700, claims that Chang and Yüan, soon after their arrival in Peking, jointly recommended that a national parliament be convened in 1911; *NCH,* July 25, 1908, p. 231, reported that of the six grand councillors, Chang and Yüan alone agreed that a full constitutional system should be implemented in as short a period as five years.
31. *NCH,* January 31, 1908, p. 283.
32. Ibid., January 24, 1908, p. 219, and May 23, 1908, p. 476.
33. Ibid., May 30, 1908, p. 545, and January 2, 1909, p. 2.
34. Kuo T'ing-i, p. 1322, and Chang Ping-to, p. 285. Chang's foremost Chinese biographer claims, more credibly I think, that the Grand Council, minus Yüan, was ordered to make up the edict for Yüan's dismissal, which had been decided upon, and that Chang hit upon the idea of an ailing foot as the excuse; however, he also reports that Chang was very upset at the arbitrary manner in which the whole affair was handled. Hsü *nien-p'u,* p. 228. A further indication that Chang was in no position to decide Yüan's fate one way or the other was a report that Chang himself was apprehensive for his own position in the day or two following Yüan's dismissal. Walter Hillier to Jordan, January 3, 1909, in FO 405/190, no. 75.
35. *NCH,* October 2, 1909, p. 22.
36. From Yüan's point of view, MacKinnon, "Yüan Shih-k'ai in Tientsin and Peking," p. 195, concludes that the relationship seemed "distant but not hostile."
37. *NCH,* November 21, 1908, p. 495; November 28, 1908, p. 524; January 2, 1909, p. 2; January 16, 1909, p. 139.
38. Ibid., August 7, 1909, p. 354, and August 21, 1909, p. 414.
39. FO 405/190, Jordan to Grey, March 16, 1909.

40. See Jordan's comments in ibid., and in FO 405/191, Jordan to Grey, July 15, 1909. The foreign diplomats were especially sensitive to a decline in the effectiveness of the Ministry of Foreign Affairs, of course.
41. Ayers, pp. 245–51, places much emphasis upon Chang's concern in this area.
42. Kuo T'ing-i, p. 1288.
43. The above items from Hsü *nien-p'u,* pp. 212–13, 218. In his last months, Chang was also hard at work designing a course of study for the education of the young Hsüan-t'ung emperor; *NCH,* May 8, 1909, p. 326.
44. Hsü *nien-p'u,* p. 213; *NCH,* February 21, 1908, p. 451, and September 19, 1908, p. 715.
45. Kuo T'ing-i, pp. 1242–43. Also see E-tu Zen Sun, "The Chinese Constitutional Missions of 1905–1906," *Journal of Modern History* 24.3 (September 1952): 251–68.
46. Hsü *nien-p'u,* p. 206. The telegram is in *CC,* 196:26–26b.
47. Kuo T'ing-i, p. 1258.
48. Ibid., pp. 1262–63. Also see MacKinnon, "Yüan Shih-k'ai in Tientsin and Peking," pp. 111–13.
49. Kuo T'ing-i, p. 1262. The draft can be found in *CC,* 197:28b–31.
50. The lieutenant governor would be responsible for constitutional government, agriculture, public works, and commerce; in addition to finances, the new commissioner for financial administration would also supervise communications.
51. Chang was already hostile to the Reorganization Office because the representative he had sent to Peking to participate in the discussions had been ignored, and the office presented the package of proposals to the provincial officials as a fait accompli. In late 1906, before his formal protests on the defects of the draft reorganization, he also denounced the speed and carelessness of its preparation in a letter to a friend. Hsü *nien-p'u,* p. 206.
52. The telegram is in *CC,* 197:19–28b.
53. *CC,* 197:19b–20.
54. This telegram is in *CC,* 197:32–35.
55. FO 405/178, "Annual Report, 1907—China," p. 3, says that Chang "took the lead" in opposition. *NCH,* January 25, 1907, pp. 175–76, claims that Tuan-fang, Ts'en Ch'un-hsüan and Chou Fu all approved the draft; only Chang and Governor Wu Chang-hsi of Kiangsi opposed it.
56. Kuo T'ing-i, pp. 1273, 1275, 1279. Also FO 405/175, Jordan to Grey, July 11, 1907.
57. Kuo T'ing-i, pp. 1281–82. For some press samples, see FO 228/1664, Fraser's selection of press extracts, April 26 and May 27, 1907.
58. Kuo T'ing-i, p. 1283.

59. *NCH,* September 20, 1907, p. 700.
60. FO 228/1664, Fraser's press extracts of October 12, 1907.
61. This was followed up in July, 1908, with more detailed regulations for the actual selection of delegates to the provincial assemblies. Kuo T'ing-i, pp. 1291, 1309.
62. Ibid., pp. 1293, 1295–96. Rhoads, *China's Republican Revolution,* p. 152, notes that "the constitutional program was designed specifically to provide a set of proper forums for public debate," and to restrict participation to these "approved channels." This is, I think, an accurate description.
63. *NCH,* August 29, 1908, p. 536, June 20, 1908, p. 749, July 25, 1908, p. 231; and Ting Wen-chiang, p. 273, respectively. The latter claim is by one of Liang Ch'i-ch'ao's friends, in correspondence with Liang in 1908.
64. *NCH,* February 15, 1909, p. 384.
65. E-tu Zen Sun, *Chinese Railways and British Interests,* chap. 4; also John Gilbert Reid, *The Manchu Abdication and the Powers, 1908–1912* (Berkeley, 1935).
66. Hsü *nien-p'u,* p. 201. The memorial is in *CC,* 68:8b–16b.
67. Kuo T'ing-i, p. 1307.
68. The edict specifically noted the lack of construction progress as justification for delegating one overall supervisor. Hsü *nien-p'u,* p. 212; Kuo T'ing-i, p. 1309.
69. FO 405/189, Jordan to Grey, July 21, 1908. Interestingly, at this time the president of the Kwangtung Railway Company was Liang Ch'eng, formerly minister to Washington and Chang's agent for negotiating the redemption of the line in 1905.
70. The edict is quoted in Hsü *nien-p'u,* p. 214.
71. *NCH,* October 31, 1908, p. 261, and November 7, 1908, p. 340; the latter claims that Chang had already announced his trip to the south, and planned to leave in late November.
72. Kuo T'ing-i, pp. 1319–20.
73. Hsü *nien-p'u,* p. 215.
74. For example, it seems that the favorable terms of the Tientsin-Pukou loan agreement, announced in January, 1908, preempted potential criticism of it on nationalistic grounds. Here I am reading some into E-tu Zen Sun, *Chinese Railways and British Interests,* pp. 133–35.
75. Ibid., p. 101.
76. This very complicated series of events is handled quite ably in ibid., pp. 101–11. Also see Reid, pp. 21–43.
77. The last minute United States arrival created tension between Chang and his old associate Liang Tun-yen, now foreign minister, who recognized that in the form in which it had come, the United States initiative could not be rebuffed. See Reid, pp. 41–50.
78. For example, on March 22, 1909, Chang telegraphed the Kwangtung

officials and gentry, excoriating them for obstructing the establishment of a Canton-Hankow general line branch office in Canton. Hsü *nien-p'u,* p. 218.

79. FO 405/195, "China—Annual Report, 1909," p. 15. Also FO 405/198, Jordan to Grey, October 23, 1909. Reid, p. 55, likewise concludes that Chang's death "removed the one man in public life who might prevent a bitter clash between Peking and the provinces."
80. FO 405/198, nos. 239 and 241, Jordan to Grey, November, 1909.
81. *NCH,* September 25, 1909, p. 723.
82. Ting Wen-chiang, pp. 273, 289; Kuo T'ing-i, p. 1322.
83. Kuo T'ing-i, p. 1311. Yüan requested its prohibition after the Cheng-wen she attacked him. It is unclear how Chang felt about the Cheng-wen she. Chang Ping-to, pp. 285–86, claims that Yüan's adherents tricked Chang into requesting its abolition by telling him that he (Chang), as well as Yüan and Prince Ch'ing, was a target of its hostility; this claim is perhaps compromised by the author's anti-Yüan bias.
84. *NCH,* February 6, 1909, p. 318.
85. Chang Ping-to, p. 273.
86. Kuo T'ing-i, pp. 1258–96, passim; *NCH,* 1907, passim.
87. See, for example, the Shanghai newspapers translated in Fraser's press extracts for the first part of 1907, in FO 228/1664.
88. Hsü *nien-p'u,* p. 219.
89. Ibid., p. 220. A General Staff Council (Chün-tzu ch'u), prelude to a modern General Staff, independent of the Ministry of War, was set up under the regent, to direct the armed forces.
90. Ibid.
91. Rhoads, *China's Republican Revolution,* p. 204, says that "at the end of 1910 the Ch'ing dynasty was still a viable regime." I agree to some extent, but what would prove to be the fatal defects of the regime were certainly clearly evident to Chang Chih-tung already in 1909.

Conclusion

1. His memorial in *CC,* 70:24b–26b.
2. *Tung-fang tsa-chih,* 6.10 (1909): 32–40, and 6.11 (1909): 53–55; *The Times,* October 6, 1909; *NCH,* October 9, 1909, pp. 67–68, 79; FO 405/195, "China—Annual Report, 1909," p. 6. However, the organ of the T'ung-meng hui in Tokyo, the *Min-pao,* published a scathing denunciation of Chang's career; "Chang Chih-tung ssu" [The death of Chang Chih-tung], in no. 25 (February 1910), pp. 16–19.
3. *Hsü nien-p'u,* pp. 224–28. Governor-General Chao Erh-sun of Szechuan praised Chang's work as educational commissioner there early in his career; Governor-General Chang Jen-chün at Nanking requested permission to erect a memorial to Chang in memory of his sometime service there.

4. Some comments by E. H. Fraser from 1902 are perceptive in this regard. Fraser, analyzing Chang as standing between the exiled radicals and the extreme court conservatives, said, "He dreams of a court purified of greedy eunuchs and . . . placemen, [and a] government advancing upon cautious, steady reform." FO 228/1457, Fraser to Satow, January 4, 1902.
5. I am indebted to Ernest P. Young for the concept that practical power deriving from control of reform programs was not a zero-sum game. I.e., after 1900 both central government and provincial elite could simultaneously expand their area of initiative and control (although presumably at some point they would inevitably become rivals).

Glossary

This glossary excludes persons who appear as authors in the bibliography. Proper names are alphabetized as if a comma follows the family name. Hyphen, apostrophe, and umlaut are ignored in alphabetization.

an-ch'a shih 按察使
Aoki 青木

chang-ch'eng 章程
Chang Chi 張繼
Chang Chien 張謇
Chang Ch'üan 張權
Chang Hsiao-ch'ien 張孝謙
Chang Jen-chün 張人駿
Chang Ping-lin 章炳麟
Chang Po-hsi 張百熙
Chang Shih-chao 章士釗
Chang Ssu-hsün 張斯恂
Chang Tsu-t'ung 張祖同
Chang Yin-huan 張蔭桓
Ch'ang-yen pao 昌言報
Chao Erh-feng 趙爾豐
Chao Erh-sun 趙爾巽
Chao Feng-ch'ang 趙鳳昌
ch'ao-t'ing 朝廷
che 摺
Che-chiang ch'ao 浙江潮
chen 鎮
Ch'en Chih 陳熾
Ch'en Ch'i-t'ai 陳啓泰
Ch'en I 陳毅
Ch'en Pao-chen 陳寶箴
Ch'en Pao-ch'en 陳寶琛
Ch'en San-li 陳三立
Ch'en T'ien-hua 陳天華
Ch'en Wen-hsien 陳問咸
Ch'en Yen 陳衍
ch'eng 城
Cheng-ch'i hui 正氣會
Cheng-ch'üan 正權
Cheng Hsiao-hsü 鄭孝胥
Cheng-hsüeh pao 正學報
cheng-i 正義.
Cheng-wen she 政聞社
Chi Chü-wei 紀鉅維
Chi I-hui 戢翼翬
Chiang Piao 江標
Ch'iang-hsüeh hui 强學會
Ch'iang-hsüeh pao 强學報
Chiang-su 江蘇
Ch'ien Hsüan-t'ung 錢玄同
Ch'ien Hsün 錢恂
Chih-chün 志鈞
Chih-hsin pao 知新報
Chih-hsüeh hui 質學會

Chih-tu chü 制度局
chih-yen 卮言
Ch'in Li-shan 秦力山
chin-shih 進士
Ch'in-wang Chün 勤王軍
Ch'ing, Prince 慶親王
Ching Yüan-shan 經元善
ching-chi t'e-k'o 經濟特科
ch'ing-i 清議
Ch'ing-i pao 清議報
ch'ing-liu 清流
Ch'ing-nien hui 青年會
Ching-pao 京報
Ching-shih wen-pien 經世文編
Ch'iu Shu-yüan 邱菽園
chou 州
Chou Fu 周馥
chü 局
Ch'ü Hung-chi 瞿鴻禨
Ch'ü T'ing-shao 瞿廷韶
Ch'üan-chieh Shang-hai Kuo-hui chi ch'u-yang hsüeh-sheng wen 勸戒上海國會及出洋學生文
Ch'üan-hsüeh p'ien 勸學篇
chü-jen 舉人
Chün kuo-min chiao-yü hui 軍國民教育會
Ch'un, Prince 醇親王
Chung-kuo kung-hsüeh 中國公學
Chung-kuo liu-hsüeh-sheng hui-kuan 中國留學生會館
Chung-kuo ts'an-yung min-ch'üan chih li-i 中國參用民權之利益
chung-shu 中書
Chung-wai chi-wen 中外紀聞
Chung-wai jih-pao 中外日報
Chün-tzu ch'u 軍諮處
ch'u-shen 出身
chu-shih 主事

En-ming 恩銘

Feng Ch'i-chün 馮啓鈞
Feng Kuei-fen 馮桂芬
fu 府
Fu Chang Chih-tung shu 復張之洞書
Fu Tz'u-hsiang 傅慈祥
fu-kuo ch'iang-ping 富國强兵
fu-yu 富有
fu-yu p'iao 富有票

Han Wen-chü 韓文舉
Han-k'ou jih-pao 漢口日報
Han-pao 漢報
hou-hsü 後序
hsi-fa 西法
Hsi-liang 錫良
Hsi-yüan (palace) 西苑
Hsia Chieh-fu 夏偕復
hsiang 鄉
Hsiang-hsüeh pao 湘學報
Hsiang-pao 湘報
hsiang-shen 鄉紳
hsieh-pan ta-hsüeh shih 協辦大學士
hsien 縣
Hsien-cheng pien-ch'a kuan 憲政編查館
hsin-ch'i 新奇
Hsin-min ts'ung-pao 新民叢報
Hsiung Hsi-ling 熊希齡
hsiu-ts'ai tang ping 秀才當兵
hsü 序
Hsü Chih-hsiang 徐致祥
Hsü Ch'in 徐勤
Hsü Jen-chu 徐仁鑄
Hsü Shih-ch'ang 徐世昌
Hsü T'ung 徐桐
Hsüan-t'ung 宣統
Hsüeh-sheng chün 學生軍
hsün-su 迅速
Hu Han-min 胡漢民
Hu Ying 胡英
Hua-hsing hui 華興會

Huang Ch'ang-nien 黃昌年
Huang Chung-huang 黃中黃
Huang Hsing 黃興
Huang Shao-chi 黃紹箕
Huang Shao-ti 黃紹第
Huang T'i-fang 黃體芳
Huang Tsun-hsien 黃遵憲
Huang-ch'ao ching-shih wen-pien 皇朝經世文編
hui 會
Hu-pei ch'üan-sheng hsüeh-wu ch'u 湖北全省學務處
Hu-pei hsüeh-sheng chieh 湖北學生界

I Nai 易鼐
i-chien shu 意見書
I-ku 貽穀
i-shih hui 議事會
I-shu chü 譯書局
I-shu kuan-chü 譯書官局
Ito Hirobumi 伊藤博文
I-yung tui 義勇隊

jen-min 人民
Jih-chih hsin-pao 日知新報
Jih-chih hui 日知會
Jung-ch'ing 榮慶
Jung-lu 榮祿

K'ang Chien-t'ang 康建唐
K'ang Kuang-jen 康廣仁
K'ang Yu-wei 康有爲
Kang-i 剛毅
K'ao-ch'a cheng-chih kuan 考察政治館
K'o-hsüeh pu-hsi so 科學補習所
Ko-lao hui 哥老會
ko-ming 革命
K'uai Kuang-tien 蒯光典
Kuan-chih pien-chih kuan 官制編制館
Kuang Ch'i-chao 鄺其照
Kuang-fu hui 光復會
Kuang-hsü 光緒
Kuan-pao 官報
Kuan-shu chü 官書局
kuan-tu shang-pan 官督商辦
K'ung Kuang-te (Lü Yang-sheng) 孔廣德
Kung-i hsüeh-t'ang 工藝學堂
kung-sheng 貢生
K'ung-tzu kai-chih k'ao 孔子改制考
K'un-kang 崑岡
kuo-chia 國家
kuo-hui 國會
Kuo-hui 國會
Kuo-wen pao 國聞報

Lan T'ien-wei 藍天蔚
lao shu-sheng 老書生
Li Han-chang 李瀚章
Li Hung-chang 李鴻章
Li Hung-tsao 李鴻藻
Li Lien-ying 李連英
Li Pao-sun 李寶巽
Li P'eng-sheng 李鵬生
Li Ping-heng 李秉衡
Li Ping-huan 李炳寰
Li Pu-ch'ing (Li Lien-fang) 李步青
Li Shao-fen 李紹芬
Li Sheng-to 李盛鐸
Li Shu-ch'ang 李庶昌
Li Te-shun 李德順
Li Wei-ko 李維格
Liang Ch'eng 梁誠
Liang Shih-i 梁士詒
Liang Ting-fen 梁鼎芬
Liang Tun-yen 梁敦彥
Liang-hu shu-yüan 兩湖書院
Liao Shou-feng 廖壽豐
Li-chih hui 勵志會
likin 釐金

Lin Hsü 林旭
Lin Kuei 林圭
Liu Ching-an 劉靜菴
Liu Keng-yün 劉賡雲
Liu Kuang-ti 劉光第
Liu K'uei-i 劉揆一
Liu K'un-i 劉坤一
Liu Pang-chi 劉邦驥
Liu Shih-p'ei 劉師培
Liu-Jih hsüeh-sheng lien-ho hui 留日學生聯合會
Lo Chen-yü 羅振玉
Lo Feng-lu 羅豐祿
Lu Ching-yüan 盧靜遠
Lu Ch'uan-lin 鹿傳霖
Lü Hai-huan 呂海寰
Lu Pao-chung 陸寶忠
Lü Ta-sen 呂大森
Lü Yang-sheng 魯陽生
luan 亂
Lung Chan-lin 龍湛霖
lung-t'ou 龍頭

Ma Fu-i 馬福益
Mai Meng-hua 麥孟華
Miao Ch'üan-sun 繆荃孫
min-chu 民主
min-ch'üan 民權
min-chu chih ch'üan 民主之權
ming-chiao 名教
Ming-kang 明綱
mo-i 末議
Mou-ch'in court 懋勤殿
mu-fu 幕府

Na-t'ung 那桐
Nan-hsüeh hui 南學會
Nan-yang ta-ch'en 南洋大臣
nei-p'ien 內篇
Niu Yung-chien 鈕永建
Nung-hsüeh pao 農學報
Nung-wu hsüeh-t'ang 農務學堂

Odagiri Masunosuke 小田切萬壽
O-pao 鄂報
Ou Ch'ü-chia 歐榘甲
Ou-yang Jui-hua 歐陽瑞驊
Ou-yang Lin 歐陽霖

P'an Ch'ing-lan 潘慶瀾
pao-chia 保甲
pao-huang 保皇
Pao-huang hui 保皇會
Pao-kuo hui 保國會
pao-wei chü 保衛局
pen 本
P'i Hsi-jui 皮錫瑞
Pi Yung-nien 畢永年
p'ien 片
p'ien-chien 偏見
pien-fa 變法
p'in-ming 拚命
Po hou-tang Chang Chih-tung Yü Yin-lin wei-shih 駁后黨張之洞于蔭霖僞示
pu-cheng shih 布政使
P'u-chün 溥儁

Rikugun Shikan Gakkō 陸軍士官學校

Segawa 瀨川
Seijō Gakkō 成城學校
shang-wu chü 商務局
Shang-wu pao 商務報
Shao-ying 紹英
Shen Chin 沈藎
Shen Hsiang-yün 沈翔雲
Shen Tseng-chih 沈曾植
Sheng Hsüan-huai 盛宣懷
sheng-yüan 生員
Shen-pao 申報
Shih Kung-pi 時功璧
Shih-hsü 世續
Shih-lu 實錄
Shih-pao 時報

shih-wu 時務
Shih-wu hsüeh-t'ang 時務學堂
Shih-wu jih-pao 時務日報
Shih-wu pao 時務報
Shinpu Gakkō 振武學校
shishi 志士
shu 署
Shuang Shou 雙壽
shu-yüan 書院
su-ch'eng k'o 速成科
Sun Chia-nai 孫家鼐
Sun Chung-yü 孫仲愚
Sun Pao-ch'i 孫寶琦
Sun Yat-sen 孫逸仙
Sung Chiao-jen 宋教仁
Sung Po-lu 宋伯魯
Sung Yü-jen 宋育仁
Su-pao 蘇報
su-wang kai-chih 素王改制

ta-hsüeh shih 大學士
Tai Hung-tz'u 戴鴻慈
ta-kang 大綱
T'an Chi-hsün 譚繼洵
T'an Chung-lin 譚鍾麟
T'an Ssu-t'ung 譚嗣同
tang 黨
T'ang Chen 湯震
T'ang Ching-sung 唐景崧
T'ang Erh-ho 湯爾和
T'ang Shao-i 唐紹儀
T'ang Shou-ch'ien 湯壽潛
T'ang Ts'ai-ch'ang 唐才常
T'ang Ts'ai-chung 唐才忠
T'ao Mo 陶模
Ta-tao hui 大刀會
ta-t'ung 大同
t'i 體
T'ieh-liang 鐵良
T'ien Pang-hsüan 田邦璿
T'ien Wu-chao 田吳炤
t'i-fa shih 提法使
Tōbun Gakkai 同文學會
Ts'ai Chün 蔡鈞
Ts'ai Chung-hao 蔡鍾浩
Ts'ai O 蔡鍔
Ts'ai Yüan-p'ei 蔡元培
Tsai-chen 載振
ts'ai-cheng ssu 財政司
Ts'ai-k'an 才堪
Tsai-tse 載澤
Ts'ao Ya-p'o 曹亞伯
Ts'en Ch'un-hsüan 岑春煊
Ts'en Ch'un-ming 岑春蓂
Tseng Kuo-fan 曾國藩
Tseng Lien 曾廉
Tseng-ho 曾鉌
tso-fu tu yü-shih 左副都御史
Tsou Jung 鄒容
Tsou Tai-chün 鄒代鈞
Ts'un-ku hsüeh-t'ang 存古學堂
T'u Jen-shou 屠仁守
Tuan, Prince 端親王
Tuan-fang 端方
t'uan-lien 團練
Tung Fu-hsiang 董福祥
t'ung-chih 同志
T'ung-meng hui 同盟會
tung-shih hui 董事會
Tu-pan cheng-wu ch'u 督辦政務處
Tu-pan chün-wu ch'u 督辦軍務處
tu-pan ta-ch'en 督辦大臣
tzu 字
Tzu-ch'iang chün 自强軍
Tzu-ch'iang hsüeh-t'ang 自强學堂
Tz'u-hsi 慈禧
tzu-i chü 諮議局
tzu-ko 資格
tzu-li 自立
Tzu-li chün 自立軍
Tzu-li hui 自立會
tzu-pan 自辦

wai-p'ien 外篇
Wan T'ing-hsien 萬廷獻
wang (destruction) 亡
wang (recklessly) 妄
Wang Chao 王照
Wang Chih-ch'un 王之春
Wang Ching-fang 王璟芳
Wang Ching-wei 汪精衛
Wang Feng-ying 汪鳳瀛
Wang Hsien-ch'ien 王先謙
Wang K'ai-yün 王闓運
Wang K'ang-nien 汪康年
Wang Ping-en 王秉恩
Wang Ta-hsieh 汪大燮
Wang T'ao 王韜
Wang Wen-shao 王文韶
wang-kuo 亡國
Wan-kuo kung-pao 萬國公報
Wei-ch'ih liu-hsüeh chieh t'ung-chih hui 維持留學界同志會
wei-hsing 闈姓
Wei Kuang-tao 魏光燾
Wei-yen 危言
Wen T'ing-shih 文廷式
Weng T'ung-ho 翁同龢
wen-jen 文人
Wu Chih-hui 吳稚暉
Wu Chung-hsi 吳重憙
Wu Feng-kuei 吳鳳桂
Wu Lu-chen 吳祿貞
Wu Ta-ch'eng 吳大澂
Wu T'ing-fang 伍廷芳
Wu Tsu-yin 吳祖蔭
Wu Yung 吳永

yamen 衙門
Yang Jui 楊銳
Yang Shen-hsiu 楊深秀
Yang Shih-ch'i 楊士琦
Yang Shih-hsiang 楊士驤
Yang Shu 楊樞
Yang Tu 楊度
Yang-wu chü 洋務局
Yao Hsi-kuang 姚錫光
Yeh Chüeh-mai 葉覺邁
Yeh Han 葉瀚
Yeh Te-hui 葉德輝
Yen Fu 嚴復
yen-lu 言路
Yü Lien-san 俞廉三
Yü Yin-lin 于蔭霖
yüan 圓
Yüan Ch'ang 袁昶
Yüan Shih-k'ai 袁世凱
Yüeh-lu Academy 嶽麓書院
Yu-hsüan chin-yü 輶軒近語
Yu-hsüan-yü 輶軒語
Yu-hsüeh i-pien 遊學譯編
yung 用
Yung Wing (Jung Hung) 容閎
Yün Tsu-ch'i 惲祖祁
yu ping tsai 有兵在

Bibliography

Works in Western Languages

Ayers, William. *Chang Chih-tung and Educational Reform in China.* Cambridge: Harvard University Press, 1971.

Bays, Daniel H. "The Nature of Provincial Political Authority in Late Ch'ing Times: Chang Chih-tung in Canton, 1884–1889." *Modern Asian Studies* 4.4 (1970): 325–47.

Boorman, Howard, ed. *Biographical Dictionary of Republican China.* 4 vols. New York: Columbia University Press, 1967–71.

Braisted, William R. "The United States and the American China Development Company, 1895–1911." *Far Eastern Quarterly* 11.2 (February 1952): 147–65.

Britton, Roswell S. *The Chinese Periodical Press 1800–1912.* Shanghai: Kelly and Walsh, 1933.

Cameron, Meribeth E. "The Public Career of Chang Chih-tung 1837–1909." *Pacific Historical Review* 7.3 (September 1938): 187–210.

———. *The Reform Movement in China, 1898–1912.* Stanford: Stanford University Press, 1931.

Chang, Hao. "Liang Ch'i-ch'ao and Intellectual Changes in the Late Nineteenth Century." *Journal of Asian Studies* 29.1 (November 1969): 23–33.

———. *Liang Ch'i-ch'ao and Intellectual Transition in China, 1890–1907.* Cambridge: Harvard University Press, 1971.

Cheng, Shelley Hsien. "The T'ung-meng-hui: Its Organization, Leadership and Finances: 1905–1912." Ph.D. dissertation, University of Washington, 1962.

Chesneaux, Jean, ed. *Popular Movements and Secret Societies in China 1840–1950.* Stanford: Stanford University Press, 1972.

Chi, Madeleine. "Shanghai-Hangchow-Ningpo Railway Loan: A Case Study of the Rights Recovery Movement." *Modern Asian Studies* 7.1 (1973): 85–106.

Chu, Samuel C. *Reformer in Modern China: Chang Chien, 1853–1926.* New York: Columbia University Press, 1965.

Cowan, C. D., ed. *The Economic Development of China and Japan.* London: Allen and Unwin, 1964.

Crowley, James B., ed. *Modern East Asia: Essays in Interpretation.* New York: Harcourt, Brace and World, 1970.

Des Forges, Roger V. *Hsi-liang and the Chinese National Revolution.* New Haven: Yale University Press, 1973.

Dutt, Vidya Prakash. "The First Week of Revolution: The Wuchang Uprising." In *China in Revolution: The First Phase, 1900–1913,* edited by Mary C. Wright, pp. 383–416. New Haven: Yale University Press, 1968.

Eastman, Lloyd. "Ch'ing-i and Chinese Policy Formation During the Nineteenth Century." *Journal of Asian Studies* 24.4 (August 1965): 595–612.

———. "Political Reformism in China Before the Sino-Japanese War." *Journal of Asian Studies* 27.4 (August 1968): 695–710.

———. *Throne and Mandarins: China's Search for a Policy During the Sino-French Controversy 1880–1885.* Cambridge: Harvard University Press, 1967.

Esherick, Joseph W. "Reform, Revolution and Reaction: The 1911 Revolution in Hunan and Hupei." Ph.D. dissertation, University of California, 1971.

Feuerwerker, Albert. *China's Early Industrialization: Sheng Hsüan-huai (1844–1916) and Mandarin Enterprise.* Cambridge: Harvard University Press, 1958.

———. "China's Nineteenth-Century Industrialization: The Case of the Hanyehping Coal and Iron Company, Limited." In *The Economic Development of China and Japan,* edited by C. D. Cowan, pp. 79–110. London: Allen and Unwin, 1964.

———. "Comments." In *China in Crisis,* edited by Ping-ti Ho and Tang Tsou, vol. I, bk. 1, pp. 179–93. Chicago: University of Chicago Press, 1968.

———, Murphey, Rhoads, and Wright, Mary C., eds. *Approaches to Modern Chinese History.* Berkeley and Los Angeles: University of California Press, 1967.

Field, Margaret. "The Chinese Boycott of 1905." *Papers on China* 11 (1957): 63–98.

Folsom, Kenneth E. *Friends, Guests and Colleagues: The Mu-fu System in the Late Ch'ing Period.* Berkeley and Los Angeles: University of California Press, 1968.

Franke, Wolfgang. *The Reform and Abolition of the Traditional Chinese Examination System.* Cambridge: Harvard University Press, 1960.

Fung, Edmund S. K. "The T'ang Ts'ai-ch'ang Revolt." *Papers on Far Eastern History* 1 (March 1970): 70–114.

Gasster, Michael. *Chinese Intellectuals and the Revolution of 1911: The Birth of Modern Chinese Radicalism.* Seattle: University of Washington Press, 1969.

Hackett, Roger F. "Chinese Students in Japan, 1900–1910." *Papers on China* 3 (1949): 134–69.

Hall, John W. "Feudalism in Japan—a Reassessment." *Comparative Studies in Society and History* 5 (1962): 1–51.

———. "The Nature of Traditional Society." In *Political Modernization in*

Japan and Turkey, edited by Robert Ward and D. Rostow, pp. 14–41. Princeton: Princeton University Press, 1964.

Hao, Yen-p'ing. "The Abortive Cooperation Between Reformers and Revolutionaries, 1895–1900." *Papers on China* 15 (1961): 91–114.

———. "Cheng Kuan-ying: The Comprador as Reformer." *Journal of Asian Studies* 29.1 (November 1969): 15–22.

———. "A Study of the Ch'ing-liu Tang: The 'Disinterested' Scholar-Official Group (1875–1884)." *Papers on China* 16 (1962): 40–65.

Harrell, Paula S. "The Years of the Young Radicals: The Chinese Students in Japan, 1900–1905." Ph.D. dissertation, Columbia University, 1970.

Hatano, Yoshihiro. "The New Armies." In *China in Revolution: The First Phase, 1900–1913*, edited by Mary C. Wright, pp. 365–82. New Haven: Yale University Press, 1968.

Ho, Ping-ti, and Tang Tsou, eds. *China in Crisis*. 2 vols. Chicago: University of Chicago Press, 1968.

Howard, Richard. Introduction to "The Chinese Reform Movement of the 1890's: A Symposium." *Journal of Asian Studies* 29.1 (November 1969): 7–14.

Hsiao, Kung-ch'üan. "The Case for Constitutional Monarchy: K'ang Yu-wei's Plan for the Democratization of China." *Monumenta Serica* 24 (1965): 1–83.

———. "K'ang Yu-wei and Confucianism." *Monumenta Serica* 18 (1959): 96–212.

———. "K'ang Yu-wei's Excursion into Science." In *K'ang Yu-wei: A Biography and a Symposium*, edited by Lo Jung-pang, pp. 375–407. Tucson: University of Arizona Press, 1967.

———. "The Philosophical Thought of K'ang Yu-wei: An Attempt at a New Synthesis." *Monumenta Serica* 21 (1962): 129–63.

———. "Weng T'ung-ho and the Reform Movement of 1898." *Tsing Hua Journal of Chinese Studies*. New series. 1.2 (April 1957): 111–245.

Hsü, Immanuel C. Y. *The Rise of Modern China*. New York: Oxford University Press, 1970.

Hsüeh, Chün-tu. *Huang Hsing and the Chinese Revolution*. Stanford: Stanford University Press, 1961.

———, ed. *Revolutionary Leaders of Modern China*. New York: Oxford University Press, 1971.

Hummel, Arthur W., ed. *Eminent Chinese of the Ch'ing Period (1644–1912)*. 2 vols. Washington, D.C.: U.S. Government Printing Office, 1943–44.

Hunt, Michael H. *Frontier Defense and the Open Door*. New Haven: Yale University Press, 1973.

Imperial Maritime Customs. *Decennial Reports on the Trade, Navigation, Industries, etc., of the Ports Open to Foreign Commerce in China and on the Conditions and Development of the Treaty Port Provinces, 1892–1901*. 2 vols. Shanghai, 1904–6.

Iriye, Akira. "Public Opinion and Foreign Policy: The Case of Late Ch'ing China." In *Approaches to Modern Chinese History*, edited by Albert Feuerwerker, Rhoads Murphey, and Mary C. Wright, pp. 216–38. Berkeley and Los Angeles: University of California Press, 1967.

The Japan Weekly Mail. Yokohama, 1894–1917.

K'ang, Yu-wei. "Chronological Autobiography." Translated and edited by Lo Jung-pang. In *K'ang Yu-wei: A Biography and a Symposium*, edited by Lo Jung-pang, pp. 17–174. Tucson: University of Arizona Press, 1967.

Kennedy, Thomas L. "Chang Chih-tung and the Struggle for Strategic Industrialization: The Establishment of the Hanyang Arsenal, 1884–1895." *Harvard Journal of Asiatic Studies* 33 (1973): 156–63.

———. "The Kiangnan Arsenal 1895–1911: The Decentralized Bureaucracy Responds to Imperialism." *Ch'ing-shih wen-t'i* 2.1 (October 1969): 17–37.

———. "The Kiangnan Arsenal in the Era of Reform, 1895–1911." *Chung-yang yen-chiu yüan chin-tai shih yen-chiu so chi-k'an* [Bulletin of the Institute of Modern History, Academia Sinica] 3.1 (July 1972): 269–346.

Kosaka, Masakata. "Ch'ing Policy over Manchuria (1900–1903)." *Papers on China* 16 (1962): 126–53.

Kuhn, Philip A. *Rebellion and Its Enemies in Late Imperial China: Militarization and Social Structure, 1796–1864.* Cambridge: Harvard University Press, 1970.

Lamley, Harry J. "The 1895 Taiwan Republic." *Journal of Asian Studies* 27.4 (August 1968): 739–62.

Lee, En-han. "The Chekiang Gentry-Merchants Vs. the Peking Court Officials: China's Struggle for Recovery of the British Soochow-Hangchow-Ningpo Railway Concession, 1905–1911." *Chung-yang yen-chiu yüan chin-tai shih yen-chiu so chi-k'an* [Bulletin of the Institute of Modern History, Academia Sinica] 3.1 (July 1972): 223–68.

———. "China's Response to Foreign Investment in Her Mining Industry (1902–1911)." *Journal of Asian Studies* 28.1 (November 1968): 55–76.

LeFevour, Edward. *Western Enterprise in Late Ch'ing China.* Cambridge: Harvard University Press, 1968.

Levenson, Joseph R. *Confucian China and Its Modern Fate.* 3 vols. Berkeley and Los Angeles: University of California Press, 1958–65.

Lewis, Charlton M. "The Hunanese Elite and the Reform Movement, 1895–1898." *Journal of Asian Studies* 29.1 (November 1969): 35–42.

———. "The Opening of Hunan: Reform and Revolution in a Chinese Province, 1895–1907." Ph.D. dissertation, University of California, 1965.

———. "The Reform Movement in Hunan (1896–1898)." *Papers on China* 15 (1961): 62–90.

Li, Chien-nung. *The Political History of China, 1840–1928.* Translated and edited by Ssu-yu Teng and Jeremy Ingalls. Princeton: Van Nostrand, 1956.

Liew, K. S. *Struggle for Democracy: Sung Chiao-jen and the 1911 Chinese Revolution.* Berkeley and Los Angeles: University of California Press, 1971.

Liu, Kwang-Ching. "Li Hung-chang in Chihli: The Emergence of a Policy, 1870–1875." In *Approaches to Modern Chinese History*, edited by Albert Feuerwerker, Rhoads Murphey, and Mary C. Wright, pp. 68–104. Berkeley and Los Angeles: University of California Press, 1967.

———. "The Limits of Regional Power in the Late Ch'ing Period: A Reappraisal." *The Tsing Hua Journal of Chinese Studies.* New series. 10.2 (1974): 207–23.

———. "Nineteenth-Century China: The Disintegration of the Old Order and the Impact of the West." In *China in Crisis*, edited by Ping-ti Ho and Tang Tsou, vol. 1, bk. 1, pp. 93–178. Chicago: University of Chicago Press, 1968.

Lo, Jung-pang, ed. *K'ang Yu-wei: A Biography and a Symposium.* Tucson: University of Arizona Press, 1967.

MacKinnon, Stephen R. "The Peiyang Army, Yüan Shih-k'ai and the Origins of Modern Chinese Warlordism." *Journal of Asian Studies* 32.3 (May 1973): 405–23.

———. "Yüan Shih-k'ai in Tientsin and Peking: The Sources and Structure of His Power, 1901–1908." Ph.D. dissertation, University of California, Davis, 1971.

Michael, Franz. "Military Organization and Power Structure of China During the Taiping Rebellion." *Pacific Historical Review* 18 (1949): 469–83.

Millard, Thomas F. *The New Far East.* New York: Charles Scribner's Sons, 1906.

Morrell, James. "Two Early Chinese Cotton Mills." *Papers on China* 21 (1968): 43–98.

The North China Herald and Supreme Court and Consular Gazette. Weekly. Shanghai, 1850–1941.

Parson, Wm. Barclay. *An American Engineer in China.* New York: McClure, Phillips & Co., 1900.

Paterno, Roberto M. "The Yangtze Valley Anti-Missionary Riots of 1891." Ph.D. dissertation, Harvard University, 1967.

Pittau, Joseph, S.J. *Political Thought in Early Meiji Japan.* Cambridge: Harvard University Press, 1967.

Pong, David. "The Income and Expenditure of Kiangsi Province in the Last Years (1860–1864) of the Taiping Rebellion." *Journal of Asian Studies* 26.1 (November 1966): 49–65.

Porter, Jonathan. *Tseng Kuo-fan's Private Bureaucracy.* Berkeley: Center for Chinese Studies, 1972.

Powell, Ralph. *The Rise of Chinese Military Power 1895–1912.* Princeton: Princeton University Press, 1955.

Public Record Office, London. Files under Foreign Office (cited as FO).

———. Files under Public Record Office (cited as PRO). PRO 30, Sir Ernest Satow's personal papers.

Rankin, Mary Backus. *Early Chinese Revolutionaries: Radical Intellectuals in Shanghai and Chekiang, 1902–1911.* Cambridge: Harvard University Press, 1971.

———. "The Manchurian Crisis and Radical Student Nationalism, 1903." *Ch'ing-shih wen-t'i* 2.1 (October 1969): 87–106.

Reid, John Gilbert. *The Manchu Abdication and the Powers, 1908–1912.*

Berkeley: University of California Press, 1935.

Rhoads, Edward J. M. *China's Republican Revolution: The Case of Kwangtung, 1895–1913.* Cambridge: Harvard University Press, 1975.

———. "Nationalism and Xenophobia in Kwangtung (1905–1906): The Canton Anti-American Boycott and the Lienchow Anti-Missionary Uprising." *Papers on China* 16 (1962): 154–97.

Scalapino, Robert A. "Prelude to Marxism: The Chinese Student Movement in Japan, 1900–1910." In *Approaches to Modern Chinese History*, edited by Albert Feuerwerker, Rhoads Murphey, and Mary C. Wright, pp. 190–215. Berkeley and Los Angeles: University of California Press, 1967.

Schiffrin, Harold Z. *Sun Yat-sen and the Origins of the Chinese Revolution.* Berkeley and Los Angeles: University of California Press, 1968.

Schrecker, John. *Imperialism and Chinese Nationalism: Germany in Shantung.* Cambridge: Harvard University Press, 1971.

———. "The Pao-kuo Hui: A Reform Society of 1898." *Papers on China* 14 (1960): 50–69.

———. "The Reform Movement, Nationalism, and China's Foreign Policy." *Journal of Asian Studies* 29.1 (November 1969): 43–53.

———. "The Reform Movement of 1898 and the *Ch'ing-i*: Reform as Opposition." In *Reform in Nineteenth-Century China*, edited by Paul A. Cohen and John Schrecker, pp. 289–305. Cambridge: Harvard University Press, 1976.

Sigel, Louis T. "T'ang Shao-yi (1860–1938): The Diplomacy of Chinese Nationalism." Ph.D. dissertation, Harvard University, 1973.

Smythe, E. Joan. "The Tzu-li Hui: Some Chinese and Their Rebellion." *Papers on China* 12 (1958): 51–68.

Spector, Stanley. *Li Hung-chang and the Huai Army: a Study in Nineteenth-Century Chinese Regionalism.* Seattle: University of Washington Press, 1964.

Sun, E-tu Zen. "The Chinese Constitutional Missions of 1905–1906." *Journal of Modern History* 24.3 (September 1952): 251–68.

———. *Chinese Railways and British Interests 1898–1911.* New York: King's Crown Press, Columbia University, 1954.

Tamada, Noriko. "Sung Chiao-jen and the 1911 Revolution." *Papers on China* 21 (1968): 184–229.

Tan, Chester C. *The Boxer Catastrophe.* New York: Columbia University Press, 1955.

Teng, Ssu-yu, and Fairbank, John K. *China's Response to the West: A Documentary Survey 1839–1923.* Cambridge: Harvard University Press, 1954.

United States, National Archives. *Despatches from United States Consuls in Shanghai.* Washington, D.C.: National Archives, 1947 (microfilm).

Wakeman, Frederic, Jr. "The Huang-ch'ao ching-shih wen-pien." *Ch'ing-shih wen-t'i* 1.10 (February 1969): 8–22.

———. "The Price of Autonomy: Intellectuals in Ming and Ch'ing Politics." *Daedalus* 101.2 (Spring 1972): 35–70.

Wang, Y. C. *Chinese Intellectuals and the West: 1872–1949.* Chapel Hill:

University of North Carolina Press, 1966.

———. "The Su-Pao Case: A Study of Foreign Pressure, Intellectual Fermentation, and Dynastic Decline." *Monumenta Serica* 24 (1965): 84–129.

Ward, Robert, and Rostow, D., eds. *Political Modernization in Japan and Turkey*. Princeton: Princeton University Press, 1964.

Wehrle, Edmund S. *Britain, China, and the Antimissionary Riots 1891–1900*. Minneapolis: University of Minnesota Press, 1966.

Wesleyan Methodist Missionary Society. Archives, correspondence from central China. London.

Wright, Mary C. "Introduction: The Rising Tide of Change." In *China in Revolution: The First Phase, 1900–1913*, edited by Mary C. Wright, pp. 1–63. New Haven: Yale University Press, 1968.

Wu, Yung. *The Flight of an Empress*. Transcribed by Liu K'un. Translated and edited by Ida Pruitt. New Haven: Yale University Press, 1936.

Young, Ernest P. "Nationalism, Reform and Republican Revolution: China in the Early Twentieth Century." In *Modern East Asia: Essays in Interpretation*, edited by James B. Crowley, pp. 151–79. New York: Harcourt, Brace and World, 1970.

———. "Problems of a Late Ch'ing Revolutionary: Ch'en T'ien-hua." In *Revolutionary Leaders of Modern China*, edited by Chün-tu Hsüeh, pp. 210–47. New York: Oxford University Press, 1971.

———. "The Reformer as a Conspirator: Liang Ch'i-ch'ao and the 1911 Revolution." In *Approaches to Modern Chinese History*, edited by Albert Feuerwerker, Rhoads Murphey, and Mary C. Wright, pp. 239–67. Berkeley and Los Angeles: University of California Press, 1967.

Young, L. K. *British Policy in China, 1895–1902*. London: Oxford University Press, 1970.

Young, Marilyn Blatt. *The Rhetoric of Empire: American China Policy 1895–1901*. Cambridge: Harvard University Press, 1968.

Yu, P. K., et al., comps. *The Revolutionary Movement During the Late Ch'ing: A Guide to Chinese Periodicals*. Washington, D.C.: Center for Chinese Research Materials, Association of Research Libraries, 1970.

Works in Asian Languages

Ch'ai Te-keng 柴德賡, et al., eds. *Hsin-hai ko-ming* 辛亥革命 [The 1911 Revolution]. 8 vols. Shanghai, 1957.

Chang Chih-tung 張之洞. *Chang Wen-hsiang-kung ch'üan-chi* 張文襄公全集 [Complete works of Chang Chih-tung], edited by Wang Shu-t'ung 王樹枬. 6 vols., 229 *chüan*. Taipei, 1963.

Chang Nan 張枬 and Wang Jen-chih 王忍之, eds. *Hsin-hai ko-ming ch'ien shih nien chien shih-lun hsüan-chi* 辛亥革命前十年間時論選集 [Selected articles on current events during the decade preceding the 1911 Revolution]. 2 vols. Peking, 1960–63.

Chang Nan-hsien 張難先. *Hu-pei ko-ming chih-chih lu* 湖北革命知之錄 [An account of the revolution in Hupeh]. Shanghai, 1947.

Chang P'eng-yüan 張朋園. *Liang Ch'i-ch'ao yü Ch'ing-chi ko-ming* 梁啓超與清季革命 [Liang Ch'i-ch'ao and the late Ch'ing revolution]. Nankang, Taiwan, 1964.

Chang Ping-to 張秉鐸. *Chang Chih-tung p'ing-chuan* 張之洞評傳 [The Life of Chang Chih-tung]. Taipei, 1972.

Chang Ts'un-wu 張存武. *Kuang-hsü san-shih-i nien Chung-Mei kung-yüeh feng-ch'ao* 光緒卅一年中美工約風潮 [The protest movement over the Sino-American treaty of 1905]. Nankang, Taiwan, 1966.

Chang Yu-fa 張玉法. *Ch'ing-chi te li-hsien t'uan-t'i* 清季的立憲團體 [Constitutionalists of the Ch'ing period]. Nankang, Taiwan, 1971.

Ch'en Ch'iao 陳鍫. "Wu-hsü cheng-pien shih fan pien-fa jen-wu chih cheng-chih ssu-hsiang" 戊戌政變時反變法人物之政治思想 [Political thought of those opposed to reform at the time of the 1898 coup]. *Yen-ching hsüeh-pao* 燕京學報 [Yenching journal of Chinese studies] 25 (1939): 59–106.

Chi I-ch'iao 戢翼翹. "Hsien-hsien Wen-hsiang-kung shih-chi t'an" 先賢文襄公事迹譚 [Talking about the life of the former worthy Chang Chih-tung], *Hu-pei wen-hsien* 湖北文獻 [Documents on Hupeh] 2 (January 1967): 19–21.

Chien Po-tsan 翦伯贊, et al., eds. *Wu-hsü pien-fa* 戊戌變法 [The reform movement of 1898]. 4 vols. Shanghai, 1953.

Ch'ing-i pao 清議報 [Journal of public opinion]. Yokohama, 1898–1901.

Chu Ho-chung 朱和中. "Ou-chou T'ung-meng-hui chi-shih" 歐洲同盟會紀實 [A record of the T'ung-meng-hui in Europe]. *Ko-ming wen-hsien* 革命文獻 [Documents on the revolution] 2 (1953): 251–70.

Chu Yen-chia 朱炎佳. "Wu Lu-chen yü Chung-kuo ko-ming" 吳祿貞與中國革命 [Wu Lu-chen and the Chinese revolution]. In *Chung-kuo hsien-tai shih ts'ung-k'an* 中國現代史叢刊 [Selected articles on the contemporary history of China], edited by Wu Hsiang-hsiang 吳相湘 6 (1964): 161–232.

Chung-hua min-kuo k'ai-kuo wu-shih-nien wen-hsien pien-tsuan wei-yüan-hui 中華民國開國五十年文獻編纂委員會 [Committee on the compilation of documents on the fiftieth anniversary of the founding of the Republic of China], ed. *Chung-hua min-kuo k'ai-kuo wu-shih-nien wen-hsien* 中華民國開國五十年文獻 [Documents on the fiftieth anniversary of the founding of the Republic of China]. Vols. 1–. Taipei, 1963–.

Fang Chao-ying 房兆楹. *Ch'ing-mo min-ch'u yang-hsüeh hsüeh-sheng t'i-ming lu, ch'u-chi* 清末民初洋學學生題名錄初輯 [Name registers of students abroad in the late Ch'ing and early Republic, first collection]. Nankang, Taiwan, 1962.

Fang Tu-lien-che 房杜聯喆. "Ching-chi t'e-k'o" 經濟特科 [The special examination in political economy]. In *Chung-kuo hsien-tai shih ts'ung-k'an* 中國現代史叢刊 [Selected articles on the contemporary history of China], edited by Wu Hsiang-hsiang 吳相湘 3 (1961): 1–44.

Feng Tzu-yu 馮自由. *Chung-hua min-kuo k'ai-kuo ch'ien ko-ming shih* 中華民國開國前革命史 [History of the Chinese revolution before 1911]. 2 vols. Taipei, 1954.

———. *Ko-ming i-shih* 革命逸史 [Reminiscences of the revolution]. 5 vols. Taipei, 1969.

Hsiao I-shan 蕭一山. *Ch'ing-tai t'ung-shih* 清代通史 [A general history of the Ch'ing period]. 5 vols. Taipei, 1963.

Hsiao Ju-lin 蕭汝霖. *Liu-yang lieh-shih chuan* 瀏陽烈士傳 [Biographies of martyrs of Liu-yang, Hunan]. N.p., 1913.

Hsü T'ung-hsin 許同莘. *Chang Wen-hsiang-kung nien-p'u* 張文襄公年譜 [Chronological biography of Chang Chih-tung]. Taipei, 1969.

Hsü Wan-ch'eng 許晚成, ed. *Chang Chih-tung chih Liang Ting-fen lun hsüeh-wu shou-cha* 張之洞致梁鼎芬論學務手札 [Handwritten letters of Chang Chih-tung to Liang Ting-fen concerning educational affairs]. Hong Kong, 1968.

Hu Chün 胡鈞. *Chang Wen-hsiang-kung (Chih-tung) nien-p'u* 張文襄公（之洞）年譜 [Chronological biography of Chang Chih-tung]. In *Chin-tai Chung-kuo shih-liao ts'ung-k'an* 近代中國史料叢刊 [A compendium of historical materials on modern China], edited by Shen Yün-lung 沈雲龍. Vol. 47. Taipei, n.d.

Hu Pin 胡濱. *Wu-hsü pien-fa* 戊戌變法 [The reforms of 1898]. Shanghai, 1956.

Huang Fu-ch'ing 黃福慶. "Ch'ing-mo te liu-Jih cheng-ts'e" 清末的留日政策 [Policy on study in Japan in the late Ch'ing period]. *Chung-yang yen-chiu yüan chin-tai shih yen-chiu so chi-k'an* 中央研究院近代史研究所集刊 [Bulletin of the Institute of Modern History, Academia Sinica] 2 (June 1971): 47–95.

Huang Tsun-san 黃尊三. *San-shih nien jih-chi* 三十年日記 [A diary of thirty years]. N.p., n.d.

Kuo T'ing-i 郭廷以. *Chin-tai Chung-kuo shih-shih jih-chih* 近代中國史事日誌 [Daily record of events in modern Chinese history]. 2 vols. Taipei, 1963.

Li En-han 李恩涵. "Chung-Mei shou-hui Yüeh-Han lu-ch'üan chiao-she: wan-Ch'ing shou-hui t'ieh-lu li-ch'üan yün-tung te yen-chiu chih i" 中美收回粵漢路權交涉：晚清收回鐵路利權運動的研究之一 [The Sino-American negotiations for the recovery of the Canton-Hankow railway rights: the late Ch'ing movement for recovery of railway rights, part 1]. *Chung-yang yen-chiu yüan chin-tai shih yen-chiu so chi-k'an* 中央研究院近代史研究所集刊 [Bulletin of the Institute of Modern History, Academia Sinica] 1 (August 1969): 149–215.

Li Kuo-chi 李國祁. *Chang Chih-tung te wai-chiao cheng-ts'e* 張之洞的外交政策 [Chang Chih-tung's foreign policy]. Taipei, 1970.

———. *Chung-kuo tsao-ch'i te t'ieh-lu ching-ying* 中國早期的鐵路經營 [Early railroad enterprise in China]. Nankang, Taiwan, 1961.

Li Lien-fang 李廉方. *Hsin-hai Wu-ch'ang shou-i chi* 辛亥武昌首義記 [A record of the 1911 Revolution in Wuchang]. Wuchang, 1947.

Li Shou-k'ung 李守孔. "T'ang Ts'ai-ch'ang yü Tzu-li-chün" 唐才常與自立軍 [T'ang Ts'ai-ch'ang and the Independence Army]. In *Chung-kuo hsien-tai shih ts'ung-k'an* 中國現代史叢刊 [Selected articles on the contemporary history of China], edited by Wu Hsiang-hsiang 吳相湘 6 (1964): 41–159.

Liang Ch'i-ch'ao 梁啓超. *Wu-hsü cheng-pien chi* 戊戌政變記 [Record of the

1898 coup]. Taipei, 1958.

Liu Hou-sheng 劉厚生. *Chang Chien ch'uan-chi* 張謇傳記 [Biography of Chang Chien]. Shanghai, 1958.

Lo Chia-lun 羅家倫, ed. *Chung-hua min-kuo shih-liao ts'ung-pien* 中華民國史料叢編 [Compendium of historical materials on the Republic of China], series A. Taipei, 1968.

Lü Shih-ch'iang 呂實强. "Chou Han fan-chiao an" 周漢反教案 [Chou Han's anti-missionary activities]. *Chung-yang yen-chiu yüan chin-tai shih yen-chiu so chi-k'an* 中央研究院近代史研究所集刊 [Bulletin of the Institute of Modern History, Academia Sinica] 2 (June 1971): 417–61.

Lü Yang-sheng (K'ung Kuang-te) 魯陽生（孔廣德), ed. *P'u-t'ien chung-fen chi* 普天忠憤集 [Loyal rage of the whole nation]. 2 vols. Shanghai, 1895.

Ming-Ch'ing tang-an kuan 明清檔案館, ed. *Wu-hsü pien-fa tang-an shih-liao* 戊戌變法檔案史料 [Archival historical materials on the 1898 reforms]. Peking, 1958.

Nihon gaikō bunshō 日本外交文書 [Documents on Japanese foreign relations]. Vols. 1–. Tokyo: Gaimusho 外務省 [Foreign ministry], 1936–.

Onogawa Hidemi 小野川秀美. "Bojutsu hempō to Konanshō" 戊戌變法と湖南省 [Hunan province and the 1898 reforms]. In Onogawa Hidemi, *Shimmatsu seiji shisō kenkyū* 清末政治思想研究 [Studies in late Ch'ing political thought], pp. 181–223. Kyoto, 1969.

———. *Shimmatsu seiji shisō kenkyū* 清末政治思想研究 [Studies in late Ch'ing political thought]. Kyoto, 1969.

Sanetō Keishū 實藤惠秀. *Chūgokujin Nihon ryūgakushi* 中國人日本留學史 [A history of Chinese students in Japan]. Tokyo, 1960.

Shao Hsün-cheng 邵循正, et al., eds. *Chung-Jih chan-cheng* 中日戰爭 [The Sino-Japanese War of 1894–1895]. 7 vols. Shanghai, 1956.

Shen Hung-lieh 沈鴻烈. "Ssu chia-hsiang nien Nan-p'i" 思家鄉念南皮 [Recalling home and Chang Chih-tung]. *Hu-pei wen-hsien* 湖北文獻 [Documents on Hupeh] 1 (October 1966): 34–37.

Shen Yün-lung 沈雲龍, ed. *Chin-tai Chung-kuo shih-liao ts'ung-k'an* 近代中國史料叢刊 [A compendium of historical materials on modern China]. Vols. 1–. Taipei, 1967–.

Shih Ching 石錦. *Chung-kuo hsien-tai-hua yün-tung yü Ch'ing-mo liu-Jih hsüeh-sheng* 中國現代化運動與清末留日學生 [China's modernization movement and students studying in Japan at the end of the Ch'ing]. Taipei, 1967.

Sun Yü-t'ang 孫毓棠, et al., eds. *Chung-kuo chin-tai kung-yeh-shih tzu-liao, ti-i-chi, 1840–1895 nien* 中國近代工业史資料第一輯 1840–1895 年 [Materials on the history of modern industry in China, first collection, 1840–1895]. 2 vols. Peking, 1957.

T'ang Chih-chün 湯志鈞, ed. *Wu-hsü pien-fa jen-wu chuan-kao* 戊戌变法人物傳稿 [Draft biographies of persons in the 1898 reforms]. 2 vols. Peking, 1961.

T'ang Ts'ai-chih 唐才質. "T'ang Ts'ai-ch'ang ho Shih-wu hsüeh-t'ang 唐才常和時務學堂 [T'ang Ts'ai-ch'ang and the academy of current affairs].

Hu-nan li-shih tzu-liao 湖南歷史資料 [Historical materials on Hunan] 3 (1958): 106–7.

Ting Wen-chiang 丁文江. *Liang Jen-kung hsien-sheng nien-p'u ch'ang-pien ch'u-kao* 梁任公先生年譜長編初稿 [Preliminary draft of sources for a chronological biography of Liang Ch'i-ch'ao]. 2 vols. Taipei, 1962.

Tung-fang tsa-chih 東方雜誌 [The Eastern Miscellany]. Shanghai, 1904–.

Wang Erh-min 王爾敏. *Ch'ing-chi ping-kung-yeh ti hsing-ch'i* 清季兵工業的興起 [The rise of the munitions industry in late Ch'ing times]. Nankang, Taiwan, 1963.

———. *Wan-Ch'ing cheng-chih ssu-hsiang shih-lun* 晚清政治思想史論 [Essays on late Ch'ing political thought]. Nankang, Taiwan, 1969.

Wang I-nien 汪詒年, ed. *Wang Jang-ch'ing (K'ang-nien) hsien-sheng: chuan-chi, i-wen* 汪穰卿（康年）先生：傳記，遺文 [A biography and writings of Wang K'ang-nien]. In *Chin-tai Chung-kuo shih-liao ts'ung-k'an* 近代中國史料叢刊 [A compendium of historical materials on modern China], edited by Shen Yün-lung 沈雲龍. Vol. 5. Taipei, 1967.

Wang Shu-huai 王樹槐. *Wai-jen yü wu-hsü pien-fa* 外人與戊戌變法 [Foreigners and the 1898 reforms]. Nankang, Taiwan, 1965.

Wu Hsiang-hsiang 吳相湘, ed. *Chung-kuo hsien-tai shih ts'ung-k'an* 中國現代史叢刊 [Selected articles on the contemporary history of China]. 6 vols. Taipei, 1960–64.

Wu To 吳鐸. "Chin-t'ung t'ieh-lu te cheng-i" 津通鐵路的爭議 [The dispute over the Tientsin-Tungchow railroad]. *Chung-kuo chin-tai ching-chi shih yen-chiu chi-k'an* 中國近代經濟史研究集刊 [Researches in modern Chinese economic history] 4.1 (May 1936): 67–132.

Yü Pao-hsien 于寶軒, ed. *Huang-ch'ao hsü-ai wen-pien* 皇朝蓄艾文編 [A collection of reform writings]. 8 vols. Taipei, 1965.

Index

Volumes previously published by the University of California Press, Berkeley, Los Angeles, London, for the Center for Chinese Studies of The University of Michigan:

MICHIGAN STUDIES ON CHINA

Communications and National Integration in Communist China, by Alan P. L. Liu

Mao's Revolution and the Chinese Political Culture, by Richard Solomon

Capital Formation in Mainland China, 1952–1965, by Kang Chao

Small Groups and Political Rituals in China, by Martin King Whyte

Backward Toward Revolution: The Chinese Revolutionary Party, by Edward Friedman

Peking Politics, 1918–1923: Factionalism and the Failure of Constitutionalism, by Andrew Nathan

Reform and Revolution in China: The 1911 Revolution in Hunan and Hubei, by Joseph W. Esherick